The Flying Years

Frederick Niven

The Flying Years

Copyright © 2012 by Indo-European Publishing

Contact:
IndoEuropeanPublishing@gmail.com

The present edition is a reproduction of 1942 publication of this work, produced in the current edition with completely new, easy to read format by Indo-European Publishing.

For an authentic reading experience, the Spelling, punctuation, and capitalization have been retained from the original text.

ISBN: 978-1-60444-743-9

IndoEuropean
Publishing.com
Los Angeles, CA, USA

DEDICATORY LETTER
to
A. RICHARDS

My dear Richards,

There is no need to remind you—far in terrestrial space though the Columbia Valley may be from Magdalene College—of September, 1933. "A magic gets hold of some days and they remain with you forever . . ." So I read—a reference to certain days in that September—in one of those welcome letters that Dorothy and you collaborate upon.

The sage-brush, as you will remember, was in full yellow bloom on the slopes of the foothills and the peaks you were going to climb were austere in distance. The saddle-horses and the pack-horses that were to carry you to your base camp had gone out on their way to the road's end, and in Wilmer, all sunlight and the ricochetting of a clicking grasshopper or two, you waited for the car in which you were to follow them. There, after talk of this and that, you asked me: "And what are you doing just now?" So I outlined to you The Flying Years of which not a word was written then. I will not excessively say that you upheld me from falling and strengthened my feeble knees. I was not so hopeless as all that either of being able to tell something of them or of finding ears, somewhere, to hear; but I did have, at the back of my mind, a melancholy whisper of "Who cares?" Your interest, your enthusiasm, silenced it. The day came of "All set." There was the car spinning away, and you called through its dust that was enveloping me, for a parting word: "Don't let the years fly too long."

I can't tell you how I appreciated that nor how memory of it has heartened me in the writing of this book that I am dedicating to you—in the hope that you will find it not too grievously lacking in what, as I outlined it to you, you felt it should contain and convey.

Yours,
Frederick Niven

Apart from the historic characters in this novel no portrait is intended of any person.

CONTENTS

Chapter One	Eviction	1
Chapter Two	Red River	6
Chapter Three	To the Mountains	15
Chapter Four	Indian Woman	21
Chapter Five	Race	31
Chapter Six	Kildonan Bell	39
Chapter Seven	In the Haar	45
Chapter Eight	Ettrick Brothers	49
Chapter Nine	At Lasswade	56
Chapter Ten	Impulse	64
Chapter Eleven	Travellers' Tales	70
Chapter Twelve	Escape	72
Chapter Thirteen	"The Great Sickness"	77
Chapter Fourteen	Blue Jays	83
Chapter Fifteen	Progress	86
Chapter Sixteen	S.D.	91
Chapter Seventeen	Blackfoot Crossing	95
Chapter Eighteen	A Collet Ring	100
Chapter Nineteen	Prairie Schooner	107
Chapter Twenty	Fiona	111
Chapter Twenty-One	Voila les Boeufs!	115
Chapter Twenty-Two	Mr. Hodges Advises	122
Chapter Twenty-Three	Photograph	133
Chapter Twenty-Four	Birth	139
Chapter Twenty-Five	Changes	151
Chapter Twenty-Six	Descendants	159
Chapter Twenty-Seven	Business	164
Chapter Twenty-Eight	Two Sons	169
Chapter Twenty-Nine	Heather	180
Chapter Thirty	Buffalo Bill	190
Chapter Thirty-One	"A Married Man's Town"	193
Chapter Thirty Two	Sacrifice	201
Chapter Thirty-Three	Blue Gentians	205
Chapter Thirty-Four	Angus and Sam	210
Chapter Thirty-Five	Voice of the Prairie	216

CHAPTER ONE
Eviction

Memory, as the years slipped past, always served Angus Munro with Loch Brendan through a web of yammering gulls, but his mother remembered it through a mist of tears.

There had come to her no omen that the Munros were to leave there. An omen would have hinted the Hand of God in it, however strangely, whereas there seemed to be only the callousness and rapacity of man. Not that any supernatural warning was needed in face of the bitter evidences, but her folk were prone to omens. Her grandmother, as she often told, when recounting the stories of the land, had been waked one night in the '45 by her brother who was, as they said, out. She had sat up in bed, staring at him in the dusk of the kitchen. The smouldering seed of the fire had blazed to a sudden puff of air—and he it was, without doubt, in that flicker of light. He shook his head to her, forlorn-like, as in a sign that something had miscarried, and then was gone. "So you see," Angus's mother would say, "my granny was fully prepared when the news came that her brother was dead on Culloden Field."

As for herself, when the news came that Angus's brother, Robin, had been drowned in the Sound, she was prepared. She took it as his father did not. Daniel Munro seemed to lose his reason for awhile, marching to and fro like a soldier on sentry-go, back and forth. At each sudden advance he appeared to be going for help; then he would halt, aware that there was no help, stand dazed a moment, wheel, and stride off again—back and forth. But Mrs. Munro spoke slowly:

"That was the death candles burning over the Sound last night," said she. "I should never have let him go this day. I was warned."

She was intimate with ghosts. Shadows, by the way, was the word for them among another folk in another land to which they were all going—the father grimly, the mother in tears, the lad with a sense of adventuring.

They were no great readers in Brendan in those days, though in the winter great story-tellers, while sleet scoured the window and night gave a hollow moan in the chimney, with narratives of the old days, myth and truth: of King Hakon; of the Norse woman with the flame-coloured hair; of Cromwell's soldiers that bided in Inverness after the wars and, surrounded there by the Gaelic speech, kept pure amongst themselves their own tongue

1

and passed on to their bairns the fine language of their time, so that, in after years, Sassenach philologists would comment on how beautiful was the English the folk of Inverness spoke; of Prince Charles Stuart; of Cluny in his "cage" on Ben Alder when it was supposed by most that he was long since in France; of the smoking out of the Macdonalds in the cave of Sciur; of the pixies and the kelpies.

Angus's father saw the change coming and was for the boy conning his book. The English they had was thus book-English, their natural speech being the Gaelic. Even Mrs. Munro learnt to speak it—and with the prettiest lilt. But the point here is that between his mother's old stories and the books that his father got for him, and a bent he had for knowing what was happening on the hills and the lochs and the sea—a sort of living with the weather— the boy (sixteen then) had his own kind of private excitement and happiness in life. He had his own gossip, too. He would sooner hear of a whiskered seal flapping onto the Black Rocks with gruff bark like an old man's cough, than any yatter of human follies and failings.

The eviction at Brendan was quieter than some. The Munros expected it. Daniel possessed a booklet—Information for Emigrants to British North America. PUBLISHED BY AUTHORITY (that on the title-page gave them deep confidence in it), Price Sixpence—and he and Angus assuredly conned it, reading all its information on New Brunswick, Nova Scotia, Prince Edward's Island, on Eastern (Lower) Canada, on Western (Upper) Canada, and were a little troubled that the Western Canada it touched upon was not the west to which they were going. They were going even beyond "Western (Upper) Canada." They made themselves acquainted, hopefully, with the value out there of the sovereign and the guinea, and discovered what an American Eagle was worth, a Spanish minted doubloon, a Spanish milled dollar, and what was a pistareen. A great mixture of coins there seemed to be in the Canadas, from the French five-franc piece to the Mexican dollar. They learnt that there were Emigrant Sheds at the landing-place for those who could not "incur the expense of lodging," in which they could sleep a night if necessary, and they made computation of how much food they should cook in preparation for their further journey into that west beyond the tabulated west of the booklet. It was cheering to note that the further one went the higher were the wages paid for labour.

Folk ate well in the Canadas by all accounts, never there, as in Scotland, on the edge of starvation. A man could kill his deer without by your leave of any, and there were crops other than of

2

poor oats and potatoes. There was even a sugar tree! Now, there was a land for you! Think on it! Yes, there was a lot of talk of "the Canadas" before they were, indeed, started on their way thither.

Their neighbours, the Grants (Jessie Grant was the lass of Angus's calf-love), were also leaving Brendan, but not for the Canadas. There were but Jessie and her mother, the father having been drowned in the boat accident that took Robin Munro. They were going to Glasgow to live with Mrs. Grant's sister, married to an ex-soldier, Cameron by name, a big-hearted man who had set up as a smith, was doing fine there, and had offered, himself, to look after them.

The events of the Highlands and the isles of that period put a kind of dolour into even the young, ageing them somewhat, gave them too soon, a sense of distrust in Life. Happiness and trouble were blent in their eyes and the elders seemed always to be admonishing them in this fashion: "There's no one can go courting these days." "There's no lad can plight troth with a lass these days."

Nevertheless, there they were—Jessie and Angus—in the silver-green shade of a birch wood by Loch Brendan, betwixt Brendan and the point, on the morning of the day of departure. To each the proximity of the other was a rare, blessed, mysterious and secret anodyne for the public woe that they could not escape.

"If I make a way in the Canadas—" Angus began.

Jessie interrupted him.

"I'm sure of myself but I'm not sure of you," she said.

What, exactly, did she mean? What was it in him, he wondered, that she was not sure of?

"Would you wait for me?" he asked her.

"I'll not say yes," she answered, "because—" she left the rest in air.

"Because of what. Jessie?" He repeated her name, urgently: "Jessie, Jessie . . ."

She sighed his name for the only reply, held her face up to him. As he bent kissing her she turned it away in some young distress, then suddenly drew him close, responding to his caresses. Next moment she abruptly disengaged herself, shook her head, her cheeks pallid.

"No promises!" she implored. "I'm sure of myself but I'm not sure of you. There's mother calling."

She pressed a hand against his breast and ran from him as though she were running also, in agitation, in deep distress, from herself. At the bend of the road she halted and looked round. There they stood looking one to the other—for an eternity, it seemed: then she turned and was gone from sight and he walked home by the loch-side, the incoming Atlantic tide toying with the seaweed fringe of Scotland along the rocks.

By the door stood a group of men, talking. It was the old talk (repetitive as that of the young lovers on their uncertainties), talk upon the plight of the people in that grandly beautiful land that the Munros were leaving.

"Yes, that is so. Join the army! Join the army!" one was saying to Daniel. "That's all for some of them."

"It's a poor consolation for a lad," he replied, "sticking his bayonet into the belly of a Rooshian, to imagine that he is fighting for his own and stabbing into his real enemies, the men who have put him and his out of house and home. The army! It might be ordered against the French next, instead of to help the Turks against the Rooshians, for all we know as it was when I was a lad. And the French were good friends to the Scots in the '45."

The old talk, the old talk. Another spoke.

"They say it's not to make room for the deer that we must go," he said. "They say that never was any thrust out to make room for deer for them to shoot. Quibbles! Quibbles! To make room for sheep it is—and then the sheep make room for the deer. They'll bring up that lie if ever we get the Commission of Inquiry that some talk of."

"Yes, and it's been going on since the '45," declared Munro. "It was different, though, when it was the Sassenach that came with fire and sword. When a man's foes shall be they of his own household it is bitter!"

Angus sidled past them into the house. Just then, from one of the further cottages up near the bracken and the heather (that soon would encroach everywhere there), came the preliminary sounds, the intermittent drones, of a bagpipe. Who could be thinking of piping over the tying of the last symbolic knots on the ropes round tin trunks and boxes? There was Mrs. Munro plucking and plucking at her under-lip, looking out of the window, perhaps at Ben Chatton or perhaps at a lone magpie veering by with some significance for her superstitious mind.

"They tell me there are places where they do not dare to do it," Angus heard his father say, "even with the rent far in arrears. And why? Because clear it is that there would be blood shed if they tried. They tell me that at some places they have answered the threat of eviction by driving the deer into the sea. Ah, well, by the grace of God some have bowels of compassion. There is a Macleod, now, when the potatoes failed, who fed his people himself to tide them over instead of turning them out. There would be no faith in any landlord left if it wasn't for one or two like him. But they are

4

not in the majority. 'It's my land to do with as I please.' That's the usual. It's bitter! First of all driven off the good lands onto poor, and then we have it flung at us, 'Would you not be better to go to a new country instead of trying to live on land like that—and be grateful if you have your passage money given you?' Well!" He came indoors. "Give me a hand, Angus, with this trunk."

They carried it out. When they went in again, Mrs. Munro had ended her reverie at the window and was drying her eyes.

"I remember a story my mother told me of a Highlander in Quebec," she said, speaking as out of a dwam.

Her husband stared at her in amazement, thinking she was about to launch a tale of some omen, but it was not so.

"It was in the days when the colonists in America rebelled against the arrogance of King George the Third," said she, "'75 or thereby. A Cameron he was. He had not joined the Royal Highland Emigrants' Regiment there but when the rebelling colonists came to assault Quebec he did do his part in the repulsing of the attack, whatever. So he was offered pay after the fight for his services. Says he, this Cameron lad who had gone to the Canadas after the '45, says he, 'I will help to defend the country from the invaders but I will not take service under the House of Hanover.' That was the spirit! Now, what was I telling you this for?" she asked herself. "Oh, yes, I know—the spirit in that. Yes, we are going, but we'll go proud."

She raised her head and with a glare dared the tears to come again.

"Perhaps the clergy are right," she exclaimed suddenly, over another thought.

"In what way?" asked Daniel.

"When they tell us it is the will of God that we go as a punishment for sins, and that any who offer resistance are in danger of hell-fire forever."

"The clergy," said Daniel, "have their livings from the landlords. They know who butters their bread."

"That sounds like profanity!" she cried out.

"I'm not talking of the Almighty," said he. "I am talking of the clergy—an entirely different consideration. They call me a heretic, and if trying to educate yourself and your issue is heresy, then heretic I am. But I'm not talking profanity."

She looked at him, troubled. His thoughts were sometimes beyond her.

The blast of a siren sounded and Angus peered out of the doorway. There was the boat on which they were to embark, splitting the dark water as a plough's coulter the dark spring loam.

The high corries answered with their echoes to her bellow, the gulls rose and volleyed in air, their silver reflections flickering among the loch's reflection of the hills.

Silently they looked their last on the shell of the home. Afternoon having come, an interior dusk was already in corners. It was as if they were ghosts visiting the place where once they had been part of the active life of earth.

"Scotland," said Munro, and again, "Scotland. Just a few sad songs and old ballads! That's all. I see it getting worse every year. God knows what the end will be. And yet—and yet—we'll take Scotland with us: a kingdom of the mind."

He stooped at the rear window. His wife stepped over and stood beside him, and he put an arm round her. By the way they bowed Angus realized that they were looking toward the graveyard where Robin lay, he who was drowned the day after Mrs. Munro saw what she called the death candles out at sea. Though he was but sixteen, Angus had some sense in him and hurried out, left them, so that when they turned they would not find him there indecently staring like a gowk of no understanding.

The surge of waves broke out on the rocks, an orderly smashing pulse of water from the steamer's wake. She was out there, come to rest, waiting for them. It was then that Daniel Munro lost his control after that grand thought of how they would take Scotland with them, a kingdom of the mind.

"To hell with Scotland!" he broke out.

There was a silence then like the silence left when the wind passes through a wood of pines. It was as if Nature held breath, as if the spinning of the world ceased a moment—a moment that belonged to horror as over a sin against the Holy Ghost.

"You should not have said that," Mrs. Munro whimpered.

"No, I should not have said that," he whispered. "I didn't mean it, I didn't mean it."

And as for Peter came the crowing of the cock, there rose the sound of the bagpipes through Brendan, in the slow measure of a coronach.

CHAPTER TWO
Red River

The odours of the new land, before they had sighted it, came out to meet them through a white mist over the sea, odours of robustiously scented forests. The steamer crawled on, calling and calling with her siren till the vapour was dazzlingly infiltrated with sunlight and then, by the sunlight, dissipated away—and there were rocky promontories glittering a welcome.

Further than Lower Canada, further than Upper Canada they were going because of friends in the country beyond, freends, indeed—which is to say, in the Scots sense, relatives. Had it not been for these the Munros would have been much in the condition of some of their fellow voyagers who had merely had their passage paid for them. Landing with scarcely a penny and bound chiefly for the neighbourhood of Toronto (that used to be called York when Angus's mother was a girl), most of them with no word of English, nothing but the Gaelic, they were in anxious plight. By the charity of their compatriots in the land, given in such a way that the name for it was changed to hospitality, these went on to their journey's end.

The Munros' freends in the Red River Settlement—the Frasers—had sent them some financial assistance. In return for that Daniel, before taking up his own land, was to help Ian Fraser on his; and Angus, no doubt, would be working out the while for wages—or such was the suggested plan.

Of the Red River Settlement Mrs. Munro had some woeful stories. She would narrate how the first Highlanders that went there had been hardly used, ordered back by the Northwest Fur Company's representatives, and might have been all homeless again had it not been for a Macleod—a smith—who made shot out of some chains, loaded it into an old cannon he found there, and defied those who would turn them back, with a handful of men at his side. Her husband had to remind her that that was a while back, in her grandmother's day, and that the Settlement had vastly changed since then—that here was 1856 and not 1815.

They went by train (not by such wilderness waterways as those people of two generations back had gone, from Hudson's Bay to Lake Winnipeg), by train to Minnesota, sleeping on the train, eating on the train, a basket of provisions with them for the journey. A young man walked through the coaches now and then with boxes of a crisp sort of biscuit new to them called crackers, and with fruit. Mrs. Munro, after one sampling of his peaches, would resolutely turn her eyes away on hearing him chant his seductive wares. So juicy were these peaches that she had to spread her handkerchief—her pocket-napkin—on her knees when eating them. Never had she known such lusciousness.

"Pea-ches! Or-an-ges!" came the young man's cry, and her head would turn and she would stare hard out of the window.

"We have our basket of sufficient food," said she, "and if I succumb to the temptation of these fruits, and this craving for

7

them, we will have to spend all ere we come to journey's end, whatever!"

Leaving the train at St. Cloud they went on by stagecoach, a four-horse coach, clip-clopping along in a rhythm that at times made the lids droop, sleepy, over eyes that would fain see all the way, clip-clopping and swaying through forests the heady odour of which excited young Angus, and across clearings where stumps smouldered, and by the side of lonely rushy lakes like dropped fragments of blue sky. Minnesota, the driver told Mrs. Munro, was a Sioux Indian word meaning "sky-reflecting water." Each night they stopped at some rest-house by the wayside. Some of the men at these places Mrs. Munro thought the most fearsome she had ever seen, grim of visage and with revolvers at their belts in big holsters. But if ever she and one of them came face to face in a doorway it was always, "Pardon me, ma'am," and hats off. And "Ma'am" it was at the tables when they passed her the cruets. They did not wear their armaments when eating, always, she noticed, before they came into the dining-room, as casually as they hung up their hats, handing to the proprietors of the places their ammunition belts with the pistols attached, as in some usage or courtesy of the country.

As she whispered to him her comments on the ways of this region, Daniel thought she was beginning to be eased of the sense of being far from home which clearly had shadowed her hitherto. But when they came to Abercrombie on the Red River and she discovered that there they had still further to go, aboard a boat, she came near to breaking down. Every roll of the train wheels, the drumming of the stage coach horses' hoofs, the thrashing of the big stern-wheel on the river boat, told her the same refrain—A far cry to Loch Brendan.

As for the Settlement: each of them on arrival promptly observed it in a different way, and in that difference you have all three measured and weighed. Mrs. Munro saw the houses as alien, they being built of logs. Munro saw them as not altogether strange, they being thatched; and Angus saw them as romantic, they being of log with thatch. The lack of a mountain-side on which to rest their eyes was dreadful to Mrs. Munro, to Mr. Munro odd, to Angus novel and exciting.

Their freends, the Frasers, welcomed them warmly. Ian Fraser, the father, was working out at the time with a wheelwright for wages, toward getting money instead of getting exchanges of goods for his produce. On the steamship International, which had brought them there, he found a job for Angus as deck-hand. Daniel, according to their agreement, began to work on the farm.

A happy family—Fraser and his wife, Hector, the son, about eleven then, Fiona, between five and six, and little Flora, age four, named after her mother. There was no impression of a cloud over life there as at Loch Brendan, but a sense of freedom to the point of wildness. With the family increasing they had added to the original house, and with a little contrivance there was room for the Munros.

Several times during the days that followed his arrival there, young Angus remembered how his father had spoken of a kingdom of the mind—Scotland, a kingdom of the mind. Surely it was so here, with the Gaelic round them, the burr of the Scots voices, and often the pipes playing about the place from one house to another. Yet looking back on those days later, there was no doubt in his mind at all that as he recalled and was aided by that phrase—a kingdom of the mind—his mother was haunted and vexed by her husband's cry of To hell with Scotland! Not a word of that had they from her, but she had not forgotten it, and being of a superstitious turn it gnawed in her, first like a recurrent and then as she did not rout it, like a chronic sickness. Indeed, she was not, as they used the word there, a well woman. It was all, for her, despite the Gaelic and the pipes, far from home.

For Angus one of the great pleasures in the change from Loch Brendan was in the food. One never had to say here, "If that's my dinner I've had it!" They were not limited to potatoes and them, perhaps, none too good because of a wet season. Fine trout could be fished, and all round about they could shoot the prairie chickens, while venison was everybody's. Hunters came in from the Great Plains with buffalo meat, and Mrs. Fraser taught Mrs. Munro both how to prepare it and to preserve it (as the French and Scots half-breed hunters had learnt from the Indians, beating in with it various berries) so that it would keep for months—for years, if need be, they said. When Ian was reading the Scriptures aloud one night and came to the words Shall hunger no more, neither thirst any more, they meant to Angus the new land. He was not going to be one of those who make a god of the wame, but it was good to rise from the table satisfied.

In some ways the people were wilder than at home, in others more kind. A man was much more his brother's keeper, if ever there was occasion for brotherly help. None asked servility but most practised courtesy. On Sunday there were church services—all in their braw clothes. You would see silks then, silk gowns, and below them the feet that peeped in and out were in moccasins as often as not, moccasins heavily beaded, that could be got in trade with the Indians for a twist of tobacco. Some folks in the Scots settlement had the blinds down all Sunday, but neither the Frasers nor the Munros believed in that.

"Keep the good light of God out on the Sabbath day? Na, na," said Mrs. Fraser.

There was not much money in the place, though wages were higher than in the east. Almost all was done in Trade—which is to say exchange or barter. It was towards getting money against the time when they would be taking up their own land, and building on it and living apart from the Frasers, that Angus had gone to work on the river boat—the International. A month or two later he was offered, and accepted, other work—on what they called the flat boats—with a Captain Buchanan, from Ayrshire. It was not but an honorary or whimsical title. He had been a blue-water sailor and captained ships round the Horn and there he was, far inland, caught by some call of this great continent's interior. In Minnesota there was wood and with the Red River settlers there was a scarcity of it, so there was a brisk trade in bringing timber from south of the line. The method of transport was to lash it together into a sort of boat in which a load of freight would be carried. On arrival at the settlements the freight was delivered to the consignees and then the boat taken apart and sold for building material. On the flat boats, with Buchanan, Angus worked till the river froze.

In the winter there were dances even those who did not dance at home in Scotland (such as some of Lowland birth, descendants of old Covenanting families) dancing out there. You would hear the fiddles going and from the doorways the voices of those who called the dances: First lady and first gentleman—balance; first lady and first gentleman—both hands; first couple down the line; and wildly went the fiddles. Second couple down the line; and merrily went the fiddles. All hands round—gaily they danced by Red River then. Strathspeys and reels, the Highland schottische and quadrilles they danced, wearing their tartans (that had been prohibited in Scotland in the '45 but were still worn a hundred years later), and glancing to the door sometimes you would see the dark faces of Indians looking in, coveting the colours. There was a wild jig, the Red River Jig, a great favourite with the Métis—French half-breeds. And now and then some Indians would give their own dances, and when the drums beat and their feet thudded out the rhythms, the queerest thoughts and emotions would come to Angus. He could hardly put a name on it. It seemed he had heard these lilts, and danced to them, too, in a time forgotten that the sound of them set him struggling inwardly to remember—which was a feeling, thought he, too ridiculous to tell to any.

All the winter Mrs. Munro had been none too well, which was a regret to them all—for most people newly arrived found the air a tonic, had a fresh joy in life. She, on the contrary, seemed to lose hold of it. Daniel suspected that much of her trouble was mental. Surreptitiously she brooded, he believed.

"I think," said he to her one day, "you have never forgotten, Kate, what I said when we were leaving—"

She interrupted him with a catch in her voice.

"What makes you think that?" she cried out. "I have never said."

"It's just a thought I have," he replied. Today he might have called it telepathy. "I believe you brood upon it."

"If the coronach had not begun right on the heels of your crying out so—" she said, admitting he was right in his surmise, but stopped there, left the rest in air.

They did not know Angus had entered, and he, hearing this, backed out, left them, much as he had retreated from them that last day at Brendan when he came on them side by side bowed to the window, peering along the slopes.

In the spring, after the ice had broken and was tinkling and crashing away down river, when the snow was off the plains and flowers were showing, Mr. Munro thought a jaunt or two might help his wife, put the colour in her lips again. So they went, all three, driving west to visit a further Scots settlement out on the prairies. The land was still wet from the thaw, the wheels drawing up mud as they revolved, and it fell in gobbets with a clapping sound, but there was nothing of the snell in the air. A fine fresh day it was to breathe. "This," thought Daniel, "should do her good."

Over a little rise (for rises there were, as they discovered on travelling, waves in that sea of grass) they came suddenly to a small lake of the kind called slough. It was not the usual ducks that clucked there but some birds, gray-blue and white, that rose, yammering. Sea-gulls here—and so far inland! Mrs. Munro put chin on chest to hide sudden tears, but her shoulders shook with sobbing.

"What is the matter?" her husband exclaimed, drawing rein. "Are you in pain, Kate? What has taken you?"

"Nothing," she answered.

"But it must be something," he insisted.

She looked up at him, biting on her lips and trying to stem the flow by pressing her eyelids closer. That was one of the last pictures Angus had of her—crying like a bairn. Here was a sad downfall for the woman who had talked of going proudly, but a far cry it was for her to home and the sea gulls weaving their silvery reflections in the waters of Loch Brendan. The life at Brendan had been hard—but it was home, and there was an end of it! She seemed like a little girl in grievous trouble.

"The gulls took me by surprise," she said in a small voice.

No need to explain why the surprise of these birds caused her to sob. Her husband and son both knew the picture that would be in her mind. Daniel put an arm round her.

"If we made money enough we might take you back again," said he. "It won't be Loch Brendan, but somewhere in Scotland—in the old land."

"No, no," she said, "you should be angry with me, not kind to me. I'm a child and should be whipped!"

That night Angus dreamt that all the blinds were down at the windows and he was trying to raise them but they would not budge. In this dream he went from one to another, from room to room, and for all his trying not a blind could he raise.

The malady that carried her off would today be called pernicious anaemia. She had no appetite, and nothing that she forced herself to eat gave her sustenance. She was always tired, though she never complained of it.

Angus, as soon as the river was open again, only a few days after that drive, had gone back to the flat-boat work, and it was but on the third or fourth trip that he knew, as they sculled into the bank, that something was wrong. It was a boy with a fishing-rod—or a fishing-pole, as they used to say, a slender, sappy tree branch with line and hook pendant—who broke the news to him, the Fraser boy, Hector, tuft of hair sticking out of a hole in his hat. He dropped the fishing-pole as the flat boat was sculled close to the bank and stared with wide eyes, no smile in response to Angus's wave. Then he clapped hands to mouth, trumpet-fashion, and began to shout:

"You're to come home at once! You're—to—come—home—at—once! I've been watching for you yesterday and today, too!"

"Something wrong," said Buchanan.

"Something wrong," said Angus.

"You're to come up at once," shouted Hector excitedly.

"What's the matter?" asked Angus as they pulled in and he made passes with a boat hook at their jetty.

"It's your mother. You're to come at once."

"You go," said Buchanan.

Angus leapt ashore and climbed the bank, Hector leaving his home-made fishing-rod lying there and hurrying after him. On the point of asking the boy for more detail Angus let the inquiries go. Hector seemed to be both youthfully elated over his task of herald and youthfully perturbed. The slapping of his bare feet and, anon, his panting, died away as Angus hurried to the house. At the door was Mrs. Fraser, head lowered, shading her eyes from the low blinding rays of the setting sun. She stepped back as he drew near.

"Go right in to her," said she, with no greeting save that. "I've had Hector waiting for you since yesterday lest you came early."

He did not ask why she was so anxious for his return. Her face told him. His mother, thought he, must be dying. The bedroom door was ajar, and as he stepped in, his father, sitting by the bed, looked up at him, his life's great agony in his eyes. Standing at the bed-foot was the doctor, a commiserate man, pity in his bearing, distress.

Mrs. Munro was in the article of death.

"She will tak' nae nourishment," the Scots physician's voice came huskily. "If she could but have taken into her blood some nourishment . . ." His voice dropped, and in a tone of sad complaint he ended, "but she will not assimilate."

She seemed to be in a coma and yet, thought Angus, there was a recognition in her eyes through the new opacity that he could not but observe with piercing concern. It was as though the candle of her life guttered, flared—and sank. She drew a breath of content, or of restfulness, then another, desperately.

"Can ye lift me?" she asked in the merest whisper. "Can ye lift me that I could see the hills?"

Munro looked at his son. Angus looked at his father. To see the hills! They bent over her to do as she asked. As they raised her she had again knowledge of where she was, lost, apparently, these last moments.

"There are no hills," she murmured. "I forgot I was here," and tears came to her eyes.

It was then, as they laid her back, that her spirit, her shadow passed, tears in her eyes that she could not see the hills of home. Someone at a distance began an evening's practice on the pipes. Perhaps she heard it and, slipping away toward unconsciousness thought that she was back in Brendan and falling asleep there.

It had been their intention on arrival, after discussion of plans with the Frasers, to take up their own land that spring, but the death of Mrs. Munro caused that to be deferred. Daniel had no heart, as well they realized, to go on with that matter for some time. So, though Ian had not continued with the wheelwright, Daniel continued to work on the Fraser farm. There was enough for them both to do.

But Munro was never to take up land there, no more than six feet of it beside his wife. Only three months after Kate had gone her husband followed her. Just a year to the day from the day of their arrival he passed away after a stroke in the hot field where he was working.

The bearers, at his funeral, made up for the abstemiousness with which, in deference to her views, they had carried Kate kirkward. There were but four of these bearers, two to a side, and with them walked four others to relieve them from time to time. Seldom was a coffin taken in a cart and the Fraser home was some way from the church. There were oatcakes and whisky before the start, and when they carried him out all were rosy. Daniel was a big man, and sooner than usual Ian Fraser, master of the ceremonies, seeing the bearers were hunched to the handles, gave the cry:

"Relief!"

The two on each side who had been but keeping slow step took their places, and the four who fell out had their dram before all moved on again. A few hundred yards on there was again the chant:

"Relief!"

The bearers fell out, and had their dram, as did the mourners, halted behind, and on went the procession once more.

"Aye, he was a great man," one remarked. "I believe he weighed twa hunner wi' the breath o' life in him; and with the kist weighing—"

"Wheesht!"

It did not matter to Angus, though. Even then there was that in him which developed in the years till the time came when he could hear what would have irked, angered, or hurt him as a lad and pay no heed.

"Relief!"

"No, no, I'll have nae mair now till we get him bedded. For the credit of the corp I mauna stagger."

"Wheesht!"

There was a great turnout, of Highland and Lowland, and when they met any French half-breeds upon the way these stood to one side and, uncovering, crossed themselves. Even some Indians, encountered riding into the settlement, reined in and sat by the road wrapped in their blankets, like men turned suddenly to painted effigies, with heads all bowed.

"Relief!"

There were two pipers ahead, at the kirk gate, and as the procession drew near they began to play. Angus felt he might have

14

been spared that. To him death needed no pageantry, no music. He feared then that he was about to make a fool of himself, but there came into his mind, "We'll go proudly," and he took hold of himself and saw his father to rest like a man, then came away to a consciousness—temporarily muted, as a new wound is often accompanied, at first, by a stunning of the nerves—of being alone (father and mother taken from him within three months), which, many friends though he had, was never rightly to leave him all his days.

The first to speak to him was Captain Buchanan, for whom he had been working on the flat-boats. Buchanan was very drunk and when he was drunk he seemed to be aware of all the sadness of life. Never did Angus see him taciturn in liquor, only plaintive and fuddedly compassionate, never what they call greeting fou. He came with a lurch alongside of Angus, who was walking home with Ian Fraser, and said he, with a hiccup:

"The Lord giveth and the Lord taketh away. We have all got to come to it. Blessed be the name of the Lord. Aye. But what I want to say tae you is something practical."

He flapped a hand in air before his eyes.

"Some other time maybe, whatever," suggested Ian gently.

"You're richt! This is not the moment," said Buchanan. "I'll come and see you the morn's morn. I want to see you special."

With a hiccup he dropped behind again. In silence Angus and Ian walked on, a faint murmur, a faint whisper of voices and shuffle of feet in the dusty road to rear. Ever and again came also the hiccup of Captain Buchanan, and when that sounded, Fraser would glance at Angus and mutter, embarrassed, "Aye—aye," or "Indeet, indeet. Yess, yess," very sad for the lad's sake.

CHAPTER THREE
To the Mountains

Ian Fraser had fancied that Buchanan was so fuddled at the funeral that his promise to call and see Angus would be entirely forgotten by him, but there he was, next day, speiring, as he would say, for the lad.

Angus was out by. He was dimly at work on some tinkering, alone in the tool shed, and there Buchanan found him, coming in at the door very sober and sedate, looking as though he had suffered personal loss, but managing, with gaze on the floor or in distance, to come speedily to the business that brought him there.

15

He had received an offer, he explained, sitting down on a keg of nails and filling his pipe with deliberation, to go to the far end of these plains that lay to west of them—"to the boat-building there," said he.

Angus thought for a moment that his caller was not sober as he seemed. Boat-building away inland on those prairies! Then he remembered that through that West country rivers ran, and that they were great enough and sufficiently free of rapids for long distances for heavier craft to ply on them than the canoes of the company—these buoyant canoes that were paddled and portaged from Hudson's Bay and from Fort William (by Rainy Lake and Lake of the Woods) to Fort Garry, and by Portage la Prairie away into the chain of rivers toward remote Swan Lake and beyond.

Buchanan was to take a man or two with him, he explained, able at the work; the pay, he added, was good.

"It would be a change for you," he declared, with a nod and a quick glance. "It would take your mind from—aye," he ended. "What say ye?"

Angus told him he appreciated his thought and his kindness. At that Buchanan rose, and staring out of the window remarked that he would like fine if they could start on Thursday morning.

"Here's Tuesday," said he, wheeled, and walked to the door.

Angus followed him. They stood there a moment or two.

"Yes, I'll be ready," said Angus.

"That's fine, then," replied Buchanan, and departed, leaving the young man to his tinkering and his thoughts.

With his employer going away from Red River he—were he to remain—would have to seek a new job, and there had always been a spell for him in that curve of sky over the space to west, as if with a still small voice it called him. He would be sorry to leave the Frasers. He had come to look upon them as close kindred rather than as the "forty-second cousins" that they were. The children had called his father uncle. He liked the callant Hector. He liked the baby Flora, and very greatly he liked Fiona, who would come to him in the evenings, book in hand, and say "Will you hearken me my lessons?" There was a Sunday when she had asked him to hearken her a psalm.

"Thus spake the sheriff—" she began.

"The seraph," Angus had corrected.

"Thus spake the sheriff—"

"The seraph."

"Oh! Thus spake the seraph and forthwith appeared a shining throne—"

16

"A shining throng—throng."

"Oh! Thus spake the sheriff—I mean seraph—and forthwith appeared a shining throng. Perhaps I had better know, if you please, what a seraph is. That might help."

Yes, he would miss the family life of the Frasers. There was a ring that Mrs. Munro had worn on her third finger, in the collet the hair of her husband's mother. Daniel's father had had it made, a fine piece of work by an Edinburgh goldsmith after his wife's death—on its inner surface the initials of his and her Christian names in monogram—and Daniel, inheriting it, had given it to Kate as wedding ring. When she died Mrs. Fraser had taken it from her hand and kept it to give to Daniel later. He, however had not worn it, put it away; but alone in the world, Angus—finding it among his father's few treasures—put it on his little finger. He had no near kin left, but the sight of that ring, the feel of it, to turn it round sometimes on his finger in those days of desolation, seemed to help, mitigated the sense of solitariness somehow. It gave him two generations of his folk for secret company.

The party consisted of Mr. Buchanan, two half-breeds (of French and Saulteaux blood), who were known only by their Christian names of Pierre and Aloysius, Tom Renwick, a fellow-worker on the flat-boats with them, Sam Lovat Douglas, and Angus.

Douglas—he who was later to become Sir Samuel Lovat-Douglas—had just arrived at Fort Garry on his way to Fort Edmonton, with a wallet of letters of introduction to factors and such throughout the land (to William McTavish, the governor of Assiniboia for the company, Mackay of Fort Ellice, Lillie of Fort Carlton, Chantelaine of Fort Pitt, Hardisty of Fort Edmonton, Macaulay of Jasper House, and Colin Fraser of St. Ann's), and hearing that Buchanan was westward bound had made arrangements with him to go with them. Douglas, in his early twenties Angus judged, was heavily built at that time, with a powerful frame—and a geniality of manner somehow suggesting rather the plausible than the candid. Clearly he was in the country on business bent, but to ask direct questions of a man was not the usage in those days. As a matter of fact Angus was not curious. If a man had no desire to disclose his affairs—then it was nothing to do with him. Yet it was to Angus that Douglas revealed the object of his journey. It was on the night they stopped at the Touchwood Hills post—that shortly afterwards was abandoned by the company and left to crumble in the weather and the seasons.

"I'm verra glad," said Douglas in that friendly way of his, "to have your company on this odyssey—and I hope you mak' weel at the boat-building. Some fools tell me that in a new land a man should take the first job that turns up. Well there may be something in that; but I'm no' eager to take the first job lest I stay in it. You see what I mean? Man, I'm ambeetious!"

The others were over at the post for company and a chat there (to the official in charge at the Touchwood Hills House, Douglas had no letter), and they were alone at the night fire. Its flames illumined the heavy forehead, the heavy jowl, the dancing and genial eyes of Sam Douglas.

"Do you know what I'm here for?" he asked. "I'll tell you. You haven't tried to pump me to find out, so I'll tell you," and he laughed. "This country is going to open up—to develop. What have we seen so far? Buffaloes by the hundred, and these two half-breeds whooping Voila les boeufs! Voila les boeufs!"

"An odd fellow," thought Angus. "He seems to be acting." (Not but what he had already a liking for Sam.) "Even his Scots burr he seems to accentuate deliberately at times—as now, when we are alone together, for example. Something a trifle humbugging about him, is there? Something of insincerity in his ingratiating manner? And yet, isn't it easier to get along with one who would fain be a good fellow than with one who is sulky and taciturn?"

Thus was Angus thinking as Douglas paused there by the fire beside him on a buffalo robe, gazing into the flames.

"Aye, buffaloes," Sam went on after a pause. "And antelope louping over the prairie, and a few bit villages of the Crees in their leather tents. But consider how the buffalo are being killed off. They are no' just for the sustenance of the Indians now. The trade that has sprung up in their robes as they call these pelts," and he stroked the one on which he sat, "is going to exterminate them; and the railroad builders down in the States are feeding the navvies on buffalo meat. Mark my words. Man, man, my mind is of the kind that is aye just a jump ahead—maybe twa jumps. There's going to be cattle grazing on these buffalo pastures before long. And there are going to be fixed habitations—fixed habitations. But what are the folks going to burn to keep them warm in wintertime? It's a cold winter here. Buffalo chips? Na. And there's not sufficient wood in the river bottoms to last them long when they come in here in great numbers, as come they will. I'm looking for coal. My mind is of the kind that goes jumping ahead! Aye, burning rocks. I heard of burning rocks from an Indian on the Missouri. They have coal there; and he told me there were burning rocks up here to north also. But it's no' safe to travel up through the Blackfoot country, as ye ken, so I went back doon the Missouri and over to

18

the Red River and Fort Garry, and I'm going to see these burning rocks in the north. That's what I'm here for, sir. I'm thinking of the future. I'm planning big."

It was young man's talk, perhaps, and as the years passed he might be more minded to keep his own counsel; but many were the young men in the land, then, engaged on affairs onerous and dangerous—factors and explorers of the company hardly more than striplings. All the difference between them and him was that they were in the service of others, and he already was, as they say, playing a lone hand.

Doubt in him suddenly intruded unhappily into Angus's liking for him when, after a lull in talk during which they but sat smoking there by the fire, the talk resumed came somehow to the subject of the stipends paid by the Hudson's Bay to its factors and clerks.

"A small stipend," declared Douglas, as though he were an aged promoter and experienced financier, "and the promise of a fair pension is the idea. You see, it makes a man work well to know his old-age is provided for if he behaves himself—and, actually, he may never live to have the pension. If I was head of a big company I'd run it on those lines. It would be benevolent, you see, to arrange for the pension—and, as I say, only a percentage would get one. That's to be considered."

"You would not, then, pay the pension to widows of your employees?" asked Angus.

Sam Douglas rubbed a hand over his face.

"That would have to be thought over," he replied, and dismissed the subject by rising to prepare his blankets for the night, the sound of the fumbling steps and the voices of the others drawing near them from the direction of the post.

Rumours of Blackfeet raiders in the region when they reached Fort Carlton ordained a continuance together toward Edmonton, with the intention of passing southward, thence, to the Mountain House; but at Fort Pitt there was a dark-eyed young man, the half-breed son of one of the factors, who was setting out across country for Rocky Mountain House. He was known to the Blackfeet. (His mother was, in fact, a Piegan woman—which is to say Blackfoot, the Blackfeet being, as Angus had it explained to him, a tribe in three parts: the Blackfeet proper, the Bloods, and the Piegans, all speaking a common tongue.) So there they said farewell to Douglas and the half-breeds, striking out west, south of Beaver Lake, by the Dried Meat Hills, Buffalo Lake, the Red Deer River's upper waters, and Gull Lake—new names to Angus, with the life of the land in the sound of them.

For some reason or another Douglas's parting remark remained hauntingly in the young man's ears.

"I hope you mak' weel at the boat-building," said Sam.

"And I hope you find your coal that you are going to make a fortune over—by and by," replied Angus.

"Oh, sooner than you think!" Douglas told him.

There seemed at the time and in the remembrance as he rode on to be an ironic note in the words, I hope you mak' weel at the boat-building. Did Douglas want, all friendly at parting, to spur Angus on, to make him think further than the day's board and bed? "Some folks tell me that in a new land a man should take the first job that turns up, but I'm no' eager to take the first job lest I stay in it." That also Douglas had said. He may have intended, at parting, a jog to his new friend toward looking ahead, planning big.

It was a little way beyond Gull Lake, coming to an eminence, that Angus had one of his experiences, these experiences that he told to no one but that went (more than other ones apparently less airy, less unsubstantial) to the making of what he was to become in the drift of the years. It was an experience of the spirit kin with that which had privately befallen him over a year before when the odours of the new land, before they had sighted it, came out to meet them through a white vapour over the sea, into which the steamer's siren bleated. By the olfactory nerves had come that one. By the eyes came this, with the gift of a secret ecstasy.

Before him the Rocky Mountains were suddenly revealed beyond belts of colour that were of woods, parklands, wedges of sky-reflecting water, twist of river, fragment of distant lake. Very much as it was with him when listening to music was it with him then, gazing on the scene before him. Music would pick and choose through the past years of his life, recover and toss to him this, that and the other: the tone of a voice, the light on a pebble, a forgotten wail of wind in a chimney from a winter storm of years back, the glance of eyes (Jessie's, no doubt), the gleam through water of a herring shoal—and leave it to him to make something of the medley.

He thought of his father's remark—Scotland, a kingdom of the mind. Scotland was not his. They would not have him there. Well, he had Scotland still, the bark of seals on the Black Rocks, the remembered smell of sun-scorched bracken, of peat-smoke beaten down in the gales. He thought of the vast Atlantic swaying like a compass disc betwixt the rise and fall of Scotland's seaweed fringe and the scent of pines, firs and cedars in the mists off Newfoundland. Of the curve of the Milky Way he thought, seen

20

from their prairie camps at night, a whirl of sparks from the Arctic shores to the Caribbean. Of the columns and whip-lashes of light, up to the zenith and gone, of the Aurora Borealis, seen after hot summer days of their journey (not only in winter as many believed), he thought as he reined in his horse and sat motionless staring from that butte beyond Gull Lake at the revelation of the Rocky Mountains.

Something happened to him beyond his power to express; something happened, wordless, like music. As though the blue of the sky had run and thickened roughly at the base, there lay the ranges, low in contrast with the height of that space of blue but— he aware of how far off they were—majestic in their serene extent. They dropped away to south, they dropped away to north, as into a quiet eternity. Here and there slashes of white showed among their purple. Here and there rocky gables twinkled like mirrors, and at one place, far in, there was a dun seething, peaks turning to cloud and clouds solidifying into peaks. A lightning flash was drawn in quick gold on that portion where peaks and clouds fused, and then came a distant sound, the faintest rumble.

But he could not stay there all day, his spirit and the sighing of the wind in the grass blending as sky and mountains blent in that section of storm on the ranges. Men and horses ahead were dwindling to the size of ants, passing away in a steady jig-jog with the rhythmic swing of long tails, the slight sway of the riders' shoulders and of the balanced packs. After that vision they would soon be at journey's end.

It was, in fact, next morning, just one calendar month from the day they started out from Red River that, cresting a knoll, they saw beyond a twist of river the towers of Rocky Mountain House.

CHAPTER FOUR
Indian Woman

It was as the summer changed into autumn in the year '57 that Angus came to Rocky Mountain House and already the place had its history, though the signs of it were splintered in wood instead of being chiselled in more ancient stone. Here were no granite peel towers, only those wooden watch bastions. Here was no Roman Wall such as crumbled through the centuries betwixt Clyde and Forth, no ruined keep such as sat by the side of the Wee Cumbrae, gazing hollow at its double on the mainland. But in the logs of Rocky Mountain House already, when young Munro came there, was a silver gray veneer of the weather that silently told him dead men's hands had hewn them and set them up. The scene in which the fort sat—with its history, recent in comparison with the history of his homeland—spoke beyond record, it seemed, spoke from the beginnings of the world, prehistoric days, the early ages. There lay the eternal mountains—higher than Grampians, if obvious comparisons were to be made—and in the twilight the bay of a timber wolf came as it were from a time before Bruce, before Hakon, of whom his mother had known the legends.

Here had come one Pangman, and on an old pine close by had cut his name and hewn the date: Peter Pangman, 1790. Here, in the days before the amalgamation of the Hudson's Bay Company (the Governor and Company of Adventurers of England trading into Hudson's Bay) and the Northwest Fur Company, Alexander Henry of the latter (known as Alexander Henry the Younger, to distinguish him from his roving uncle) had fuddled a party of Piegan Indians with whisky into which he decanted laudanum, making them incapable of going on toward the Rockies to intercept David Thompson, who was then on his way to trade with their enemies through the passes. And what would David Thompson, Angus wondered, have thought of these methods, listening to it all and hearing, anon, of that curious man of brain, heart, and sinew who refused to serve liquor to the natives?

The factor of the house entertained them often with these old stories as the evenings drew in, telling of how Thompson once, importuned by his friends to take kegs of rum to trade away off in the land of the Kootenays, stampeded the horses so that they dashed under tree branches, smashing the barrels, then wrote a letter—that would get back to his partners he knew not when, nor by what hands—telling of the accident and, glad that he had found a way not to debase the natives with fire-water, sat down to his lonely evening fire in the glow of resinous pine-knots to read a chapter from the pocket Bible he carried along with him. There was a legend of him having arrived at the Mountain House once from one of his expeditions beyond the mountains, that had been in winter, downcast greatly at the treatment accorded to the sledge-dogs—a humane man.

"What was he like to look at?" Angus asked, and was given a description of him—broad shoulders, deep-set eyes, high forehead and across it his fair hair cut bang-fashion.

The ghost of David Thompson, the shadow of David Thompson, moved for him always thereafter against the background of these silver-gray logs. There was also a peppering of history in them, gouged holes that had been made by no woodpeckers' beaks but were souvenirs of occasions when Cree and Blackfeet, unhappily arriving simultaneously, fought round its walls.

At the fort they had fires of coal—which Douglas had gone seeking; and there were men whose duty was to go to the outcrop a little way back and pick it out, pack it to the House. As for the burning rocks: Angus discovered that the Indians called them so not because they at any place, so far, mined and burned coal themselves, but because there were certain areas ignited no doubt by bush fires, that smouldered away, glowing by night in deep crevices and raising their pillar of smoke by day. Had Sam Douglas read more in the journals of the old explorers he would not have needed an Indian's account of burning rocks to send him on his quest. That coal was in the land had been known and noted by travellers long ago—Franklin, Peter Fiddler and Mackenzie among them. Seams had been smouldering to the knowledge of white folk for a hundred years, and according to the legends before that, time out of mind.

Less was Angus impressed by any feeling of lack of history in the land than by the sense of the prehistoric there.

News of the outer world—near and far—they heard and discussed. The territory of Kansas was still, it seemed, a troubled place to live in with the settlers from the free and those from the anti-slavery states at loggerheads, drawing their guns over their differences. There was trouble in Europe, as always. There was war between France and Sardinia, France and Austria. There were wranglings over the provinces of Nice and Savoy. They heard of that fracas and, anon, that it was over, then that another was brewing in Sicily; and Victor Emmanuel and Garibaldi were discussed on the banks of the Saskatchewan. More distant, sometimes, seemed to Angus the people of these discords and bloodshed than the folk of Venus (if folk there were on that planet), setting in a clear sky beyond the Rockies.

When the Blackfeet came north to trade there was ceremonial, the factor going out to meet them with a gift of tobacco. As sharing salt to the Arab was whiffing from the same pipe to them. The chief would accept the gift, fill his sacred pipe, and the sub-chiefs and the factor would smoke, with a dignified observance in the pointing of the stem, even in the manner of handling it and in the direction of its circuit—with the sun—"Much as we white men," remarked the factor, "have a ritual in the birling of the wine round the table."

In the earlier days—of the Northwest Fur Company, when rum was much used in trade—there was great care exercised in

23

letting the Indians, of whatever tribe, into the Fort. A few at a time they passed into the trade-room and up in the galleries company employees were secreted with primed rifles at hand. When the rum was in the tomahawk was often out. The Indian had to be taught to like the spirit, and when the extensive use of it was discontinued he had a grievance—that he was not given it. He would demand, with murder in his eyes. Dreadful and dowie doings there had been in that place of lonely grandeur. To avoid these clashes of tribes at enmity the company's officers tried to keep the trade of the Plains Cree to Forts Edmonton, Pitt and Carlton (the woods Crees went chiefly to Carlton and à-la-Corne), of the Eastern Assiniboine to Qu'Appelle, of the Saulteaux to Forts Ellice and Pelly. Rocky Mountain House, by the company's desire, was for the Blackfeet confederacy and for the Sarcees (who seemed, by their speech, to be a southern band of the Chippewyans—the Tinnhes—of the northern lakes), and the Western Assiniboines, generally called the Stonys. But Crees still came there at times, even as roving Sarcee and Blackfeet would dare to go as far as the core of their northern enemy's lands—Fort Edmonton.

Never, so far, either at Red River or at the Mountain House, had Angus been homesick for Brendan, because of the melancholy of crushing conditions of the life of his people there. Yet a day came on which, at the sound of a place-name, he had—if but for a moment—a pang at his heart, a realization of being far from home, and he understood how his mother would ache for Scotland despite their misery there. There arrived at the Fort a man with a marked Highland accent who, on being asked whence he came, replied "Dunvegan," which Angus took for Dunvegan in Skye, and had a vision as of all the Hebrides with trailing mists, quiet glens, and sea lochs huzzaing with a homing tide.

"Dunvegan," said he—homesick.

"Yess—north of Fort Edmonton, on the Peace River it iss."

"Oh, I thought you meant Dunvegan in the Isle of Skye."

"No, no, I've never been in Scotland. I was born in Glengarry—Upper Canada," he added quickly, with a laugh, noting a look of puzzlement on Angus's face.

He was descended, no doubt, from others cast out of their homes as his folk had been—and the brief homesickness passed.

In talk of those who had been before him in these parts he learnt much of their marital affairs—their blanket marriages, their prayer-book marriages, their registered unions: the varieties of marriage observances and plain concubinage. High-placed men, he heard, in the service of all the trading companies—the old Northwest Fur Company, the X.Y. Company, the Hudson's Bay

Company, had taken Indian women as wife or as concubine—and some, when their time of living in the west was finished, left women and half-breed weans behind, while others took theirs east with them.

Tom Renwick voiced plump and plain the view that if a man must have a woman he might as well visit the Indian camps and find some temporarily obliging and clean squaw without any legal proceedings whatever. There were older men present and Angus wondered how such a suggestion struck them. There was a marked silence—and it occurred to him that perhaps they were considering that Tom's view was a sound one, but that it would have been better for a junior not to have expressed it.

"This young man's dogma," said the factor, wagging his head at Renwick, "is apt to lead to trouble. You be careful, Tom, of acting upon that conception in some of these Indian villages."

"I wasn't thinking of it personally, sir," replied Renwick.

"Hum!" said the factor.

"I believe that with a white-man marriage," Buchanan remarked, "a squaw has a tendency, as time slips along, to be dictatorial. Marry one according to their own rites and it's no' so bad. I'm told. She'll be aye a wee bit uncertain if the white man feels wholly bound. Give them a ceremony before a priest or a clergyman and there is, I doot, that tendency. A squaw with a marriage certificate in her hand is apt to become heap big chieftainess."

"That applies," the factor pointed out, laughing, "to some white women, too. I doubt if it is typical."

"They are, of course, savages—les sauvages," said Buchanan.

"Daniel William Harmon said—" began the factor.

Daniel William Harmon: Angus had never so much as heard the name, yet the factor spoke it as though almost to quote an authority. Some, in Angus's position, might have damned Mr. Harmon and his opinions at a venture, but instead of that he reminded himself that little did he know of this west to which he had come; and desiring to know more he was all ears and his gaze was eager on the speaker's face.

"Daniel William Harmon said that hospitality to strangers he had found to be among the Indian virtues, and that he had been treated with more real politeness by them than is commonly shown to strangers in the so-called civilized world."

"Well, Harmon certainly knew both," said one of the clerks.

The factor went on to talk of one and the other—giving them their names, Harmon and Sir Alexander Mackenzie among them—who had married Indian women, and these not eastern Indians long in touch with white people, but Indians of the Great Plains; and that talk sooner than he had any premonition (premonition, in fact, he had none) was to be turned over and over in Angus's mind.

When the snow was beginning to creep down on the range of the Rockies westward with that amazing straight line as though ruled along the mountains where upper whiteness and lower green met, Buchanan, Renwick and Angus went off to the hunting of white-tailed deer in the wooded country.

Over gray and brown pebbles a stream came down through the forests. The place belonged to antiquity. The stands of deciduous trees among the evergreen conifers were yellowing, autumn having come, and Indian summer might hold all in exquisite trance for a month or more. As they rode down to that stream, their pack-horses laden with the kill of deer, there was an odour of burning wood, red-willow smoke. There, in a natural meadow, a green gusset by a curve of the hurrying water, was an Indian encampment, a cluster of tepees, the leather ones of that epoch.

There had, by the signs, been a meal recently eaten in the open. No smoke came from the tepees, but a fire crumbled into ash before them, sending up, as is the way of red-willow well alight, more of odour than of smoke into the air. A mere sift of blue, a haze of blue, ascended from that natural meadow in a thin long wisp, and was caught by the draught of the stream's passage, drawn away trembling above its flow, a pennant of blue twining above the twinings of the creek so that its further course could be traced some distance by that gauzy riband among the tree-tops. Little did Angus realize how even that, remembered in days to come, would importune him till it was as though a voice called in his dreams, Come back.

He and his two companions rode down to the water's edge. The Indians had been hunting also and in the creek-bed were many hides held down by stones. Others, pegged to the ground, or stretched upon upright wicker frames, the women were scraping clean. By the lodges sat the men, some idling after the hunt, one making arrows—running the shafts back and forth, to assure them straight, through a stone in the centre of which was a circular hole. The horses of the white men whinnied to the horses of the Indians. The horses of the Indians answered back, looking up from their grazing, displaying white splashes on broad foreheads and Roman noses—these descendants of Arab sires.

The Indians scarce looked up. They might, by their manner, have been unaware of indication that anyone was coming, going on with the straightening of arrow shafts, the chipping of fat from hides. The three men paused at the creekside, their pack-string loping ahead and craning necks to drink, then the saddle horses craning down, so that the riders sat forward, hands extended with the reins. They knew these people and, as the animals drank, when one or another of the band glanced toward them they raised their hands in the customary signs of greeting, either the palm held upward—the sign of peace (a hand with no weapon in it)—or with the first two fingers elevated and slightly oscillated, the sign for two people, friends, together.

The pack horses, having drunk, waited with dripping muzzles for direction, and were driven by Tom Renwick through the stream on to the meadow and across it, past the camp to the further ford. Buchanan reined in a moment to hail an elderly man, Chief Red Shield.

"Hullo, Chief!" he called. "You get deer?"

"You bet!" replied Red Shield, his face wrinkling in a smile.

Buchanan rode on, pointing a finger at two children that balanced at the lodge door sucking their thumbs, staring at him, and—"Boo, boo!" he chanted at them, an old squaw looking from the solemn children to the jocund white man and rippling laughter.

That was the day when Angus first saw Minota.

In some impulse he glanced round and there, a little way up the creek, was an Indian girl dressed in the manner of the time, which was part native, part white, with fringed deerskin kirtle over deer-skin leggings, and a print flower-patterned bodice from the company's trade-rooms. Her head was bound with a blue bandana, thick plaits of hair hanging on either side. Hand on hip, head canted, she was watching him; and when their eyes met she did not look away.

Angus smiled at her and after a moment, when it seemed she was not going to respond, she did, then looked toward one of the elder women at work upon a hide. To her, then, Munro turned and was just in time to realize she had seen and was pretending utter engrossment in her task.

Quiet he was, following Renwick and Buchanan through the forest that flounced these slopes, aware of the smell of balsam in the dusky hush, seeing the tree shadows rippling over the backs of the two in front, rippling over the horses' haunches, keenly alive to scent and sound, the click of a hoof on a stone in the dust of the forest floor. The roar of the creek had fallen away. Surely the silence of that forest was older than the Roman Wall. As he rode he thought of Sir Alexander Mackenzie, of whom he had often heard with his Indian woman, and of Harmon, whose name was new to him, with his.

Next day when they were in camp the horses, tearing grass close by, became restless, raising their heads, snorting.

"Somebody coming," said Buchanan.

There between the tree boles above them was a movement. Laughter came down, rippling laughter of Indian women, the deep brief laugh of a man. It was their friends again, Red Shield's band. Pack ponies titiuped past, laden with rolled hides. Young men following them, swaying loose in their saddles, gave response with a waggle of two fingers to the salutes of the white men. A squaw rode slowly by on a deliberate piebald that had no doubt been as it were the nursery horse of many children. She smiled. Looking after her they saw a cradle hanging on her back, a small face there, eyes staring out at the receding landscape.

Anon came Red Shield, a fine figure, sitting erect, foursquare. He not only was a chief—he looked a chief in his fringed buckskins, and with his plaited hair (the braids), bound at the ends with little brass rings. He halted to talk to Buchanan, and as he did so the horses of those behind behaved as usual when one stopped ahead—immediately took the opportunity to turn aside and snatch at the special herbage of their fancy.

There was the girl of Angus's admiration and considerations—swinging out her rein-hand to ride past Buchanan and Red Shield.

"Your horse wants to stop and eat," Angus said.

"Yes," and she showed white teeth in a smile.

That was all. He wondered if that was all she knew of white-man speech, yes and no.

"Your people seem to have got plenty deer for moccasins," he remarked.

"Yes—and the skins are very good this year," she replied.

The clarity of her voice, the precision of her utterance, made him glad he had not spoken to her with the usual sort of pidgin-English.

"What is your name?" he asked.

"Minota," said she. "My father is Chief Red Shield," and she inclined her head toward him.

"Oh, your father is Chief Red Shield. I have seen him once or twice at the Mountain House."

He was suddenly aware of a young man manoeuvring a half-broken horse past them. It seemed to him that there was anger on the rider's face. He stepped aside to give more room, said "How-do," but the Indian was surly.

"He does not speak English," explained Minota.

"Where did you learn it?" Angus inquired.

"My father taughted me," she answered, and then in her eyes was shadow of a doubt of her pronunciation.

To him it was well enough. Red Shield, he had been told, was one of the ablest chiefs of the Crees thereaway.

The old lady who had observed their exchange of smiles the day before was upon them then. Minota flicked the rein ends over her horse's haunch and it moved on.

"How do you do?" said Angus to the old lady.

"How—do—you—do?" she responded, stately.

"I hope we will meet again," Angus said, turning to Minota.

"I expect so," she said.

The chief shook his lines and the cavalcade passed, leaving an odour of new-tramped, new-crushed pine, fir and tamarack needles, an odour of horse-flesh.

"A fine old fellow that," said Buchanan.

"And Angus is thinking a fine young lass," said Tom Renwick, sitting on his heels by the fire. "Eh?"

"Yes. Not bad," admitted Angus.

I expect so: what, precisely, did she mean by that? Had she seen in his eyes what Tom Renwick had evidently seen? Did she mean only that wide though the land through which they roamed they would no doubt forgather again? He was surely in love to be probing for deep implications in casual remarks.

They did meet again, at the Port, several times before the snow fell, and on each meeting the deeper was Angus enamoured of his copper-coloured maid with the dark, lustrous, candid and somehow pathetic eyes.

A letter from Ian Fraser, received just the day before one of these visits of the Indians, for some reason—he could not tell how or why—had the effect of restraining him, though but temporarily. He was back, in memory, with that happy family, saw the plates in their racks round the kitchen that was like an old Scots interior, heard again Ian at his work singing in his fine natural voice the old ballads; hearkened Fiona her lessons—and her psalm!—and was doubtful if he should act as he was here moved to. He had seen enough of Minota to believe that all he had to do was to ask her, and she would be his woman. He turned about and about on his finger the ring that had been his mother's, the hair of his grandmother in its collet, and asked himself (asked, almost it seemed, the ghosts of his people) if he was wise.

He did indeed believe that, by an Indian's view, by an Indian's ways of courtship, he had gone far already. He had seen

29

the young men at the preliminaries of their courting, which was but making eyes at the girl of their choice till she either too often turned her back with a finality of disdain or indifference and it was realized as hopeless to proceed, or raised her eyelids in passing and smiled, when the next step was to waylay her in the dusk and cast a blanket round her. There they would stand, these young lovers, by the hour, no one paying any heed, not even the wild striplings of the village.

Yes, in all the meetings he had had with Minota her eyes (after the first talk) had told him with a lovely darkening or misting in them, like the darkening of pools of water under a passing cloud. She gave herself to him in that misting of her dark eyes.

The end of it all was that in the spring young Angus Munro (just nineteen then) took his woman—it was never my wife; my woman it was—to the factor, her father and mother with them, to have an entry made of his union with Minota Red Shield in the company's books.

He did not ask himself insistently why that was all, why he did not go to the mission and have a white man's marriage. He silenced the inquiry by telling himself that some white men took their woman to wife without even the formality of an entry in the books, no more formality than the present of a gun or a few horses to the father.

What was the depth of his love? What was the depth of hers? Her eyes had clouded when, her promise to be his woman given, he had said that they had better have it written down at the Fort; but she had not asked, instead, for a prayer-book ceremony. Minota would have gone with him even without that. He offered neither gun nor horses to old Red Shield. She did not want that; her father, she said, did not want that. That savage, Chief Red Shield, and his squaw looked upon it as an honour to have their daughter wed to a white man. Minota's mother was a sonsy woman, coming to the age when those of her race have a tendency to broaden in a very definite "middle-age spread," a sonsy woman with genial eyes and a happy laugh. She was a Stony (which is to say an Assiniboine of the west, a Rocky Mountain Assiniboine) whom Red Shield had met once at the House when both her tribe and his were camped close-by there to trade.

No—no gun, no horse for the girl but, not as the purchase price, merely as a gift—as the phrases went, a prairie gift, a gift cut off, a gift in itself, meaning not given in hope of any return or exchange—he presented Chief Red Shield (on the sober advice of Captain Buchanan) with a silk hat, a secondhand top hat, with a second-hand ostrich feather round it, for the trade-room at Rocky Mountain House had a queer miscellaneous stock of goods.

CHAPTER FIVE
Race

Within the palisades were two or three cabins from an earlier period, uninhabited, and in one of these, new-caulked in chinks between the logs, with a Franklin stove from the trade-room, Angus took up house with Minota, making the third at that time in the Fort with an Indian woman. He had moved, as it were, another step away from Loch Brendan. This log cabin was not like those at Red River, thatched, but had a roof of split cedar—cedar shakes.

Speedily his Cree talk improved. He discovered that there was not only pidgin-English but pidgin-Cree, and that many white people who imagined that they spoke Cree spoke only that. Minota unfolded for him the tenses of the verbs, and he learnt how pliant were the sentence formations, how full the vocabulary, and that often with one word could be conveyed what necessitated the use of half a dozen English to express. He came to respect les sauvages more and more.

As she taught him her language his mind often went back to Sabbath evenings in Scotland, Sabbath evenings at Red River, and the voice of his father (or of Fraser) would be with him again, reading in the Scriptures. For to the same simple, elemental, eternal things did the Crees go for imagery as the Hebrews. The winter is past, the rain is over and gone, the flowers appear on the earth, the time of the singing birds is come and the voice of the turtle is heard in the land, might have been one of Minota's songs. Like as a hen gathering her chickens under her wings was pure Cree, it struck him. When she taught him the sign language even more did he recall the voice of his father rolling out the Hebraic metaphor in the candlelight at Brendan. If one would signify in the sign language I am happy, so Minota showed him, one made the signs for day and my heart, meaning: The day is in my heart. There seemed to be no giving of orders in the talk of the hands. There was no Do that, no Do not do that. Instead there was I think it good for you to do that, or I think it not good to do that.

The names of the months, the moons, she told him, beginning with the moon before winter; the moon when the leaves fall: the moon when deer rut; the moon when deer shed their horns; the moon that is hard to bear; the moon when the buffalo cow's foetus is large; the moon of sore eyes (because of the sunlit snow then); the moon when the geese lay eggs; the moon of growing grass; the moon when strawberries ripen; the moon when the buffalo bulls are fat; the moon when the buffalo cows are in season; the moon of red plums. She showed him games, gambling games with little pegs, peeled wands: and one that was simply cup-and-ball Indian fashion.

Well though she could speak English she could read neither print nor script, nor did she know the Cree syllabics devised at Norway House by the Methodist missionary there, James Evans, for her people. Pictograph she could have translated, with the symbolic colourings among the figures represented, but not these symbols. The Woods Crees speedily learnt them but the Plains Crees, roving about in bands, buffalo hunters chiefly, had not the same need to leave missives behind as those who split up into small parties and families for their hunting and trapping in the Land of Little Sticks. The day was to come when Angus would regret that he had not taught her to write.

Like most white men he had looked upon savages as signifying something ceaselessly vindictive and treacherous. Red River had corrected that. Like most white men he had looked upon the religion of his people as the only true faith—and discarded that view while living with Minota. Very tenderly he came to think of her as she lost her shyness before him and revealed what lived behind these dark, deer-like eyes, behind that soft-moving and graceful exterior. She reminded him at times, by reason of her innocence, her naïveté, of his mother, and occasionally, with her heresies, of his father. She could not understand, for example, simple though it is to the civilized mind, how the company that sold firearms to the Crees was the same that sold firearms to the Blackfeet, Blackfeet and Cree being hereditary enemies. The shareholders in armament firms that gaily, in our days, manufacture lethal weapons for any who will buy she could not have understood.

There were moments when, in place of feeling that he had condescended, or descended, in this alliance, he felt that he was in the presence of something far superior. She was credulous, pathetically so, he thought often, but that credulity, he realized, was from her honesty and truthfulness. She told him of the Blackrobe that came to the Piegans southward with what was called the seventh day ceremonials.

"And one day," said she, "a Piegan went out to hunt, and the Blackrobe saw him going and called to him that it was the Rest

Day. The Indian laughed at him and—" her eyes were solemn as she continued, "he was killed that day by a grizzly bear. So the Blackrobe stood up before all the people and told them that God had sent the bear to punish that man, and the next time he rang his bell and called that it was the Day of Rest he had a great gathering in his lodge for the ceremonial. Do you think," she ended, "that God would send a grizzly to kill the man for not resting on His Day?"

Angus shook his head slowly, saying nothing.

"After that Blackrobe left them he went through the Flathead country and there he baptized a great many, all under the water in a river. And after he had baptized them they went on a war party against the Crows and got many horses, without any being killed. The Blackfeet heard of it and waited for him to come back and got him to baptize a lot of them, and then they went out horse-stealing into the Gros Ventre country, and it was the most successful raid they had had for many snows."

She looked into his eyes.

"You think there is nothing in it?" she asked, trying to read his thoughts.

He was in a quandary similar to that of parents who have had formal religious upbringing and wonder, grown to years of questioning, whether they should bring their children up to a belief in all the old stories or not. She pressed the point.

"You think there is nothing in it?" she repeated.

"I do not know," he said.

It was clear to her he would not say any more than that. Of her own people's medicine men she had been rendered somewhat skeptical. They demanded much when they came to shake their rattles, beat their drums, blow their whistles and sing over sick people. She thought that many men and women could do more for illness with herbs and certain roots made into plaisters. Not but what she herself knew of a medicine-man who did a wonderful thing. He cut with a flint a crack in the side of an ailing woman, sucked some of the bad blood there, spat it forth, and lo, he had sucked a little frog from her inside.

"Did she recover?" Angus asked.

"Yes, she recovered at once, and her man gave the medicine-man ten ponies, for he was very fond of her."

She told him the medicine-men were paid chiefly with ponies and buffalo robes. But when anyone was dead their powers ended. The good Father Lacombe at Fort Edmonton had power even after men died. That beautiful black horse he rode he had received from a widow for getting the soul of her dead husband out of purgatory.

"All round us is mystery," said Minota.

Angus nodded slowly, listening.

"Yes," he replied.

"We have the same belief," she said.

There came to Rocky Mountain House news of the Sepoy Mutiny. What was it all about? they wondered. The first emotion was, no doubt, that whatever its cause, enemies of Britain, and rebels, must take their punishment. But soon there was sympathy at the Fort with the mutineers when they heard more. Living among a people prone to superstitions and respecting these if for no other reason than that the amenities might continue and Trade go well, the general view was that British arrogance had made a mess among the Sepoys. Angus, after hearing the talk, explained to Minota thus: Much as in the way that the Crees will eat dog, a dish that is abhorrent to the Blackfeet, it was bad medicine to some of the people away off there to touch pig and to others the cow was sacred. A new sort of rifle was issued to these people, the cartridges of which needed to be greased, and they had found out that the grease used was that of pig and cow. They objected, and their objection was unheeded—hence the Indian Mutiny.

"Could they not have let beaver fat, or some other fat, be used?" asked Minota. "That would have put the matter well."

"They would never think of that," replied Angus, deep in him a hatred of tyranny, of the arrogant.

He would talk to her of his early home on Loch Brendan, of how his people had been driven first from fruitful soil to barren soil by the salt-water edge, and then harried even from that. Her eyes had fear in them.

"There are some of my people," said she, "who think that the day will come when we will be treated that way by yours, but I cannot think so. I think there are many more good than bad white people, enough good to keep the bad from doing that to us. I think if they tried to my people would die fighting. Did your people fight?"

"Not where I was. Our medicine-men said we were to go and that if we offered resistance we would sizzle in hell."

"You do not believe in hell fire?"

"I—do—not!" he replied.

The year slipped past. There came the moon when the deer shed their horns, December, and preparations were made for Christmas Day (Big Sunday) with Oregon grape branches in place of holly. The doings of Big Sunday somewhat puzzled the innocence and directness of Angus's woman. According to an old usage of his Highland home he set a lit candle in the window on Christmas eve, and hearing the significance of that—a light for the dead to see—Minota took it much more seriously than he. All night she was hushed, thinking of, as she called them, the shadows seeing that signal—his father, his mother, his brother who had been drowned in the big water. Angus had difficulty in explaining to her that he was not sure if the shadows would really see. She thought they would—and they left it at that.

At the Fort the Nativity was celebrated in the usual way. Braw claes were worn as they had been worn on high-days and days of celebration all across that land, from the Great Lakes and from Hudson's Bay to the Pacific, from the beginnings of the fur trade. A prospector from the mountains (there were many such in the land, much gold having been found the year before far west in the Cariboo Country, by white men who had wandered all that way from California) drank so much rum that he died of alcoholic poisoning next day. Minota was troubled over that.

"Did they get drunk," she asked, "at the last feast before He was nailed up on the cross?"

"I should hardly think so."

"My father once got drunk and spewed in the lodge and was very much ashamed. I think Jesus Christ would not like His friends to get drunk and be sick on their last feast together. It was a cruel way to kill Him," she added. "That is a sad story."

The new year came and the new year slipped along. The moon of the sore eyes was none too bad because of a warm wind (the Chinook) which wiped the snow away. The moon when the geese lay eggs came, geese and ducks honking over, driving their wedges into the north: and Minota sang:

"The ice has broken in the rivers,
The geese and the ducks fly over,
All day—and even at night."

But with the spring she grew restless. Her people were moving out of their winter camps, setting up sweat lodges by the river sides and taking baths both wet and dry, as she explained— that is to say, steaming themselves in the low brush cages (the sweat lodges), with hot stones thrust in to them, and then either cooling outside wrapped in blankets (a dry bath) or plunging into the river afterwards (a wet bath).

The desire to move was agony to Minota. One morning she

asked Angus if he would object if she went on a visit to her people who were going from the woods to the plains soon.

"Why, no," said he.

She was troubled lest he should think she loved them more than she loved him, but after more parley and mutual assurances of devotion, and assurance of understanding from him, she took off her white woman's clothes, attired herself in the deerskin kirtle and leggings, wrapped herself in a blanket, and prepared to go. On the point of departure almost she remained. Her people, said she, would come into the Fort some day, and she could see them then. So it was his part to beg her to go and tell her he knew how she felt. As he spoke she looked long in his eyes, loving and troubled.

After she had gone, Tom Renwick must needs chaff him about his woman.

"Well, your woman has gone back to the blanket!" he said.

Angus felt he had either to take that remark as friendly jest, or to fell him. He wished that Tom's smile had been pleasanter as he spoke, to make the acceptance of his speech as a joke more easy.

"That's it," he answered, "that's it," and lightly laughed as one does when humouring another with whom for this or that reason he has to associate and would bide with amicably, though at heart he would fain see far.

Minota came back within a month, after many sweat-baths, smelling of sweet-grass which she carried in a little sack hanging from a thin raw-hide string round her neck.

In the moon when the strawberries ripen there was a suggestion by Buchanan that they might soon have finished all their work there and have to go to Fort Edmonton; and then arrived at Rocky Mountain House—Sam Douglas. He had been far beyond Edmonton into the mountains by the Howse Pass and Tête Jaune Cache Pass. He had made thorough survey of the foothill country between the ranges and Edmonton, wintering (for his first year) with Macaulay at Jasper House and (for his second) with Colin Fraser at St. Ann's. He was well content. There was coal "almost anywhere," said he. He was going back to the Old Country to "interest capital," and had come to Rocky Mountain House because he had been told there might be those there who could convoy him to Fort Brenton on the Missouri River.

No! Impossible! Attempts had been made to open a transport route that way—and failed. The Blackfeet to the south contested the passage of all. Even in mid-summer when they would be out on the plains none could risk that traverse. Angus could see, at that, that Douglas was perturbed. He evidently had no desire to cross the thousand miles to Fort Garry alone. The Crees were friendly, but there was always the risk of coming on some Blackfoot raiding party in their country. He smoothed a hand over his head, meditating. Angus laughed, surmising Douglas's cogitations.

"Yes," said he, "you have a fine, fair scalp-lock trophy there to deck the lodge of a Blackfoot on the South Saskatchewan!"

"That's just the trouble," said Sam, "that and the loneliness. I am not a man that can live alone. I've been alone enough of late, since last we parted. I was alone in the mountains till I heard voices there. Oh, man, man, I have heard the water-kelpies—and no use to assure me it was but a boulder rumbling down in the spate, or the freshets, as some of them say here, or the rise and fall of a wind that made the creeks cry loud and then hush. No, I canna thole the loneliness."

"When the voices of the dead are heard," explained Minota, "those who have been to the Catholic Mission make this sign," and she showed him. "The Methodist ones just pray without a sign. We pray and make the sign of I pity you to them, like this—or like this, I bless you."

The grace of her motions held Douglas's eye with admiration, and then—

"Aye," said he. "Well, I think I would make all the signs."

She agreed to that suggestion.

"The more signs the better," said she.

"Would you," began Sam, turning again to Angus, "think of accompanying me across the plains? In fact, I was wondering if you would come all the way with me, seeing the boat-building is nearly finished. Since seeing the coal fires here I have been thinking that evidence of a person living here would be of great help. They might look upon me as a mere promoter, ye ken, but if I had one of the men of the land wi' me—"

There came to Angus what, in Minota's absence with her people that spring, had often come to him. He saw, he heard, he smelt the old land. Often, while she had been away, he had looked at the Rockies to west and seen a peak there like Ben Chattan that stands over the head of Loch Brendan. The forests along the slopes he had, by half shutting his eyes, turned into heather and moors. At Douglas's suggestion he saw, in memory, the seaweed fringe of Scotland undulating to the tides that pound in from the Atlantic, in his reverie saw the silver reflection of the weaving gulls in the dark waters of the loch. The wood smoke and coal smoke odours of the Mountain House were changed to the smell of smouldering peat.

"I would pay all expenses," said Douglas. "We could even

arrange something in the manner of a stipend. You have conned your book"—(it was his father's phrase too,)—"and you could be of great service secretarially, too, I have nae doot." He always broadened his speech when he was engaged upon a special pleading.

Angus turned to his woman.

"Minota," said he. "It is as you felt in the spring when you had to go and see your people."

"I know it," she replied.

"If I went, what would you do till I came back?" he asked her.

She did not answer at once and Sam, with a manner as of stealth, clearing his throat, stepped to the door, looked out, the girl's dark eyes gazing after him—reproachfully, it seemed.

"I could arrange for you to have everything here you would want while I was away," said Angus.

She shook her head.

"No. It would be easier with my people. Here—" she hesitated.

Douglas went strolling out, his hands clasped behind his back.

"Some of the white men while you were away," she began, then hesitated again. "I could wear a protection string," she said, "though with my people I think my conduct would be enough; no one would ever learn that I wore one. With the white men—some of them—especially on Big Sunday, or at the new year, well, they would not then respect even a protection string. No, I would go to my people until," she looked at him with doubt in her eyes, he thought, "you come back."

Angus wondered if among her people would be some, like Tom Renwick, who would jest at her that her white man would never return. That look of doubt on her face hurt him. He had an inspiration how to wipe it away. On the impulse he withdrew the collet-ring of his forebears and, taking her hand in his, put it on her third finger. He had compromised between a Blackrobe ceremony and the less ritualistic Indian ceremony of marriage—which was none at all, unless the delivery of a string of horses at the father's door be called ceremony. He had only had the union entered in the Company's books. If she had desired more, now did he abruptly atone.

She was surely his by the light in her eyes then. Had he never before realized how deep was her devotion—her fealty—he knew it at that moment.

"I will wait for you." she said, "till you come back from the country of your people. I will wait for you—with my people."

CHAPTER SIX
Kildonan Bell

So there he was, a mere satellite for the time being, it seemed, of Sam Douglas, that young man of far-seeing plans, aware of little but the misery of farewells and that it was too late to change his mind.

The horses (it had pleased Sam to hear, while Angus was busy on the packing, that they could be sold at Red River with profit) stepped out briskly. Soon, as the ocean encompasses a ship, land dropping astern, the rolling country received them and that Backbone of the World, the Rockies, was dwindling down the sky to west. Their route was to be southeast, toward the great plain across which, picking up the loom of the Eagle Hills like a guiding pharos, they would pass on by the elbow of Battle River to the old Fort Garry-Fort Edmonton cart-trail.

Like Lot's wife was Angus that first day out, constantly slewing in the saddle, hand on his horse's haunch, to watch the sinking of the mountains. These undulating belts, the colour of smoke, along the foothills he had ridden through. He knew them for what they were. Always in this land there was an impression, whether on flat prairie, rolling foothills, or among the mountains, of immensity. It was not due merely to the scope of the immediate view, for in the forests were often narrow gulches in which one could only see, between tree trunks, trees on the further slope set precipitately and densely. Nor was it the result of studying maps of the continent. The prairie wind whispered of space and space again beyond where the blue crystal cupola rested lightly on the horizon; and in the ranges there was the consciousness, in every dell where a creek shouted under debris of fallen trees and moss hung in tassels on the branches of living ones, that there were a million such dells, scented so of cedar or of balsam, on and on, terrain of the deer, the bear, the beaver.

Angus recalled, when they came to the headwaters of Red Deer River, queer legends that Minota had to tell. Away down there near where Red Deer River flows into the South Saskatchewan, she had said, there were strange stone animals of enormous size, huge lizards of rock that were sometimes partially exposed after a gale that sifted the sand from them, or a cut-bank crumbled. Odd the inventions of les sauvages, he had thought—and would remember those stories of hers on a day to come, hearing of the discoveries of geologists there. At the time, memory of her talks about those queer creatures merely added, to the sense of spaciousness, that of mystery, as they rode on, drawing near to the swerve of land called High Butte.

They had been advised at the Mountain House to swing to the north of the butte, coasting round its base, but Angus sent the pack-horse up athwart its southern slope, looking back as he followed them to see the Rockies bobbing upward again. Near the summit in the thin whistle of the wind he halted for some moments.

Sam Douglas, no doubt, realized the cause of his companion's meditative silence there.

"It's no place for a woman," Douglas suddenly declared. It was a statement beyond question by his tone.

Angus was about to reply. "You mean a white woman?" but that would have been foolish. Obviously that was what was meant by Douglas, who then plunged into a rambling dissertation on the life of the forts where he had been, and of the settlements in their neighbourhood. There was no law, or if there were law there was no one to enforce it. Up at Edmonton murderers had been pointed out to him, murderers free and unconcerned said he. There was a Cree there, for example, who had slain two Sarcees that had been visiting his family. They had fallen in love with his daughter—"Or his sister, was it?" rumbled Sam. "Anyhow, the fellow's name was Tahakooch, and when these Sarcees prepared to leave he went out on the trail with them, dropped behind, shot them both, and came back to brag of it, swagger of it before whites as well as before Indians."

Then there was a raid he had heard of in which a band of one tribe of Indians had killed one entire band of another, men, women, and children, except one or two young women whom they had carried off. And the prospectors who were washing for gold dust on the Saskatchewan headwaters, and even over by the Peace River, when they came in—"Well, some of them," said he, and paused. "I like a dram whiles. I can tak' a dram. But drinking! Hech, sirs! I've seen drinking now. No, no place for a woman—" he paused again, "yet," he added, "but twenty years to come—you mark my words."

"Uh-hu," said Angus, and turned his back on the scene for which he had deflected the horses upward there. With lowered heads the string went dropping down the eastern slope of High Butte.

They passed on into that sea of grass in which for days on end, in a phrase of the plainsmen, they were out of sight of land, no lone butte even raising far off a purple knob in the immensity. Angus had a mental image: a great hand was dropped in water and made a wide gesture in air, flicking down the drops of Fort Ellice, Fort Pelly, Touchwood Hills Post, Fort Carlton, Fort Pitt, Fort Edmonton, with three sprayed residual drops at the end, of St. Ann's, Jasper, and the Mountain House—in a sweep across a thousand miles.

There were days when they saw—as far as eye could reach—humped dots moving slowly by the hundred all in the one direction, and they even rode through these herds of buffalo without creating a stampede. There were days when they travelled, with a flirt-flirt and frou-frou of saddle leather, between western sky and eastern sky and at night looked not only up but forth at the stars as do sailors at sea. Once or twice they came upon parties of the buffalo-runners from Red River and Qu'Appelle, Scots and French half-breeds. Once or twice they came to camps of Cree Indians upon their summer hunt, the tents all set up like white candle extinguishers in the long wrinkle of some coulee, the horses grazing round about—bays and buckskins (with or without the prized black streak down the spine), blue horses (the kind called smokies), pintos (skewbald and piebald), horses glossy black and horses silver gray. Or they met bands on trek, travelling villages jogging along with trailing travois raising the dust. These encounters were the chief interest of the traverse for Angus.

For Sam Douglas the most interesting episode had to do not with any met or overtaken on the way, but with a cloud. No bigger than a man's hand it seemed at first, sailing serene, how near or how far hard to compute, ahead of them one blazing day.

"An odd cloud that," he remarked, "different from the others."

A long gaggle of geese served to show that it was far off for these distant pin-points in none of their divagations disappeared into that cloud. What they were about it was difficult to conjecture. They appeared to be but exercising their wings above that segment of the world. Now they showed as an immense arrow, moving definitely to north, then suddenly they changed to a mere thread wavering irresponsibly in the ether. They were not travelling anywhere, had either risen in alarm or but for the pleasure of flight. The thread undulated in another direction, was again arrow-shaped; and always, beyond, was that cloud, the hue of which differed from that of others adrift and, by reason of the difference, seemed ominous.

41

It dipped to the prairie's edge and there it broke in a glittering descent, a thousand flashing points of light. They talked about it in their camp that night; and in their camp next day they talked again of it, having come to an area of the plain where the grass was beaten into the earth. Arrived at Fort Ellice, chatting of their experiences with the factor, Mackay, and Chantelaine of Fort Pitt (who was there for a night on his way back after a visit to Fort Garry), Douglas spoke of that region of bruised and beaten land.

"That was hail," said Mackay.

"There must have been a midsummer hail-cloud emptying itself there," said Chantelaine.

Douglas turned to Angus.

"That was yon cloud!" said he solemnly.

He had many questions to ask regarding these hailstorms on blazing August days.

"I have heard of the stones," said Chantelaine, "as big as marbles, even as big as bantams' eggs."

"It would hurt to get a crack on the head with one!" observed Douglas. "Do they happen often?"

Not often, he was told, and both men were of opinion that only certain districts were thus afflicted.

"Lots of people in the country for years have never seen one," said Chantelaine.

"Well, that's good hearing," declared Sam. "I suppose the buffaloes' shaggy foreparts protect them if they don't know the weather signs and clear away. But their hindquarters are not so well covered. I should think ordinary cattle—"

"They don't last long," said Mackay. "It is just a cloudburst of hail and over."

"But look what one storm can do in the time! Suppose hail came down like that in a wheat-field—"

"There are no wheat-fields here," said Chantelaine.

The subject was in Sam's mind next day as they rode on by Snake Creek toward Bird Tail Creek.

"Hail insurance," he suddenly boomed.

"What's that?" asked Angus. "What are you talking about?"

"I was just thinking that some day all these plains will be what they call smiling farms! Look at how the land has been manured through ages by the buffalo. Look at the grand, growing soil, man. It's too good for cattle, I'm thinking, a grand country like this. And when that day comes an insurance against damage to crops by hail—the way they have marine insurance and life insurance—would be a good thing. No doubt lots of people would say they would take the risk without paying insurance. These men back there said the midsummer storms are localized and don't happen often. But a fright or two, here and there, for one or another of the smiling farmers, would make them listen to a man of a persuasive turn. Aye, that's far ahead, however, but to be taken a brief of in the notebook so to speak."

"You are jumping ahead again," remarked Angus.

"Yes, a jump or two—as always. But those days are not so far off as some might imagine. I'm going to tell you something between ourselves. Last year there was a man—by the name of Hector—a civil engineer—away back there in the mountains looking for a way through for a railway. And the winter before there was another man, Palliser by name, who spent the whole winter (and he must have his courage) with the Blackfeet Indians, so that they could become friends and he could move about through their country at his ease—and he was on the same job. All last year he was at it, looking for a route for a railway."

"We heard rumours to that effect at the Mountain House," Angus began, "but—"

"But! Oh, yes, there will be but upon but for awhile, I have no doubt, but it's coming. You and me, Angus, if we live, are going to see changes in these parts."

Leaving Ellice, they went by the valley of the Assiniboine which flows into the Red River at Fort Garry, and so anon came to that small settlement to which, two years before, Daniel Munro, Kate and Angus had driven in the spring, the mud dragged up by the wheels and plip-plopping behind as the horses squelched on the way—passed near the settlement (the hoofs of their horses leaving a pennant of dust that day), coasted the slough where the unexpected gulls had been too much for Mrs. Munro. On the traverse they had, as was easy enough, lost track of a day, neither of them sure as they rode down the Assiniboine valley whether here was Saturday or Sunday. When houses began to show ahead, rectangular scrabblings on the low skyline, the sound of a kirk bell came to them on a light wind out of the east.

"So it is the Sabbath Day," said Douglas. "I wish I had taken a bet on't!"

Together they rode to the Fort to discover when the International was to go up the river. Hearing that she was not expected down for two days, Douglas remained there with the officer in charge (to whom had been one of his letters of introduction), while Angus started out upon the road for the Frasers'.

It was growing dark by Red River, scents and sounds stronger than the visible, but along the road day lingered as though the dust held it. Lights were beginning to show in windows and stars in the sky when he came to the old place. He had the impression as of having been dreaming, lying out under a tree somewhere, or in a haystack—a strange dream of broad prairies, of boat-building by a distant river, of the singing of an Indian girl in a cabin there—as a voice came out to him, Ian in the porch tapping the beat with a stick:

"A vine from Egypt thou hast brought,
Thy free love made it thine;
And drov'st out nations, proud and haut,
To plant this lovely vine.
"Thou didst prepare for it a place,
And root it deep and fast,
Then it began to grow apace,
And filled the land at last.
"With her green shade that cover'd all,
The hills were—"

The singing and the tapping ceased as Mr. Fraser rose to meet the tall shadowy form that advanced. A light from within shone on Angus's face.

"Well, well, it's Angus Munro! Come and see who's here!"

There they all were again, Mrs. Fraser unchanged in the pleasure of the meeting gathering him to her and kissing him as though he were a son.

"How you young folks do grow!" exclaimed Angus, but twenty himself. "Fiona, Fiona! If you go on like this they'll have to train you to a bean-pole! Let me see, how old are you now?"

"Nine."

"Not too old for me to kiss?"

She leapt to him in her lithe, quick way, kissed him, then linked her hands over one of his shoulders while Flora embraced him and hung, and swung, to the other side.

They passed indoors to the remembered twinkle of the homemade candles shining on the plates in their racks. At that Hector came in.

"Here's Hector," said Mr. Fraser. "He's the foreman now! That's what his mother calls him, whatever."

"Oh, yes, they are shooting up. Let me see, it is just two years since you've been gone."

"Just two years," replied Angus as they sat down—and marvelled at how much had been in his life in that time, back here at this little settlement that looked out on the curve of western sky

44

and the plains as the shore-side villages look out to sea. He had been to the end of it and was back again.

His eyes rested on Fiona, blindly it seemed, as the thought came to him how far away was Rocky Mountain House. Where, he wondered, was Minota then, as the dusk which had deepened to night here at Red River ran beyond Assiniboia, Saskatchewan—and on.

"You must have a lot to tell us of where you've been and what brings you back," said Mrs. Fraser.

One thing, he considered, he could not tell. There were unions of white with red folk round them there to be sure. Even the tallow of the candles lighting this scene came to them from the half-breed buffalo hunters. And yet—he imagined himself talking about Minota: a shadow would come in Mrs. Fraser's eyes and she would turn to her husband while he, to hide his stare of regret or unbelief, would look at the floor. There would be a silence broken only by Ian's unconscious whistling, or hissing between his teeth, of some ballad or psalm tune, in a way he had when pondering something sad, calamitous, beyond mending.

Next day Angus took an opportunity to slip away alone to the kirkyard of Kildonan to see the stone that (as he had arranged before going west) had been set up for his father and mother—a melancholy occasion. Standing there he felt again a deep loneliness—and thought of Minota. Voices had a way of haunting him, and hers was with him then, singing one of her short repetitive chants, about the grass sprouting, the geese and the ducks flying over—all day and even at night. There rose in him—there rose in him—a wish that he had for wife one of his own race. Little more than a month ago he had left her, loving her, yet here came this thought surging up and angering him with its shabby disloyalty.

"It seems he has something on his mind," Mrs. Fraser said to her husband that night.

"He went out this afternoon to the kirk where his father and mother lie," answered Ian.

"Oh, that's it, is it?" said she.

CHAPTER SEVEN
In the Haar

Had anyone told Angus Munro during that last winter at Rocky Mountain House that in the next year he would be hearing the carts rattle in the streets of Edinburgh, and seeing the room of a Lothian Street lodging hazed with a penetrating night mist, he would have known that the runes were being read awry!

First he had been in Glasgow, where Sam Douglas had interviewed many wealthy bodies, bailies and merchants, toward financing his confident coal-mining project, and at most of these meetings Angus was present.

"We have been bitten already by that country," said one shrewd Glaswegian, shaking his head, and began to talk of a transport company that was to take emigrants into the Cariboo gold-fields—a hollow fraud, he called it. "I came near to having the ignominy of being upon the board of that company," he went on, "but did not like the look of it. It had its map of the western continent, with a line showing the route from Ottawa to Minnesota and the Selkirk Settlements—Red River—and on across these prairies o' yours to the Rocky Mountains, and through them to some river flowing west."

He opened a drawer and searched in it.

"I thought I had their map," he said, "but I must have destroyed it in disgust. Their stage-coaches, they proclaimed, ran from the Red River to the mountains, and beyond that they had boats. What was the end of it? Suits against the company by folks who had found there was not a conveyance for them beyond Selkirk. I've just heard an extraordinary story about one party that they bamboozled and that didn't come back to take them to law." (Sam seemed to be all attention). "At their own expense they went on across the plains, through the mountains, and there had their own boat—made it, mark you—and they had to do what's called portaging: you'll both ken what that is, acquaint with that speculative country. At one place between close banks they decided that two might venture down with the boat lightened, instead of dragging it over land, and the others portage. Well, these got to the end of their carry and there was the boat, smashed to bits. One of the two men that had dared to run down was clinging to a rock, and him they rescued. The other was lost. When they came to look through his things for his relatives' address they found that he had his log-book entered up in full, aye to the very end. The last entry was, Arrived at the cañon—and was drowned."

The bailie's contempt for the humbugging company was forgotten as he talked by reason of his interest in that strange story.

Sam Douglas was but half listening, despite his rapt air. Stage-coaches! Why not? Why not stage-coaches across the great plains? The Sam Douglas Transport Company; or The Great Northwest Express Company: he tried over to himself various names as he sat there and the bailie talked himself down a side-turning to the end.

"Ah, weel," said Douglas, "let us get back to the coal-developing project. There is nothing fraudulent in that."

"I'm not saying there is," the other retorted, "but there is plenty of time before we invest in it."

"I'm no' so sure," said Sam. "I think you'll be coming to me sooner than you have the faintest thought, and wheedling me to get you in on't. However, however, I'm no' here to plead. I'm here to give you a chance to be in on a good thing. We'll no' tak' up your time, seeing how you feel."

There were many incidents of that sort, weeks slipping by, and no one jumping at the chance that Sam brought them. At the end of three months Angus considered how many of Douglas's letters to likely investors he had copied, and examination of the file he kept was depressing. Here was many a cast and never a bite.

They had been back close on half a year when Sam went on a visit to some relatives (like Angus, he had no near kin), and Angus thought to take passage on The Clansman while he was gone and revisit Loch Brendan, but, instead, stayed in their lodgings writing to the Frasers, to all his friends at Mountain House, and to Minota—her letter addressed care of the factor, who would read it to her.

Sam came back from his rest with renewed eagerness and his notebook full of names of "likely folk" in the capital. But after another few months in Edinburgh, where Douglas had no better luck, Angus began to feel as though imposing upon his good friend's hopes. Yet, not himself unhopeful, remembering the coal fires at the Mountain House, his faith revived on hearing that several of those whom Sam sought to interest in his plans had also heard that a railway route was being sought for out there. "Oh, yes, we admit that!" they would say.

There is no place like Edinburgh for book-shops, and when left to himself Angus spent much time in them, or turning over the volumes in the dips at their doors, needing no recollection of his father's advice to con his book. He had learnt the love of reading. A whole year fled thus, with an astounding celerity, Douglas and he back in Glasgow again with two offers of splendid chances for those seeking sound investment. One of these was for immediate not a postulated early reaping: The Great Northwest Express Company—to be going on with.

"These bodies have nae ambition beyond keeping their money in the bank," said Sam at last. "It's a wonder they trust it there and don't keep it in an auld sock under the bed! We'll try the Sassenach. I have some introductions."

So to London they went together, and there the result of all the appointments and conferences seemed depressing to Angus but to Sam were eminently satisfactory.

"We have them interested," he said "We have them interested. They have not bitten at once—but they will bite, and with a snap, just when something happens to convince them. Oh, man, if these railway engineers could only submit reports of a route we'd have them. They are taking an unco while out there. I believe they are fishing when they should be surveying!"

The words were jocular but something in the tone made Angus think that Sam was dissatisfied and so thinking he felt again that he was living on another's dream. He began not to like his position.

Here they were well into the second year of this hopeless hopefulness. They returned to Edinburgh and Sam, sprucing himself even more than usual, went off for the day on private business.

All that week Angus could not get from his mind a wish that he could hear from Minota, or from Captain Buchanan. Feeling the lack of news from her it occurred to him that he had been home a year and a half and had not written to Jessie Grant. After his mother died he had written to her and had received a letter of condolence couched in very friendly—old friendly—terms. After his father's death he had written again, thinking guiltily that it was only the sad events that drove him to letter-writing. Her reply to that did not come for a long while, for it had to be sent on to the Mountain House from Red River. In it she told him of her mother's death, writing from a new address. Her uncle—Cameron, the blacksmith—had moved from Glasgow to take over a better business at Lasswade, near Edinburgh. That had arrived after his union with Minota, and answering it, sending his condolences, he had found himself (he had to admit it) writing as one penning a duty. He felt far from Jessie and that not only in space. Your old friend he had inscribed himself. He should go and see her, seek out the house at Lasswade.

He wished Sam would come back. He felt downcast. He had a feeling that something grievous was about to befall. Nonsense! It was the haar (that fog off the North Sea) creeping up over the city, creeping even into rooms, that depressed him. And then Sam returned.

"There's a letter for you," said he, heeling off a boot by the side of their lodging fire. "I was at the bank today."

48

On leaving Rocky Mountain House it had been arranged that letters to Angus should be forwarded in care of Sam's bankers, and in his letters to his friends he had asked that the old direction should be used—never knowing where they might be.

He opened the envelope, and—"You will be heartbroken to hear, as I am grieved to communicate to you—"

These were the first words his gaze alighted on. His eyes puckered to the sheet as he read, his face ashen gray, for that letter told him that his Minota had, as she had intended, gone back to her people the day he left, and that everyone of the band was dead of the measles.

"It is, as you may know, a new malady to the race and they have no resistance to it in their blood."

Sam, putting on his slippers, remained humped forward, staring at his friend. Something was wrong. Angus sat back, then rose and walked across the room as if for help, wheeled, marched back again, stood stock still and re-read the letter.

"There is ill news," said Sam, more than perturbed.

Angus opened his mouth to speak and could not. He was stricken dumb temporarily because on each attempt to speak tears instead of words were about to come. He would not weep and could not speak. He sat down again, just nodding his head to Sam.

CHAPTER EIGHT
Ettrick Brothers

Angus was twenty-two and had had the feeling, for long, of a sort that many men do not experience till gray hairs come—a feeling of having lived his life. At times, in fact, it was as though he had known more than one life: an early one by the shores of Loch Brendan, then, to the wailing notes, the slow surge of a coronach, an end of that; another on the Red River and an end to it with a voice halting him on a blurred road, intermittently intoning, Relief: another in a west that had, remembered in Lothian Street, the quality of dream lived between the freedom, the spaciousness of an ocean of grass and the grandeur of the ranges, a life he had ridden away from of his own accord, though doubtfully and with many a backward look.

Again, recovered from the shock of the news of Minota's death (though haunted by the thought that nowhere yonder by the

Saskatchewan she moved any longer), he began to think of his position with Sam Douglas and to feel himself as—well, in an excessive fashion he called himself sponger, though had he called himself so to Sam there would have been ructions. Neither to the Great Northwest Coal Company, nor to the Great Northwest Express Company did any investors attach immediate importance. There were no more appointments with nibblers. There were, eventually, no more letters to copy. It seemed the end had come; and one day when Sam went off again on private business, Angus trudged into the country to think upon his position, for easier could he deliberate under the sky than under a ceiling.

At Morningside the sight, suddenly, of the range of the Pentlands recalled to his mind the westward view from the Mountain House, immense though the difference. He was sick for the upper waters of Saskatchewan, the upper ripplings of Red Deer River. He tramped on, meditating, and when the pee-wees were calling by Fairmilehead he came to a decision to begin—here, in Edinburgh—a new life. Home again in Lothian Street he awaited Sam's return and came to the matter straightway, the more minded to do so because, for once, there was a look of depression on the older man's face.

"I've been thinking, Sam," said Angus.

"You have been thinking," said Sam, taking off his boots by the fireside.

"Yes. I can't live off you any—"

"Bide a wee! Bide a wee!" Sam cried out, and raised a hand, holding a slipper, which he waved. "We'll pull in our belts and try again."

"No. I've been thinking and I have decided to make a fresh start. I'd like to go into the bookselling business."

"The bookselling business! You that has—"

"I've done with the wandering life."

"Oh, you have! Well, yes, I see. I suppose—" Sam bent to put on his slippers and said no more.

"Yes," Angus exploded.

"My own plans are awful unsettled," Sam confessed, "and if you are really decided on that—"

"I am."

"Well, I can give you an introduction to the Ettricks. Nothing like having wires to pull, nothing like having introductions. My folks knew old Ettrick. He was better than the sons." He stretched back in his chair. "To be quite candid, I don't know what my own future will be. Ye ken, Angus—or I don't know if I ever did mention it—I'm orphaned like yourself. I have nae

50

recollection of my mother and the dimmest of my father, and sisters and brothers have I none. Whiles when I get a whiff of a certain brand of tobacco I kind of see the old man less dim. I presume he smoked it. Aye, aye. It was my guardian I went to see the day. He was against me travelling, but when I turned twenty-one I took the gate. He said to me, says he, the day, when I went to see him, A rolling stone gathers no moss. Folk that spit proverbs at ye give me a scunner. 'No, sir,' says I, 'but it can get a certain amount of polish,' and says I, 'Bide a wee and yell see the moss.' He gave me a lecture on living on capital and hope in a fool's paradise, and finished up wi' a Latin tag, too—rusticus expectat dum defluat amnis, 'if ye ken,' says he, 'what I mean.' Says I, 'Fine I ken, but I prefer Nil desperandum!' Aye. The man is nevertheless right that I am not, for the moment, forging ahead, or making hay while the sun shines, or such like. Yes, I'll call and see the Ettricks. No, I'll write to them to make an appointment with you. The firm used to be Ettrick and Bruce; old Ettrick retired, Bruce died, and the Ettrick sons, growing up, made it difficult for the son of Bruce, and finally annoyed him out of the business. I'll no' say they are estimable, but they have a grand business. And, frankly, in life I have found it does not matter whether folks are estimable or not so long as we get from them what we want. Nor does it matter what names they cry us. Oh, well, perhaps I speak too plainly at times. Fine fellows, fine fellows—in their own way, no doubt. You'll get on with the Ettrick brothers."

So a day or two later Angus coasted the castle rock's base and mounted to the Ettrick Brothers' bookshop where William, the elder, received him—no, not graciously, fawningly. Angus was dubious of him at first sight: a man of middle stature with tow-coloured hair, wearing spectacles through which he either stared with eyes wide open or behind which, closing them, he revealed white lids to obscure the evidence of his emotions from those to whom he talked. When Ettrick cast back his head, displaying the white lids in a pose that gave his nose a porcine cast, Munro had the impulse to explain that since his friend Mr. Douglas wrote his own plans had been changed. Perhaps, it would have been better had he followed that impulse instead of telling himself that he should not judge a man at first sight. What Ettrick had to say, with all these accompanying facial changes, did of itself, as the interview progressed, cause him to wonder if here was his place.

"Do be seated, sir," William Ettrick turned and bellowed to one of his staff: "You, bring a chair for this gentleman. And what can I do for you? You are a friend of Sir Lovat Douglas's son," which, by the way, was the first Angus had heard of a title for Sam's father.

"I came back from the west with Mr. Douglas and I have been thinking that I would greatly like to go into the bookselling business here."

"Quite, quite," and the eyelids drooped. "You are considering partnership?" The eyelids rose a little and William Ettrick peeped sidelong at the young man.

"No, not just that," Angus replied.

Ettrick started, drew erect. Some thought passed in his mind that set a sleek smile on his face.

"You might find the money later, perhaps?" he suggested.

"I doubt it. I really want to get work in a bookshop."

"Ow!" said William Ettrick. "Ow!" and he blinked rapidly. "I must have misunderstood Mr. Douglas's letter. By the way it was couched I had the impression you—well," he interrupted himself, and the fawning manner that had been decreasing slipped clean off him. "As a matter of fact, we could do with another assistant."

He glanced at Angus, annoyed that he should, by reason of the wording of Sam's letter, be sitting instead of standing.

"You want a stipend?" he asked.

Angus stared.

"You see, as a rule," explained Ettrick, "beginners learning the business consider themselves lucky to be with us without the boot being on the other foot and them paying for the tuition. I'm afraid I could not offer much to start with. You see, it's reading books that gives you the idea to go in for the business, according to Mr. Douglas. You have no knowledge of the commercial?"

"None."

"Are you living with relatives in the city?" William asked, dropping his eyelids again and peeping from under them.

"I don't understand," replied Angus.

"It's plain enough, surely," said Ettrick. "If you are living with relatives you would not need as much wages as if you were living alone."

"Oh! No, at present I am staying with Mr. Douglas. He is not a relative."

"Not a relative. Quite. Well, I'm busy now. I have given you a lot of time. I'll talk it over with my brother and we'll write you."

He raised his head, closed his eyes, and Angus realized that he was expected to go.

"Thank you," he said. "Good day."

There was no answer.

Within the week there he was on next to nothing of a salary

with a promise of an increase after a year's trial, if all went well—
"which would be fair to both parties," said Mr. William Ettrick.
And hardly was he installed when Sam Douglas announced that he
was off to the west again, this time on behalf of a group of business
men, at their suggestion, to inquire into the possibility of large
scale hydraulic workings of the gold-fields in the Cariboo, such as
were being undertaken in California at the locations of the old
"Forty-niners."

"They had no fancy for either of my plans—neither the one I
came to them with nor the other that I evolved when I was
listening to yon loquacious body, you mind. But me being here
they have looked upon as a lucky chance for one of their own
notions."

"When do you go?"

"At once."

"So soon?"

"Yes, it's all fixed up. I go round the Horn this time to New
Westminster at the mouth of the Fraser River. Well, I do at least
see the world, which is not exactly the main matter, but it's fine."

So next day Angus was alone.

It was not permissible for the staff at Ettricks' to take home
even second-hand books to read, but all did; and so, though
merely to be in the service of such men gave an effect as of
ignominy, they being what they were, that misery could be looked
upon as a secondary matter by an avid reader. Besides, there were
customers who atoned.

"We have personages come into our shoap," Angus one day
heard William tell another assistant, "and I would be glad if you
would have a more deferential manner. I notice you have a
tendency to be kind of jack-easy whiles with the customers."

One of these personages, to whom Angus took a great liking,
was John Hill Burton, the historian. For some reason Hill Burton
soon selected Munro always to attend to his wants and would often
talk long with him over some book he had bought, leaning back
against the shelves, the young man at attention before him because
of Ettrick's eyes prying and peeping to be sure he was being
deferential. No sooner had Hill Burton gone, one day, than there
was a bark from William.

"Munro!"

"Yes, sir?" and Angus quick-stepped to the table at which
the senior partner sat towards the rear of the shop.

Ettrick opened his eyes wide, showing the whites all round
the pupils (no other way could he look directly at anyone), then
dropped his lids and elevated his chin.

"You are here to serve customers, not to collogue with them," he remarked.

There being no envy in Angus he did not suspect that here was, perhaps, at least partly, foolish jealousy at work. Ettrick's fawning advances Hill Burton had so often cut short that at last William, on his entrance, pretended complete engrossment over papers on his desk.

"I—beg—your—pardon?" said Angus.

"Well may you," replied Ettrick, addressing his pewter inkwell. "I saw you cracking with Dr. Hill Burton—a distinguished personage. You may drive folk from the shoap."

"He wanted to talk. I could not tell him not to."

"He wanted to talk? How could a man with his brains want to talk wi' the likes of you? You have, too, I notice, somewhat of a Hieland manner as though it's less in your line to handle quartos, let alone duodecimos, than to use a hoe."

"Or a claymore," suggested Angus.

"Eh?" snapped Ettrick, and looked up, his eyes blazing, but on meeting Angus's gaze he shut close his lids and so, head back, spoke to the air. "Remember you are a servant here and not the equal of the customers. What were you talking about to Dr. Hill Burton?"

"He was asking me about the Indians of the West. He had been reading in a book of De Quincey's—whom he knew, he told me, when De Quincey was still alive and living in Edinburgh—"

"Well, he'd have to be still alive for him to know him! There's intelligence for you—and you go cracking wi' the customers. Well?"

Angus cleared his throat.

"In this book," he said, speaking slowly, "De Quincey had mentioned a volume by a Mr. Weld on life in Canada, and there was a sentence he had quoted: The sweet laughter of Indian women. Mr. Burton—"

"Hill Burton, Dr. Hill Burton."

"—remarked," went on Angus, "that he had often heard that the North American Indian seldom laughs and wanted me to tell him if that was so."

"Which means," said Ettrick, looking unnecessarily shrewd and sly, as though proud of his simple acumen, "that you have already in your cracks with him mentioned you were out there."

"Yes."

"Be careful. You may collogue too much and drive customers away. That's all."

"Thank you," said Angus in indignation as he turned away.

54

William opened his eyes and stared at that retreating back more directly than ever could he look in anybody's face, pondering the tone of that Thank you and wondering if his assistant was being impudent.

Angus was only receiving what all received. It was part of the Ettrick policy to seek occasion for fault-finding. William kept a little black book with alphabetical index in which he entered against the names of the members of his staff all sins committed by them, however venial. Let any dare to approach him with a request for a promised increase of salary and out would come the Black Book. That was its main object. He did not (unless customers were in the shop) modulate his voice when playing the Angel Gabriel behind his table, ominous Black Book in hand. That very day Angus and the rest saw one of the assistants arrange his tie, take a resolve, and advance to the desk. His voice was slow and meek, as was fitting in a serf, but clearly, bitingly, after a pause and the opening of the drawer in which the Wee Black Book lurked, they heard William reply.

"I wonder at your impudence!" he exclaimed. "I see here that to begin the year you arrived—I said nothing of it at the time, let you off considering the season—with a bloated look on your face. You had been drinking. Can you deny it?"

"Well, sir, in my own time, you see—"

"Your own time? What do you mean by your own time? Can you conduct yourself in your own time so that in my time—I don't suppose you'll dispute that when you are in the shoap you are in my time—you look like a boiled lobster before the customers! You are a married man, are you not?"

"Yes, sir."

"Huh! And I see here that you failed to attend a customer who came in till he had to come to you and interrupt your reading in a book, in my time, I hope you will admit. Oh, no, no, ridiculous. My advice to you is to be careful. Instead of getting a rise you might be out in the street without a character. You understand me?"

"Yes, sir."

"Good. The best I can say is that I'll watch your conduct and you can come to me in a matter of six months. We'll see then."

"Thank you, sir."

No; here was no place for Angus.

Back in his lodgings he felt he needed a cleansing from the Ettrick establishment. He could not get it out of his mind: William at his table rising to salaam to important patrons with a depth of bow graduated according to their positions as personages—and not even seeing his staff when chancing to meet any of them on the street; and the younger brother, Robert, showing his tow-head behind a tall desk, where he kept the ledgers, bent over them, peeping under his brows at the assistants. Sometimes he would turn his back, stare out of the window, looking this way and that as though interested in the weather. Angus, seeing him at that, had thought he must play gowff and was hoping for a dry course; but soon he was informed by the others that when Robert behaved so he was but watching them in the window, using it as a mirror—as, indeed, he might easily, a neighbouring house-wall being only a few feet away there, helping to turn the pane to looking-glass. He was slighter than William, with a high, narrow forehead that, when he frowned to and fro in the shop, as at times he did, showed a ladder of creases, often as revolting as the white lids of his brother. Angus did not like the Ettricks.

Well, he would forget the Ettricks in a book. He had taken home with him that day—it was a Saturday—a volume of De Quincey, jogged to it by that talk with Hill Burton. And the book in turn jogged him to a Sunday's visit, the historian having told him that the "English opium-eater" had lived, while in Edinburgh, in Lothian Street and, not only that, but that De Quincey stayed for a time in a cottage at Lasswade.

Lasswade: that was where the Camerons lived. He would make his Sunday outing to Lasswade, find that cottage, and see Jessie Grant again. And damn the Ettrick Brothers and their Wee Black Book!

CHAPTER NINE
At Lasswade

Tramping into Lasswade on the Sunday afternoon, Angus halted a man upon the road to ask if he knew the De Quincey cottage, thinking to see it first and then seek out the Camerons and Jessie.

"I'm a stranger here," said that one; and the next one he accosted with his inquiry replied: "De Quincey? No, there is no man with a foreign-like name living in a house—"

"This man is dead. About four years ago he died, I believe. I wanted to see the cottage where he stayed."

"Dead! Oh, I dinna ken the name. I've only been here twa-three years masel'. Never heard of him." But Cameron he knew. "Och, aye, farrier Cameron he likes to be called. Ye see the harled wa' along the street, with the twa big doors?"

"Yes."

"That's the smiddy, and it's just by that—the first hoose set back a bit. Ye'll see it as soon as ye get by the smiddy."

Getting by the smiddy, there was the house. Coming from it were blasts of some musical instrument in an odd fashion, with notes sustained too long and then hurried ones as in atonement. In the garden was Jessie Grant.

She was standing on the red-brick path that led to the front door, looking at the flowers, looking first at the blue stonecrop border to one side and then at the yellow on the other, and did not so much as glance round at the sound of steps in the street. When he halted she turned. Their eyes met and—

"Angus!" she cried out, running to greet him as he opened the gate.

What turned the preliminaries from an embrace into a hand-shaking there was no telling, whether the sudden cessation of the blasts within, suggesting that someone might look out of the window, or the possibility of Sunday peepers behind blinds in the cottages across the way—or some other restraint, hesitancy, as they found themselves face to face again.

"I knew you the moment I saw you," she said, "but you have broadened and filled out. Come in, come in."

She led him into a little parlour that was for Sunday and special use. There was her aunt, Mrs. Cameron, rising from a harmonium, hurriedly removing an apron which she had on over her best frock. Yes, yes, she had often heard of him, and here was a real pleasure to meet him.

The smith was called in from the kitchen—or it may have been from the rear garden—an enormous, deep-chested, huge-fisted man, tusked with the military moustaches of that period and mossy with half-whiskers. He crushed Angus's hand in his and seemed satisfied with the crush in response, appraising the young man's build sternly, tucking his chin back and with two flips sweeping his tusks as from moustaches into moustache—one horizontal swirl of thick fur over his mouth.

"Be seated, be seated!"

All sat down in the parlour with the harmonium, Cameron obviously not at home there, diffidently balanced on the mere edge of a chair. By an exchange of glances between him and his wife it appeared that they had the impression that these two young people had been sweethearts in their immature nonage, Mrs. Cameron looking sentimental and Cameron roguish.

"And what are you doing here, Angus?" asked Jessie.

"I'm working—you'll be astonished to hear—in a bookshop in Edinburgh, the Ettrick Brothers'."

"In Edinburgh? So you decided to come back to Scotland. How long have you been there?"

"Let me see," he began. It felt to him a long period. "Just three months," he said.

"And you thought to look us up," said Mrs. Cameron, "as soon as you got settled."

"Eh? Er—yes."

"Did you get the job directly you arrived?" asked Jessie, and he thought how like her it was, how she was still the same as of old—to be interested so.

"No. I came back—how time flies!—over two years ago," he answered.

Jessie stiffened in her chair. The glow on her face that had made Cameron and his wife glance one to the other—she sentimentally, he quizzically—ebbed.

"Indeed!" said she, and in the oddest way turned her head and stared at the carpet to one side of her, so remaining as though suddenly smitten with wry-neck.

"Did you come to Edinburgh immediately?" inquired Mrs. Cameron, who understood the meaning of her niece's contortion.

"No," replied Angus.

Mrs. Cameron looked at Jessie and was glad she had asked the question, seeing the girl, at his reply, recovering of the wry-neck attitude.

"No," he repeated. "We were in Glasgow first. I came over as a kind of secretary to a man who was trying to float a company for opening up coal mines in the West."

"I see, and you had to stay with him in Glasgow all that time," said Jessie.

"Oh, no," said Angus. "We were through to Edinburgh, and then to London, and then back to Edinburgh again, the time slipping along—"

"And too busy to look us up!" said she.

"I didn't seem to have a moment for anything, but copying letters," said he, "and going with him to business appointments. I thought of visiting Brendan once when he took a day or two off, but I didn't."

"It's just as well," observed Cameron. "I hear there's not a stone left standing there. The houses are all demolished."

Angus imagined that Jessie's manner then was due to thinking of what had been done at Brendan, considering that it was no use to weep or wail over it. Her head was turned from them, her gaze was out of the window at the cottages across the road with the geraniums on the sills, blank and a trifle hard. But he misread her pose and misread her private thoughts. He did not notice the tapping of one of her feet on the floor, and had he done so would not have known it was by way of outlet for an annoyance she felt that he had been more than two years in the land, and three months at his work in Edinburgh since apparently resigning his position with the man he had come over with, and was only visiting them then! Sixteen (for they were of an age) they had been at the eviction: now they were twenty-two. His last letter—from that place called Rocky Mountain House—had been different from the earlier ones. She could not have told precisely in what way, but there it was, a difference, as of a voice in it.

"Well," broke out Cameron, "I have sometimes wished I had gone to the Canadas—or Canada, as I hear them cry it now—when I was a lad instead of 'listing."

"You didn't like soldiering?" asked Angus.

"Yes, and no. You have never any privacy, of course. You're always among others and yattering, yattering. There's always some lad that knows everything has to get up and harangue. You have to learn to sit in a crowd and hear nothing. In fact, I sometimes think that has an effect toward bringing on deafness—training yourself not to hear. But I liked the horses. I learnt my trade in the army. You see, I liked the horses."

"Yes, yes."

"And when I was feenished sojering I started up as a farrier and fine I have gotten on. No back to the Highlands for me. I set up first in Glasga. Aye, there's a lot of Hieland in Glasgow. Yonder at the Broomielaw on the Saturday nicht the pipes going and naething but the Gaelic round you—"

"You have been to the kirk today?" interrupted Mrs. Cameron. "I suppose you went to service before you started oot?"

"No," replied Angus.

She looked crestfallen at that.

"He's none the worse o' that," declared her husband. "The Reverend Hedges Greenfields is a fine preacher. Not but what we've been to kirk. It's a habit I got into. Church-parade, ye ken— State and Church! But they never preach from the text Thou shalt not kill in the kirks the sojers march into. They have maybe either a sense of humour somewhere or a sense of some kind of faint probity."

"Oh, Walter, Walter!" wailed Mrs. Cameron. "Whiles ye speak most dreadful and profane."

"That's not profane," he answered, but throwing back his

head he laughed. "Aye, we have church-parade every Sunday morning and in the afternoon she aye sits doon at the kist-o'-whistles. Even some kirks, in fact—havena them, will not have them on principle, inventions of the devil." He rolled an eye at his wife. "I sometimes wonder," he said slyly, "if the neighbours think so. I'm jokin', I'm jokin'," hurriedly he added, noting her sorrowful expression. "Aye, some congregations refuse to have them. They have the Precentor as of auld."

Up he rose, strutted to the big chair and standing behind it made a motion as of striking a tuning-fork, then in a deep voice declaimed:

> "'They bored a hole through Simon's nose
> And put a string through it . . .'

Sing!"

Alone he sang the words solemnly, his wife looking sad, Jessie laughing. Again he declaimed:

> "'The higher that the ploom tree grows
> The sweeter is the fru-it!'"

and warbled in falsetto:

> "'The higher that the ploom tree grows
> The sweeter is the fru-it!'"

"This is blasphemy!" his wife exclaimed.

"Blasphemy?" said he. "The better the day the better the deed and the song, the psalm, the hymn, and the chant."

"How often have I to tell you," she cried out, "that the meaning of that is that the better the day is the better should our deeds be?"

There is no doubt, thought Angus, he was being speedily inducted into the home here, his mouth closed but a smile fixed upon its edges. For Mrs. Cameron's sake he would not laugh out loud; for Cameron's sake he would not look as though impervious to his fun.

The farrier sat down.

"You will stay and have supper with us?" said Mrs. Cameron.

Angus turned to Jessie as for a seconding of the invitation, if only by a look. As he did so she reminded him, shockingly, of William Ettrick. Her eyelids drooped; she looked at the carpet, then out of the window. Her aunt was puzzled and in a fidgeting, a fussing, a little sudden flurry, glanced toward her husband.

"Certainly," said he. "We'll break bread together."

"It's quite a walk back," began Angus, Jessie still intent upon the cottages across the street. "It's a long walk and I have to be up early in the morning."

"Well, we'll have a dish of tea now," suggested Cameron. "On the Sabbath we aye have a dish of tea. And we'll have some of thae scones I smell burning."

Up rose his wife crying, "Oh, my! Oh, my!" and dashed from the room.

No one spoke for a few minutes. There was a profound silence. Angus was no deep student of character. He felt toward others emotion of like or dislike, but never burrowed down for the springs of an action, inquiring for every jot of impulse behind deed or speech. He did not realize that Jessie was annoyed that he had been over two years in Scotland and here was his first visit. The man he had been with had gone away, she gathered, or Angus had left him: and he had only come (so she mused) to call on them because he was lonely. That added to her anger. She could not, for pride's sake, as in complaint tell him she considered he might have come to see them sooner. She could not say, as in scorn: "Not till you were lonely did you remember us!" She sought opportunity to show her disdain otherwise.

"How did you get on with the aborigines oot there?" Cameron asked at last.

"Very well."

"Are the damsels attractive?" and the ex-soldier flipped his moustache.

"I liked them," Angus replied.

He was aware of the attention again of Jessie, her gaze returned from the street outside.

"You liked them!" she exclaimed.

"Yes."

So he liked the native people out there, did he? Very good!

"I have been reading in the papers," she told him, "about a massacre of white folk by Red Indians. I can't say I would find much to admire in them. Men, women, and children they killed— near to the number of a thousand."

"Eight hundred," he said, having also read of it. Cameron, who had noted the vigour of Jessie's speech, noted a little pin-point of glitter in her eyes, looked from her to Angus and arranged his moustache.

"Just eight hundred, was it?" she said. "I suppose you think that's no' so bad!"

"I can assure you," said Angus, "that when Indians do that they have been goaded to it."

"You must think a lot of them to take up their defence for killing bairns—weans, braining babies, so the papers say. You canna assure me that they are a fine folk after that."

"They must have been goaded to it," he repeated. "And there are many cases of white men killing Indians—men, women and children. Do you know that in some parts bounties have been, and still are, given for Indian scalps, just as if they were poisonous snakes."

"These massacres in Minnesota," she declared, "make me understand it."

She said so not out of her true nature but in pursuit of her desire to punish him for having been so long in Scotland and forgetful of her. But how could he take her speech save as expression of her view? He was horrified.

"We white folk are none so grand," he said. "Are you aware that in Tasmania the settlers had a drive against the natives clear across the island, shooting them as they went, till they had wiped them all out?"

"Tasmania!" she replied. "That is not Minnesota. Have you to fly to Tasmania for defence of your friends?"

"No," he answered, and was suddenly angry. He showed it, to her gratification. "I have not to fly to Tasmania. I can stay here, in Scotland. I'll tell you one thing, and that is that if an Indian comes into your house and smokes a pipe with you, you can let him sleep there at your ease. He'll not get up in the night and slay you. I'll come back from Tasmania, or Minnesota, nearer home. You may have heard of a massacre in Glencoe. And those who planned it ate the salt, so to speak, and smoked the pipe, so to speak, and then got up and massacred—"

At that moment Mrs. Cameron returned to the room, carrying the dish of tea—the tea-pot, with its helmet-like cosy over it.

"Bring in the scones, like a good lass," said she.

Up jumped Jessie to fetch the buttered scones; and as they munched and drank a little smile of content was on her face as she looked at Angus—he clearly showing, she thought, that she had annoyed him.

Tea over, he decided it was time he went back.

"It's quite a walk," he said again.

All came to the door with him. As they stood there Jessie

suddenly beamed, showing a friendly smile to someone passing by. They glanced in the direction of her wave and saw two young men saluting her, walking as though very conscious of being in their Sunday clothes. Mrs. Cameron gave her niece a puzzled stare, evidently unaware that the girl was as friendly with these two as her smile and wave might signify.

"Haste ye back, as the saying is!" It was Cameron who said that, flinging up his tusks with one hand and crushing Angus's right with the other.

"Yes—now you've found us out," remarked Mrs. Cameron.

Jessie said nothing, but as she took his hand she opened wide her eyes—so wide that again he thought of William Ettrick—in a rigid stare.

"It's fine to have seen you again," said he, and added, "Jessie." Then, on the doorstep, he nearly apologized for having, perhaps, answered her back as he ought not to have answered a woman, in that matter of the massacre that she had mentioned.

"It is nice to have seen you again," she replied, "and I hope you do well at the book-selling."

Striding away he had a feeling of disappointment, disappointment over life in general. His mind went back to the birchwood by the Grant cot in Brendan, and he recalled how diffidently there, feeling a doubt, he had spoken: "If I make a way for myself in the Canadas—" and how Jessie had interrupted him, replying that she was sure of herself but not sure of him.

"She was right then," he told the ridge of Pentlands.

They had met again—and they had quarrelled. Farrier Cameron (something likeable about that man, thought Angus) had known that their talk was truly in the nature of a quarrel by the way he looked. Yes, and but for the entrance of Mrs. Cameron (something likeable about her, thought he) with the teapot there was no knowing to what burning height the argument might have blazed. He could not forget, when he showed annoyance and his voice hardened, Jessie's smile then, a veneer as of malice on her face.

He breathed deeply of the evening air and marched on, the pee-wees rising and crying as he passed, in a field that the dusk was beginning to claim, beyond a fail-dyke. The silhouette of the Pentlands showed for awhile to west, making him again think of the Rockies five thousand miles away. And more of Rocky Mountain House and Minota was he thinking than of that cottage at Lasswade when, at a rise of the road near Liberton, he saw the lights of Edinburgh sparkle before him.

He returned to his lodgings wishing he had not gone to Lasswade—had deferred the visit.

"And I didn't see the De Quincey cottage!" he thought as he was taking off his boots.

CHAPTER TEN
Impulse

He did not haste him back to Lasswade. Impulse was lacking. With one or two members of the Ettrick staff he made friends, but was more often, in his own time during that period, in the company of books. Every Sunday, rain or shine, he was afield, generally with at least some nominal objective, standing stone or Covenanter's grave, heard the music (specially melodious it seemed to him) of Eddleston Water and the rustle of the trees at Habbie's Howe, evading argument, being alone, as to which of the two howes was the authentic one of the poet Ramsay's laudation.

From a hatred of the Ettricks, that by its intensity had a bitter effect upon himself, he passed to an easy contempt for them. When the year of his trial (trial, he would sometimes think, was indeed a fitting word) ended he dared to remind William.

"I am aware," said Ettrick to the inkwell, "that you have been in our service a year, but I am too thrang with other and more important matters at the moment. You can approach me some other time."

It was in the month of August, the year before, that Angus had begun that service, or servitude. No holidays were given to employees in their first year. Here, however, was his second beginning, another August near an end. The question of increase of salary being shelved—

"When would it be convenient for me to take my week of holidays?" he inquired.

"Holidays! You have to be here a year for that."

"I have been here a year," replied Angus.

"Oh, but you are thinking of the calendar year," said Ettrick. "Only in that sense are you into your second year. You have nae title to a holiday till you are in the second twal' month of service."

"I am into it now," said Angus.

"True enough, but you are not going to take holidays the moment it begins. Here's August near an end. I can't have any of the staff going away in September when the students and the advocates are in and out any day. That's oot o' the question. In the other matter—approach me later, should it slip my memory."

Time passed and, restless in the back of his mind, Angus realized that here he had no continuing city. Out of a mere curiosity to discover how slippery Ettrick's memory he left the matter of increase of stipend in abeyance, making no approach. It will be amusing, thought he, when the increase is granted, to have a little discussion on the equity of making it retrospective—with arrears payable as from the commencement of the second year.

It was just a year and six months to the day from his beginning in that bookshop (and, "I'll give him till tomorrow," Angus decided, "and then again approach") when, passing along Princes Street after lunch on his way back to the Ettrick house he saw, progressing slow and stately in that stately thoroughfare, three feathered Indians. Tall men enough they were, made gigantic by reason of their war-bonnets. All the people on the street meeting them moved to one side to give them way. Their slow march added to the effect of grandeur. Their mouths were tight shut, but Angus could see the twinkle in the eyes of one—he who walked in centre—at the sensation they were creating, though all pretended to be unaware of it, strolling deliberately, with eyes looking straight ahead.

Before Angus knew what he was about he threw up a hand and waved it left and right, signifying a question to follow: Who are you? he signed. They halted, and the one in the middle made the sign of Ioways.

"When I see you the day comes into my heart," signed Angus. "Nearly four snows back I came here from the prairies and the mountains and my heart is heavy here."

Never surely did the polished windows of the Princes Street shops reflect so exotic a picture: three Indians in full regalia and a young white man "talking" together, talking with their hands in wide, flowing gestures.

"You come with us and see pictures," signed one of them, and as he raised his arm in the gesture for come a coup-stick hanging from his wrist by its rawhide thong—which is after the fashion of a sword-knot—swayed to and fro. Gamins gaped at that.

What pictures? wondered Angus, but as they wheeled he fell in step with them. Away they went, the three magnificently attired savages and the tall white man, looming along Princes Street. They turned into Hanover Street, progressed up the incline to George Street, and, as the view of the hills beyond the Forth showed, one signed: "That looks good to me," perhaps in a courteous suggestion

65

that though prairies and mountains might be far off this young man's heart need not be heavy.

"It looks good to me, but my eyes see the prairies when I meet you," Angus replied.

The three eagle-like faces under the three eagle-feather bonnets were turned to watch the signs, and as he ended they laughed, friendly laughter. Had Hill Burton chanced to come along then he would have had an answer to that question of his on the day when he and Angus collogued too long for the peace of mind of William Ettrick.

To see the pictures. It was explained to Angus when they came to a doorway, on either side of which were placards upon tilted boards.

Exhibition
of
North American Indian Portraits and Scenes
also
Portraits and Scenes from the Guianas
And the Amazon
by
George Catlin

Never had there been a note in the Wee Black Book, against Angus's name, of unpunctuality in attendance. But the Ettrick establishment was as good as non-existent, though a clock in the hall, as they entered it, struck two. That sound gave him no jog. Upon the walls hung paintings of chiefs, of squaws, scenes of Indian life—a buffalo-hunt in summer, a buffalo-hunt afoot on snowshoes over a rolling plain of pale blue snow with indigo shadows.

One of his companions made the sign for Wait and passed into a sideroom, while those in the hall who had been viewing the pictures were all nudging and whispering and keeking sidewise at the two who remained with Angus. He had not long to wait. The Indian returned with an elderly white man, clean-shaven, with aquiline features, eyes at once sharp and kindly.

"How do you do, sir?" said he. "My name is George Catlin," and he held out his hand.

"My name is Munro."

"Come in, Mr. Munro. I hear you talk the sign language," and Mr. Catlin gave a little of it himself.

The three Ioways signed that they would go back to their viewing of the big village and see Angus later.

There, in that anteroom, on the walls of which were pen-and-ink and pencil drawings, these two sat talking of the west, talking of Indians in their own land, and of visits to Europe of a party of Ojibbeways from Canada that Mr. Catlin had presented to the Queen and Prince Consort at Windsor, of these Ioways from the United States who had just arrived at Leith after going up to Dundee—

"Ioways on a coastal boat from Edinburgh to Dundee!" said Angus.

"Yes, it's odd to think of," agreed Catlin.

Next day, he said, they would be off for London again on the way to Paris to visit Louis Philippe, who many years before had visited many tribes from New York State to Louisiana. They talked till the sightseeing trio came in at the door and Angus, thus interrupted, bethought him of time.

"I should have been at work at two," said he.

He had been sitting with his back to the wall, and as he rose a picture there delayed him. It was in pencil, or chalk, a drawing of an Indian, very drunk, looking over his shoulder and waving a whisky bottle. He wore an army coat, an officer's, with epaulettes, and out of the tail-pocket of it protruded another bottle of whisky. He was shown in a teetering pose with an inane grin on his face. On his head, ludicrous, was a high plug hat. Angus stared at it, thinking of old Red Shield and the gift he had given him of the second-hand silk hat, surmounted by a feather. He who in his own garb would appear splendid, in these trappings was pathetic.

"Well, I must go," said Angus.

As he shook hands with the three Ioways each made that sound which is usually reported as Ugh, but is as much or as little like that as Hein? is like the crescendo of sound at a sentence's end beloved by both German and French. Try to say Ha! through the nose with the mouth shut and you have it.

Catlin walked to the door with him through the hall.

"This has been a great pleasure," said Angus.

"Pleasure has been mine, too, I assure you," replied Catlin. "It has been a great talk. I'll be back in New Jersey again—where my home is—before long but our chat makes me feel I would like to go out west once more. But some places that I went to ten years ago in safety I could not risk visiting now. Broken treaties, rascally traders, the bottle . . . Well!" He held out a hairy-backed hand in farewell.

Smiling affably, at twenty-past three of the afternoon, Angus entered the dignified premises of the Ettrick Brothers. There were one or two customers in the shop at the time but

William could not await their departure. Catching Munro's eye he beckoned to him.

"What makes you late?" he asked of the inkwell on the table. "You are an hour and twenty-one minutes behind time."

"I was at an exhibition of pictures," said Angus.

William Ettrick was dumbfounded.

"You—you went to an-an-an ex-hibition of pictures and left others to do your work—you, that has been of the opinion you deserved an increase of stipend! You went to an ex—" Abruptly his expression changed as his attention was directed beyond Angus. "You are wanted," said he.

Angus, turning, found John Hill Burton at his elbow. Ettrick rose and bowed.

"I hope I am not interrupting business," said the historian. "I just wanted to look in and tell you, in case you have not heard of it, that there is a very interesting exhibition of pictures, of great ethnological value I should say, whether of high artistic merit or not, in the city just now."

"This," answered Ettrick on his assistant's behalf, "is very amiable of you. I appreciate your condescension."

"Thank you, indeed," said Angus. "I have seen them—just today. As a matter of fact, that was what Mr. Ettrick and I were talking of. I was telling him about them."

Ettrick cleared his throat in a succession of rasping sounds.

"Did they not make you remember your old life in that remote west?" asked Hill Burton.

"Yes, indeed. I was just on the point," said Angus, "of explaining to Mr. Ettrick that so greatly did they do so that I felt I must go back. I was, in fact, just on the point of giving Mr. Ettrick my resignation."

"Ah-ha! Impulse! Impulsive youth! Well, it is better perhaps than canny youth. When the arteries harden, impulse is not synonymous with action. I fancy that in history one could find many a case of impulse well followed. And what is impulse, what is volition? There's a subject I'm interested in—philosophically. Did you ever consider volition, Mr. Ettrick?"

"I am no student of philosophy. I am among books, but candidly I have such a busy life that—" William Ettrick cleared his throat again in a series of little rasps.

"Did you ever" (Burton turned to Angus) "do something of your own volition without enjoyment?"

"Yes, and I can remember my father and mother leaving for Canada of their own will and yet—"

"Ah, but that would be in the Clearances?"

"Yes."

"Quite. That's a kind of footnote to this inquiry."

"As for myself, then," said Angus, "I do remember well that though I left the west of my own will—and that not at all as making the best of a bad job—I did turn about and about, like Lot's wife."

"Casting a longing, lingering look behind," observed Burton, and might have continued pressing for data toward some philosophic theory he was no doubt at that time perpending, but Ettrick put him out, standing by with head a little askew, an equivocal smile on his face and his eyes almost shut. "When do you leave?"

"Just as soon as it is convenient for Mr. Ettrick to let me go."

"I shall miss you," said Burton. "I had better say good-by lest youth and your impulse carry you off before I come in again."

They shook hands warmly, William standing by and bowing, bowing.

"Very condescending of you, sir," he murmured, "very condescending, I assure you."

Away went Hill Burton out of the shop and out of the young man's life, but always to be remembered so—top-hat on his head, tapping with an old stick as he went, a little bowed with the stoop of a scholar, out of the tail-pocket of his surtout coat his kerchief hanging.

Angus watched him go and then, turning, found William Ettrick levelling upon him a steady and considering scrutiny—promptly veiled.

"You can go this night," said Ettrick to the planks at his feet. He cast back his head, opened wide his eyes, and continued to the ceiling, "So be it is understood that you go this night of your own volition so that you'll not expect your stipend to the month's end."

"I am volitioned to go tonight," replied Angus.

"Very good. I will tell Mr. Robert to give you your salary to date."

Angus went round saying good-bye to the staff.

"Are you discharged?" asked one.

"No. I have resigned."

"Have you got a character?"

"Only my own," said Angus, "for better or worse—such as it is."

He astonished Robert Ettrick, the salary to date having been paid, by offering him his hand in adieu. The junior partner looked at it a moment and then, as one compromised into a deplorable declension, granted his moist palm flabbily to the departing servant. Angus stepped to William's table.

"Well, sir," said he, "I am leaving now."

Up rose Ettrick, elevating his head.

"Well, well!" said he. "I'm sorry to part with you. But you ken your ain ken best, ye ken, as the saying goes. I think you were getting along very well and shall have pleasure in telling Mr. Douglas so, should I have the opportunity at any time."

He put hands on hips, balanced up and down on his toes as he spoke. Then he held out his hand.

"Good-bye to you," he said. "I wish you every success. If, at any time, you should want a character I'll be most happy to oblige."

It was Angus then who was dumbfounded.

"Thank you," he responded. "Good-bye to you."

William walked halfway to the door with him and there turned back with a gracious, dismissing sweep of his arm.

Angus walked along the street, a smile on his lips. He swung on his way as though treading on air. He was free. The light on the high chimney-pots of Edinburgh, gold-leaf of the sunset, was exquisite to his eyes that evening. The impact of the sparrows' excited chirpings against the walls of the courts was crisp and pleasant. Bugles blowing up at the castle played a fanfare, tossed out as it were a salute, to his liberation. He more than smiled. He laughed to himself, unaware, as he went on, so that passersby laughed, too—not as nitwits laugh at those who to them seem nitwits but infected by his gait and gaiety, cause of which they could not know.

CHAPTER ELEVEN
Travellers' Tales

When he came to his lodgings there was a cloud of tobacco smoke in the room and in the midst of it sat Sam Douglas, back from the Cariboo country, awaiting his return.

With his wonted ebullience (when the surprise on the one hand, and the fun of surprising on the other were over) Sam had great news to relate.

"It's a grand world," said he, "and I've had a most interesting time. Man—that country out there is going ahead, and going to go ahead beyond present belief." He dug down in a pocket for his tobacco pouch to recharge his pipe. "Oh, by the way," and he pointed the stem of it at Angus, "do you know what I saw on the west coast? I told myself I must mind to tell you that. I saw some peaches—and ate them, too. 'Where do these come from?' says I.

'Right here,' says the man I had them from. He told me about them. 'Here's the kind of thing to interest Angus Munro,' thinks I. It seems that boats coming round the Horn often stop for fresh water at the island of Juan Fernandez off the coast of Chile. There are peaches there, grand peaches, and they'd take some baskets of them, too. Well, it's stones of these that began the peach-growing by the Oregon River."

"Well!" exclaimed Angus—and had a private memory of other luscious peaches.

"I knew you'd say that. I've minded to tell you about them. And now there's something else. Camels! Yes, camels to west of these mountains you saw from the Mountain House."

"Camels!"

"I've seen them. You know that Cariboo country is dry and sandy, and some man who had been away down in the southwest, on the borders of Mexico, noticed that the American army was using camels there, specially imported for packing across the deserts. What does he do but import some to the Cariboo. They sent the pack mules up there crazy. The trails of that country are whiles narrow on the cañon's sides, and if the mules saw the camels acoming at such places they even leaped over the cliff—and the horses, too. The men with them sent a protest to government, but nothing could be done by law for them. There was no Act against using camels. They could, however, ask the camel-folk to be good enough to consider the advisability of discontinuing the use of the beasts. So they took them off the road, just let them loose in the hills. They seem to stand the winters not so bad. I wonder if the bears and the wolves turn a somersault at sight of them."

"Camels—there!"

"I knew that would catch you, camels—yonder. I thought of you often there. On the Fraser River I wondered how you were getting on at the bookselling. Man, yon is a roily river pouring down the silt and the gold. They have stern-wheel boats on it, the same as the International. Captain Buchanan, your old friend, is piloting one of them. He sent his best to you. They butt their way up it with the safety-valve fastened down whiles to make their way up the gurly riffles, with steam on away ahead of the guarantee— and just laugh at the chance. They have the spunk to do it."

"But what brings you back?" asked Angus.

"The news, the news!"

"What news?"

"Well, the Imperial Commission of Inquiry into a railway route over the prairies, and through the mountains to the Pacific coast, got a veto of the scheme from the engineers. But now the Red River Settlement folk have sent a memorial to the government here—last year they sent it—asking for another inquiry, so that there can be a railway in British Territory from what we used to call the Canadas to their settlement, to save all that kinking through Minnesota and then down the river. You see what will happen? It's coming. It will not stop at the Red River. All the talk of Confederation points the same way. They'll get their railway to Red River anyhow, to start with: and then there will be towns to think of beyond. I once thought of the Great Plains as pasture for cattle, with the buffalo being slaughtered the way they are. Then I thought, seeing how the buffalo herds have manured that soil for ages, and seeing the grass on it, of farms there. Yon hailstorm in mid-August (ye mind?) gave me a jar, but now I'm—"

"Three jumps ahead," said Angus.

"Yes. We ken each other gey weel! That's what I'm back for. I've left two good men out there to carry on in the Cariboo and I'm home to interest capital in the idea of commissioning some man—myself!—to buy land where the townships will be marked along that railway route. There will be a fortune in it—buying the town lots and selling them."

Would Sam Douglas have hauled down the flag had someone gifted with prevision told him then that his railway would not be across the plains for over twenty years? The chances are that he would not, would only have doubted the alleged gifts of that seer.

"And how," he inquired, having explained his presence, "goes all at the bookselling?"

"I left the Ettricks—for good—tonight."

"Indeed! Did you not get on with them?"

"Quite well. We parted good friends. It was an impulse I had."

"What are you planning to do?"

"Go back to the west."

Sam threw back his head and laughed.

"Captain Buchanan said you would."

CHAPTER TWELVE
Escape

The steamship International was thrashing her way down Red River. Sam Douglas and Angus Munro leant against the rail watching the diminutive rainbows fluttering behind in the spray above the stern-wheel.

Sam had been unable to interest anyone in investment in town-lot purchases. In the end he had lost his temper.

"I am not pleading with you," he announced. "I came to let you in on a certainty. Don't come to me in a year or two and say I didn't give you the chance."

They told him he was premature. As he had to return to the Cariboo gold-fields—and intended to do so overland instead of round the Horn—he had asked Angus to bide a wee while he made these unrequited sallies, so that they could go west together again. In those days of waiting volition had not come to Angus to visit the Camerons and Jessie to say farewell to them. A year and three months he had let slip since his first visit without calling on them. He told himself—thinking it, perhaps, a duty or a courtesy to go to Lasswade before sailing—that they knew he was at the Ettricks', and that if Jessie wished to see him she could have found him there. The quality of his first visit, as he recalled it, made it his only one.

The overland route Sam had decided upon because of having met, in the Cariboo, a Dr. Cheadle and a Lord Milton who had travelled that way—they who were to be spoken of in years to come as the first Canadian tourists, the first to make that transit neither for gold nor furs but just for fun. It was not an easy route. It was, in fact, that one of which a Glasgow bailie, years before, had spoken, the route of the haunting memorandum, Arrived at the cañon and was drowned. But adventure did not dissuade Douglas. So here were Angus and he on the International that thrashed down Red River chased by the little broken rainbows in the foam of the stern-wheel.

Suddenly Douglas spoke.

"I wish I had never seen this damned country!" he broke out.

Angus stared.

"What do you mean?" he asked. "When you smelt balsam off the Saint Lawrence you did not talk that way. All through the Minnesota woods you've been more like one coming home than away from home."

"That's just it," explained Sam. "I would like to live in my own land, but I am becoming unfitted for it by reason of knowing this one. I wish I had never seen the damned country because, visit by visit, when I return to my own I realize more clearly that I could never stay there. They are too conservative over there. You offer them the chance of a lifetime and with never a word of thanks they say, We will give the matter our consideration. Consideration!"

He moved from the rail as he spoke and they returned to the pacing of the deck that the sight of those pursuing foam bows had stopped. They came to a halt again under the wheel-house, looking ahead. The river might have been but a lake by its aspect and straight before them its end. The steamer swerved and another stretch was revealed. There was the sound, also, of the front window of the pilot-house opening and the skipper leant out.

"Come up in the wheel-house, gentlemen," he called, "and see the sunset from here."

Sam saluted him and they stepped to the door, beyond which was the ladder to the pilot-house. Sam grabbed Angus's elbow.

"What was I telling you?" he murmured. "That's it! That's part of the grip of this land on me—'Come up in the wheel-house.' I wish I had never seen the damned place, for I can never feel rightly happy again in my own."

"Hullo!" exclaimed the captain as they entered, recognizing Angus. "When was it you were a deck-hand with us? Let me see—nine years ago, I should think."

"Close on that," said Angus.

"And I know your face, too," continued the captain, looking at Sam.

"I came down with you eight years ago and went up with you five years ago," replied Sam.

"Well, sit ye down," they were told.

They seated themselves on a form beside the companion-ladder and got into talk of the years between with fragments of their doings and fragments of the life of the river in that period, the skipper to one side of the wheel on a high stool and to the other a deck-hand, both smoking cheroots.

"Aye, it's a great country," Sam declared, rising and stepping close to the window to look down at the water ahead. "It's grand to be back."

At Fort Garry they landed, Douglas going to the factor there; but Angus went on through the French half-breed settlement of Winnipeg to Kildonan, by the lower fort—the "stone fort."

Fiona spied him first and dashed to meet him through the golden haze of that afternoon, shouting back to those within, "Come and see who's here!" She ended the run with a final leap and flung an arm round his neck. She would be turned fourteen then, full of youth. She wore a great straw hat of her brother's. The brim of it came in contact with Angus's forehead and it bounced off as he bent to kiss her. They stooped together to pick it up, with a crash of colliding crowns.

"Did I hurt you?"

"No, it's all right. Well, yes, of course it hurt but it's of no consequence. Oh, it's grand to see you again!"

It was, for Angus, grand to see them all. Flora was shooting up, though not as tall as her sister. Hector was more than hobbledehoy, a youth with roguish eyes. Close on a week Angus stayed with them.

The place was always in a stir with their shouting one to another, from house to byre, from stable to the fields. Everybody was at work all day and all were happy. The Fair was held while Munro was there, and Mrs. Fraser, who had promised to bake cakes for it, appeared not to find that extra labour in the hot kitchen too much for her.

A great day was Fair Day, with exhibition of produce, of bulls and cows, of calves and pigs, with prize-givings and sports— tossing the caber, putting the stone, sword dances to the skirling pipes, Highland flings on the grass, and horse races to which the Indians came in. Angus was watching them with Fiona to one side and Flora to the other, holding an arm of each. Ian was leading home his prize-winning plough-team. Hector was in the horse race.

"Go on, Hector! Go on!"

Fiona and Flora were leaping up and down like jumping-jacks, and as the dust swirl went by dashed away from Angus to crane closer. There came a voice in his ear.

"As I told you," murmured Sam, "I wish I had never seen the damned country. This—this, too—would haunt me there, but isn't it hot?" and he mopped his brow, then returned to a little party he had left to make that comment in passing—a party of the Company's employees and ex-employees, many of these by that time retired in the Selkirk Settlements, as they usually named the region, among them one who had gone to the west on the first boat John Jacob Astor sent there—Alexander Ross, his wife, an Okanagan Indian from beyond the Rockies, on his arm, very much grande dame in her attire and bearing, "a fine bird as well as carrying fine feathers," Sam told him afterwards, talking of those he had met there.

The morning after Fair Day, Angus saw an unexpected side of Mrs. Fraser. Never had he known her thus. Her voice was harsh. All day long she flyted at Hector, at Fiona, and Flora on sight, even glared at her man when he came in whistling.

"You come to deave me with your whistling!" she exclaimed.

75

Fraser winked at the young folks, and they nudged each other with their elbows. Suddenly Mrs. Fraser, seeing that, sat down in a chair and laughed, holding her sides.

"I'm tired out," she said, "with all the work of the Fair."

"Certainly we know the cause, whatever," replied her husband, laughing too.

A few minutes later she was up and blazing at her family again. Next day it was—

"Well, Mother, how are ye feeling today?"

"Now, don't mak' fun o' me, you young folk," she begged. "Nor you either, Angus."

Memories—memories to carry away out into the Great Plains: Fiona, who looked after the hens, hurrying across the dooryard with a tilted stream of them craning like race horses behind her in hopeful pursuit, feeding-time drawing near; Fiona and Hector milking in the long dusky byre, her cheek resting against the red and white of a cow's flank, looking up at Angus's entrance with merry eyes. He found another milking-stool and sat down to help.

"She'll hold it!" Fiona called to him. "That one will hold it from you. She'll only let me milk her."

At the sound of a steady rush-rush into the pail, Hector looked round from the cow he sat by.

"It's good you hadna a bet on it, Fiona!" he said. Nothings, nothings to remember . . . no, much to remember—happier memories than those of the Ettrick bookshop.

It was not the time for the departure of one of the great brigades that, miles long, undulated over the waves of that grassy sea to west, rippled by the hour past poplar groves, dipped into coulees, twined up their sides like a mighty snake; but with a brigade that surely sent up sufficient sound from its ungreased wheels, they set out—Sam and Angus—for Edmonton, by that dapple of forts splashed across a thousand miles, Ellice and Carlton (the Touchwood Hills Post then abandoned), and Fort Pitt.

At Edmonton, Angus promptly decided what was to be his means of support in this land that had called him back. Prospectors were arriving there with gold-dust and nuggets from the rivers, Saskatchewan, Smoky, even the more distant headwaters of the Peace. So there he bade adieu to Sam and saw him ride away on the Jasper trail in the direction of the mountain passes.

But before he began his labours on the sand-bars, Angus made inquiries for any he had known before there. Buchanan and Renwick had gone to Edmonton to the boatbuilding, but left a

76

while back, Renwick moving eastward and Buchanan westward. Of Tom no word returned; Buchanan—as Sam discovered—was on the Fraser River.

It was truly rather for more news of Minota than for the sake of seeing any old friends that he had made these inquiries. Here, in this part of the west, memory of her was with him in the scents and the sounds. The Company's people recalled well that the Red Shield band was exterminated but where, out in their wanderings after the buffalo, none could inform him.

He decided to go to the Mountain House—there might be those there who could tell him more—before beginning upon the work that was to give him sustenance, if not fortune, in the land that had called him back. But no more was known there than had been written to him. The letter he had sent to her, care of the factor, had been delivered. Someone, he hoped, had read it to her. If only he had taught her to read and write. If only: the distant sound of a river's passage, the rising and falling sigh of wind in trees, were like a threnody for her, his dear sauvage!

CHAPTER THIRTEEN
"The Great Sickness"

There were many men drifting into Fort Edmonton then and building cabins nearby, to winter there, of a type new to those parts—men young and old, some who had been in California in the great gold excitement of '49 and in the Cariboo country in the excitement of '60.

The rudiments of their calling it was not hard to pick up, and for the next three years, both above and below Edmonton, Angus was looking for colour and finding it, washing gold-dust and nuggets with considerable success. The Ettrick establishment must have been to him even more tedious than he knew, for all the while he was relishing his new life not only for itself but for the escape it gave him from all that may best be symbolized as the Wee Black Book. Coming into Edmonton at the beginning of the winter of his second year he found all talking of troublous doings by Red River. The Métis of Winnipeg, by Fort Garry, ever since Confederation, two years before, had been anxious regarding their status. Transfer of the Northwest Territory from the Company to the Dominion agitated them. The transfer had been fixed for that winter and such was the news, these French half-breeds and descendants of half-breeds, of the old coureurs de bois, refused to recognize the new rule. The arrival of survey parties in the Red River Settlements had further excited them. They challenged the entry of the Lieut.-Governor, took possession of Fort Garry, hauled down the Union Jack, hauled up their fleur-de-lys and shamrocks.

Angus was troubled for the safety of the Frasers, but the general opinion was that the Scots would not be involved, though later, renewing his fears, came news that the British-Canadian settlers at Portage la Prairie were up in arms at that exchange of flags, talking of an assault on Fort Garry to drive out the French half-breeds and their leader, Louis Riel, and switch the bunting again. It's nothing, it will soon be over, was the general view. In the spring came the news of the repulse of those who would retake the fort, the capture and execution, by Riel, of one of the leaders. A military force was toiling west, by Lake of the Woods and Rainy Lakes, from Fort William to quell the insurgents who, it seemed, since that assault on their fort had merely sat there, in occupancy, under their flag. No need to worry about Kildonan, however; so he went back to his placering in the Upper Saskatchewan sands, and on his first return to Edmonton he heard that all that fracas was over. The soldiers had arrived, Riel and his men had walked out. That was all. And there ended, for Angus—the whole affair like thunder over the horizon—what was called the First Riel Rebellion.

Other news came, from another quarter, from southward. The Blackfoot Confederacy were not taking the influx of prospectors as lightly as were the Crees. A band of Piegans, under a chief called Black Weasel, was contesting the passage of the miners through their lands. So far what had befallen had been considered as the fortune of war, the chance of the frontier. Prospectors attacked Piegans, and Piegans attacked prospectors. Then a man of the fur company at Fort Benton did what no fur company employee should be so foolish as to do. He lost his temper with a young raiding Piegan and took his fist to him.

"It can't be done," said Macaulay at Jasper House.

The fat was in the fire. The young man told of the assault to his people and they came into the fort and settled the matter with the crack of a rifle. So an example had to be made. Out from the military post, Fort Shaw, went a Colonel Baker, one of General Sheridan's officers (he whose slogan was that the only good Indian is a dead Indian), to find the Black Weasel band. He failed to do so, but decided that any band would serve. He took his force charging one dawn into the sleeping camp of Bear Head and made the example there, killing men, women and children to the number of a hundred and fifty or so, set fire to the lodges, and rode proudly away.

"It's not the first thing of its kind," said Hardisty at Edmonton, and took from his shelves one of the volumes of Alexander Ross's journals.

He searched briefly for a page, found it and, pointing to a paragraph, handed the book to Angus.

"Passed a deserted Piegan camp of thirty-six lodges rendered immemorial as the place where ten Piegan murderers of our people were burnt to death—" Angus read.

He handed it back moodily. He was, in memory, back-in a cottage of Lasswade and Jessie Grant, with an inexplicable eagerness, a smile that was as a veneer of malice, was taunting him with the Minnesota massacre. He wished he had read the Ross journals (they were published before the time of that visit), for then could he have the better countered her attack with that reference to white men burning their enemies to death. No matter! He waved away again the cottage at Lasswade, annoyed at himself that across the years that talk could rankle.

"It's all deplorable," said Hardisty. "These Blackfeet, these Piegan, are none so bad, properly handled. They are good hosts. Palliser, and others before him, away back to Anthony Hendry, have told us that. The marvel to me is that they can, and do, distinguish between white friend and white enemy. The marvel is that they don't think, as Baker did, that all that matters is the complexion—and bang!"

"It may make things worse," remarked Angus.

"It may make things worse," agreed Hardisty.

Angus returned again to his placering, entirely at ease regarding the Frasers, realizing that those who said it was but a storm in a teacup at Fort Garry had been right. He decided to go downstream, built a raft and set out, trying here, trying there, at likely bars and bends, living chiefly on the land, staying a day or two at one promising place and then, rocker and shovel aboard, pulling again into the current.

Where Vermilion Creek flows into the North Fork he halted a day or two and was amazed at the number of ravens he saw flapping by. He had a sense—inherited, perhaps, from his mother—of the sinister ahead. A raven or two was all in order, but there were too many black wings for a man alone, even one who had sloughed the fancies of his ancestors. There came into his head:

"In behint yon auld fail-dyke
I wot there lies a new-slain knight . . ."

Too many corbies! And it is not good for a man to be alone.

A notion came to him to float down to Fort Pitt, get horses there, ride to Kildonan and winter with the Frasers that year instead of again staying at Edmonton. So he passed out into the flow of the river and duly arrived at Fort Pitt—and gloom.

He read it on the faces of all as soon as he got there. Soon he heard the cause: smallpox was on the prairies.

"It's bad," said the factor, "very bad. We've heard that its extent is from Missouri to Saskatchewan. The Blackfeet are dying like flies with it. Neither measles nor smallpox can these people withstand—both comparatively new to them. I believe the first great smallpox epidemic was no further back than '37."

Even as they were speaking an eerie outcry came to them. They had the manner—all there—as of men turned to stone. They stepped to the door and listened and looked. There was a sound of chanting drawing nearer, weird, repetitive, that rose and fell so that one could not be certain at first whether it came so as the rise and fall of the little winds decreed or by reason of the manner in which it was intoned.

"There they come!"

Riding up the rise to the fort were those who sang—a slow-moving cavalcade of Indians. As they came closer there was something fearsome in their voices.

"It's like people singing in their sleep," said Angus.

"Or in fever," replied the factor.

"For God's sake, look at what comes here—at this one in the lead!" exclaimed one of the clerks.

They were all armed, though this was no war party. They did not shake wavering war-whoops into the air. It was a phalanx of the moribund that rode up to the fort. This was a funeral cortège: they sang themselves to death. Behind them, flapping heavy, were ravens against the blue. An odour preceded them. The first wave of it came sickeningly; then those poor folk were all round them in all stages of the disease. They rode slowly (the very deliberateness had its horror) all round the fort, in among the buildings before any there could think what to do.

Close to Angus passed a squaw with her face woefully swelled, her eyes apparently unseeing. On her back was a child, pouched in the slack of the blanket she clutched round her, in the act of having convulsions. Some of them had the pustules all over their bodies, others had got to the last stages, their faces so bloated that hardly could one see the features, the eyes sunk away in the swellings. Still, in a kind of herd hypnotism, they raised their melancholy recitative.

Angus stood at the door of the old trade-room staring out at them. Behind him was a man who seemed not to be a member of the staff but some traveller halted there on the way.

"This is hell we are in!" he was exclaiming, walking up and down.

Angus, very troubled, turned to him.

"Oh, for God's sake! You don't help by telling us that," he snapped.

"Hell," repeated the man solemnly. "Hell we are in," and he continued to pace back and forth.

The Indians were riding into the place. They dropped from their horses. They came to the factor, who awaited them anxiously, came beseechingly, not combative, spreading their hands wide and drawing them back to their bodies in the sign for Pity us. They said, "Take this from us." They asked him, as though superstitiously believing that here was punishment for sin, "What have we done to get this?"

From inside the trade-room came the voice of that man: ". . . hell we are in . . ."

"You white men know much. Our medicine-men can do nothing," the Indians pled. "White men brought it. White men can take it from us."

Angus stared from one to another, wondering then what these were about. They were rubbing their sores against the walls. He thought at first it was because they itched, then realized it was not for that. They had clearly come there with an object; they had had an Idea. One and another would burst a pustule on him or her and smear the matter on walls, outhouse latches, or door handles. He listened acutely to the chanting:

"The white man gave it to us.
The white man gave it to us.
Take it back to the white man.
Leave it with the white man.
Leave it with the white man,
Then we shall be well again."

That was the chant with which they rode. They made no show of anger. None suggested to kill a white man. They were possessed but by that one thought: The white man gave it to us; take it back to the white man.

There was a feeling as of nightmare at high noon in talking to these people who, had they been of his colour (thought Angus) would surely have all by then been abed—and dead abed. What

81

amazing vitality kept them in their saddles! When one dismounted he fell and could not rise. Some, it would appear, had succeeded only by some superb effort of will in coming so far and, having arrived, the will snapped. They lurched from their horses and where they fell they lay. The red trickles of haemorrhages were on their saddles.

"Are you in pain?" Angus asked one after another, and all replied, "No—no pain," which eased, a little, the horror, the pity of it.

"We are sending runners to Fort Edmonton west," the factor told them, "to Fort Carlton east, to see if at either of these places there is any medicine for the disease."

"If you give me a horse I'll ride one way," said Angus.

"The messengers are off already," replied the factor.

So Angus moved over to tell others who were not near and might not have heard. One to whom he spoke—no visible part of him without sign of his malady—listened the more eagerly, no doubt, because Angus addressed him in Cree. Then—with no intention of infecting him, that was clear, but in gratitude—the man shook hands with him. The feel of that palm was dreadful, but Angus did not snatch his own away.

Having done what they had done (smeared latches, sills and walls), the Indians were prepared to listen to the factor who went among them, advising all to go into camp and lie quiet there. Above all, he warned them, none should take a sweat-bath and leap into the river, which was their cure for many ailments. They had found that out, it appeared. They did not need to be told. On the South Fork the bodies of those who had followed such treatment were drifting downriver as sometimes the buffalo, that crossed at bad places and could not climb a bank, were seen wallowing along, Blackfeet bodies were spinning down the flow, into the Cree country.

Next moment there was the crash of a gun within the fort. Angus thought that some had begun to kill and hurried indoors to see what had happened. It seemed that one of the Indians had stood before a mirror looking at his face. He was a young chief, very vain, known as Handsome Man. He saw his bloated features in the glass, began to weep, then put his rifle-butt to the ground, withdrew his moccasin before those inside could see what he was about, and pressed the trigger with his great toe.

". . . hell we are in . . ."

"For God's sake, shut up!" cried Angus.

As they had come they went, keening high and plaintive, singing their death-songs; and as the band departed, moving down to the river, one after another caromed out of the saddle, unable to balance, when the horses, dropping their heads to the descent, went mincing down the slope. Where they fell they lay, the extraordinary vitality at end.

All of two hundred miles to Edmonton, all of two hundred and fifty to Carlton—even if there were medicines there what would they avail? It was too late. Nevertheless, in both directions runners were off in hope of aid.

The sun sank. The stars came out and the Milky Way was a whirl of uncounted, uncountable sparks across the sky. But the air of the prairie was heavy with the odour of the Great Sickness, and on the rolling hills by the river banks all night long rose the ululating laughter of the coyotes.

CHAPTER FOURTEEN
Blue Jays

So he did not go on to Fort Garry. He might take the sickness with him, he considered, on his clothes even if, for himself, he escaped. A few days he remained to help there in the melancholy duty of burying those dead who had fallen close by, while the whimper and babbling of coyotes and the bay of wolves sounded through the land.

The messengers returned from east and west empty-handed. The raft on which he had floated down river he left by the bank for the service of any who cared or for the spring freshets to carry away and, buying pack and saddle horses, turned back to Edmonton, thinking much of Minota. Measles or smallpox—it was all the same to these people, both but recent afflictions to their blood.

He decided, the intention of wintering at Kildonan abandoned, to go west into the hills and build a cabin for himself by one of the tributaries of North Saskatchewan where he had, earlier, found colour sufficient to warrant that. The usage of many of packing out in the spring through the mire of the thaws to their gold-getting, packing back with the first snows to hibernate in cabins near the fort, was not to his mind. He joined the company of those who were even then dotted solitary, fellows in method but far-sundered, along the ranges west, memorials of whose occupancy of sequestered valley or high rocky basin may still be encountered by the chance traveller—a roof fallen in years ago

83

surrounded by the ant-ridden logs, or dust of logs that were once cosy walls, in tell-tale parallelogram.

Nearer to Jasper House than to Fort Edmonton was his chosen location. There was time still before the snows, though there were hints of yellow among the stands of trees. He had known of winter hardly coming until Christmas week; he had known of it setting in by October, making a sudden end to Indian summer, swooping abruptly with blizzard instead of coming by slow degrees. He had, in fact, the roof on his cabin before even the snow of tamarack needles was falling. A snowing of needles: that seemed the only way to describe the drift of these frail yellow splinters.

Time flew. At Edmonton there were books (it surprised, for some reason, many visitors of those days to see the factor's library) and Angus had brought some with him. Macaulay of Jasper House had books also, and told him to help himself. When the first snow came (a mere sifting of white on that yellow carpet of the forest) came also two blue jays. Perched on a branch nearby, erecting their crests, they gave him a raucous Hullo! He acknowledged their call by tossing to them some scraps of food.

The snow vanished, as in a turning back of the year, and the jays vanished also. Squirrels were frequently springing their rattles at him as he worked, wood-chopping. Their granaries were no doubt full, their busy days over for the season. But even so, after that first white powdering there was a sense of waiting, expectancy, tranquil expectancy, resignation, in that green domain. Then came a morning when he awoke to a new light in the shack, a trembling radiance. He looked out. The woods were filling up with snow. The flakes came quaking down. All night, thought he, they must have been falling. The boughs of the pines were bent with the load upon them. There was a screech without: the blue jays had returned.

They remained in the vicinity for his company, his eleemosynary scraps, one so little timid that when, on mild days, he let his door stand open it would come perkily in. To begin with it demanded. Anon it took. It would perch on the table when he ate and with a beady eye upon him snatch the morsel he tossed across to it, gobble it down or flirt away with it, a blue flash of wings in the doorway. Cold days coming, necessitating the closing of the door, he chipped a small hole in it, put a landing perch beside that both inside and outside, and then awaited evidence (or lack of it) of a blue jay's intelligence. In the way of men alone he ridiculously scratched with a knife-point IN—OUT on either side of the hole.

The jay, greatly daring, after several decisions to do so, that were suddenly vetoed when half in and half out, adventured at last. By week's end it was in and out as it pleased. It became bolder. It would leap upon a piece of meat on the table and, taking firm hold with its claws, insert its vicious beak and with a backward jerk tug off slivers. Sometimes so great a chunk did it wrench away that in the hole, fluttering off with the portion, it had difficulties. The meat would fall, Angus would go to pick it up, and the jay would fly screeching round the cabin till he opened the door—and out it could dart.

Once, in midwinter, when there was blue sky above and sunshine, he went to Jasper House on snowshoes, for converse with his kind, through woods intensely quiet, all the streams frozen and happed over with the drifts. The trail he left behind showed deep mauve shadows in the faint blue of that world. Now and then a laden tree would quiver and toss from it the weight it had been bearing. For a moment beside it was a ghost tree, or a jet, a falling jet of rainbow-tinted points. A little sigh as it fell—and the silence deepened again.

Half a mile from home on his return there came a shriek and two flutters of dark blue. There were his friends, or his beggars, to welcome him.

"It's only your insides you think of," he told them, but nevertheless was gratified by the reception.

The shortest day came, and each morning's light seeped earlier into his cabin. The jays, without, rose at dawn, and at dawn they clamoured to be fed. Morning after morning they screamed him awake. To pay no attention was of no avail: they but screeched the louder. The forward one alighted on its perch and rapped at the plug he had put in the hole to prevent a whistling draught overnight. He fed them with exasperation.

"You can support yourselves perfectly well without me," he complained. "Why don't you get your own breakfasts and come to dinner instead?"

And then—

One morning he was drawn from profound slumber by that domineering yell. Half awake, half asleep, the screams continuing, he rose, opened wide the door. The jay, alarmed—perhaps it had expected only the removal of the plug—dashed against his breast and at the impact, sleep still in his eyes, he caught it and (of his own momentary volition) wrung its neck.

He sat down, fully awake then, with the dead bird in his hand, sat so long that he found himself quaking with the cold, rose, shut the door, built up his fire and, standing there, looked at the stiffening corpse on his table in misery.

Outside, the bird's mate shouted anxiously. Having done what he had done, there was more to do. He went outside. There was the other bird on a bush, with demented eye, yelling on and on. Angus crossed to a bank where the snow had fallen away, thus exposing the soil, found there some stones that he could kick free from the frost that held them to the earth, and the first one he threw was aimed well. The partner of the bird he had murdered dropped without another sound.

He buried both together in the bank where he had found the stones. The silence of the forest round him was then almost unbearable.

CHAPTER FIFTEEN
Progress

Often he remembered George Catlin walking with him to the door of that hall in Edinburgh, saying, "It's changing, it's all changing . . ." For always there was some drear news when, having shut his cabin door and trudged through the woods, he arrived at Jasper House.

Blackfeet and Cree were constantly at war then. Each lay in wait for the other round the prairie forts in a chronic feud, the revenge of one but the reprisal, it seemed, for the revenge of the other.

"I hear," said Macaulay at Jasper House, "that some Plains Assiniboine and Crees, out together after buffalo, came on a Piegan camp near Cypress Hills in which were only the old men, the women, and children, the able-bodied men out hunting, and wiped them all out except one lad who escaped and got down to one of the free traders' forts. I think that's what started this trouble. We are beyond little horse-stealing forays now. It's bloody war all the time."

As the factor spoke, Angus was moodily back in the Cameron parlour at Lasswade. "Jessie would be delighted to hear of that," he thought. A pity he did not realize that she had been but trying to annoy him because of his dilatoriness in seeking her out, realize the obliquity of her attack. He could then have lightly laughed Lasswade into Limbo.

On one occasion he went to Edmonton and the place was changed. Foreboding lurked strangely even in the shadows under its eaves, in the echo of the voices and steps in its gateways. Men of a type new to him were there. They seemed to be, in verity, what his mother imagined that some she had seen in doorways of the way-houses of Minnesota were. He looked on at an exhibition of their shooting, evidently in response to some challenge following a vaunt. One stepped from a group and, with a quick glance to see that no one was beyond him, held up a fifty-cent piece between thumb and finger. His partner marched away fifty paces, wheeled, and on the instant shot the coin into the air full centre. Then, when another who watched the display cried out, "Well, you've done it, but all the same I would not like to be the one to hold the half-dollar," the marksman glanced at him and, as he turned his head, shot the cheroot from his mouth. The glitter of his eyes, alert for any resentment, was steely as a poised lynx's.

The Company's staff told Angus of callous killings there. Whisky smugglers were on the way to being cynical lords of that region. Fortunately, they told him, when the Indians get drunk—and drink-crazed, in their way—they kept to themselves. The bacchanalian screams could be heard all night at times, off in the woods—and occasional shots. As he listened to these stories he recalled that queer man who was at Fort Pitt when the band with smallpox rode in, he who walked to and fro in the trade-room, declaiming: "This is hell we are in."

He heard (appropriately to that memory) that shortly after he had left to go west to the mountains a military man, Captain W. F. Butler, had arrived on government service, bringing with him medicine chests against a recurrence of that plague, and leaflets and booklets of advice in case of an epidemic. The illustrations in these reminded Angus of some proselytizing, terrorizing pictures Minota had once shown him dealing with afflicted souls instead of bodies. Captain Butler had also been bearer of official papers to certain factors and others in the land, giving them judicial rights, power to try and convict law-breakers.

"But what's the good?" they said. "What's the good of creating Magistrates or Justices of the Peace when there is no force either to maintain law or to arrest for infringement?"

Yes, it would appear this was hell they were in. Certain lakes nearby had been christened Drunken Lakes because of the orgies that took place in their neighbourhood. Yet there was a line of demarkation. Hell did not extend to the foothills. The North Trail, that wound along their verge, was its western boundary. The Mountain Assiniboines (the Stoneys) seemed to be escaping this demoralization.

Angus was not sorry to be gone again from Edmonton westward. With Macaulay he discussed the changes.

"A variety of causes," Macaulay suggested. "The buffalo are going, so they fight over their hunting more. And it's a case now, with some of the traders, of no thought for the morrow. Certainly that's the attitude of the whisky peddlers. They don't care if the goose with the golden eggs is killed. They demand buffalo robes for carriage wraps in the east. I hear also that the navvies building the railways down south are fed on buffalo. Beef contractors are killing them wholesale. Some white men—so an Indian told me the other day—will kill a buffalo for no more than its tongue, that's all, and leave the rest to the wolves. As for the Indians themselves, there is a sort of racial depression."

"No wonder!"

"No. It's deep. The smallpox was heap big depression for them. If things go on this way they are going to be a poor pock-marked race of drunkards if nothing is done to stop it. That last outbreak must have brought them down to a quarter. I can understand it. You know the tendency of many white men when hard luck follows hard luck. And what do some of these so-called whisky peddlers give them even under the name of whisky or rum? Ammonia and blue-stone water, and water that tobacco has been steeped in, and a jolt of rum to top it off."

"No!"

"Yes! Any concoction will serve. But even when they peddle genuine stuff—and even if they water it—how does an Indian drink? By the pint, by the quart. You hear people say that they can't carry their liquor, that a smell of the cork will set them raving. I doubt it. They don't know the meaning of a nip. The whisky smugglers have forts such as none of the old Northwest forts were like—double-walled, some of them. And do they let their customers into the trade-rooms even in small groups? No, sir! Their trade is almost entirely in buffalo robes: a robe is pushed in at a wicket and a jug of watered rum, or whisky—if not worse—is pushed out in exchange. When the band is raving the peddlers sit tight inside with loaded rifles."

"It's hell!"

"It's hell. I hear that Father Lacome has sent an account of the condition of affairs to Ottawa and that two Methodists—the two MacDougalls—have done the same, and that man Sandford Fleming, who has the job of surveying a railway route across the prairies and through to the Pacific, has done the same."

Something familiar in that to Angus—that railway. He wondered if Sam Douglas was still over the ranges in the Cariboo gold-fields, wished he would write. But the passage of letters through the land was uncertain.

He went back to his cabin in the mountains, and to his placering there, as one going to a sanctuary. Yes, he was glad

Minota had not lived into these days: A pock-marked race of drunkards if nothing is done to stop it.

The following year when he went to Fort Edmonton he was prepared to be attacked on the way by some of the new element, he obviously a returning prospector. But no, they had not yet gone as far as that. He bellied up to the blower—which is to say, he had his dust weighed on the scales, blown onto the scales, as the custom was, with a diminutive bellows. A placer miner from the Saskatchewan river was behind him and fell in talk.

"Well, it's a great life," he told Angus. "I've got my money in the bank, the sandy bank of Saskatchewan. I go for three months and dig some out and come and belly up to the blower, and blow it. These Indian women are fine. By, God, these people have no morals at all! They are so keen on liquor that a buck will come along to my shack and peddle me his squaw to get the price of a jolt of rum. They have no morals at all."

Angus turned away.

He moved back to Jasper House, stayed a night there, talked awhile (in the sign language) in the morning to a party of Sarcees who were there trading, and then went his way. A month later, lonesome suddenly, he returned to the post. Always dismal news! A party of whisky traders down in the Cypress Hills had massacred a band of Assiniboines there after having sold them all the whisky they had.

"After trading?"

"Yes, peddled the stuff right in the open away from their fortresses and then lay round the camp on a bluff, and when night came, and the tepees were lit with the fires, riddled them with bullets."

"What was the idea?"

"I've been trying to arrive at that," replied Macaulay. "I think I've got it."

"What?"

"Fear. It is all very well in one of their strong forts to play that game, but out in the open, if a horde of drink-crazed Indians come demanding more and there's no more to give—or if the Indians have no more robes to offer in trade—what then? That's the only explanation I can think of. Fear. They gave them the liquor and then, when the orgy got into full swing, they got scared. Fear, cowardice, and cynicism deep as the Pit. That's all I can think of as explanation. It's bad enough. I would hate to think it was done just for hellery and fun!"

That was the end of it. Cleric and layman, priest and parson, Hudson's Bay factor, surveyors, and free traders of another sort let Ottawa know of the progress of civilization on the great plateau.

It was in a letter from Fiona that Angus had the first news of the result of these pleas, a long letter beginning with the family gossip and passing on to tell of a change at The Stone Fort (Lower Fort Garry, Kildonan way), how a military force was installed in half of it, and drilling there. "That dreadful massacre in the Cypress Hills," she wrote, "was what brought the decision to police the plains . . ."

Angus looked up.

"They're going to police the plains," said he.

"Oh—it's in your letter, is it? I was going to tell you. That news is a bit tardy now. They are policing the plains—the Northwest Mounted Police. I had word by the man who brought in the mails from Edmonton. The Redcoats are there and there's another body of them away down somewhere in the Cypress Hills. The J.P.'s and the magistrates won't have to look upon themselves as impotent much longer."

No letter from Sam, who was often at that time in Angus's mind. Again there was talk of the railway coming through. That man Sandford Fleming, they said, was not going to be beaten.

It was not till the following year that there was news from Douglas. Opening the letter, Angus was puzzled. It was headed Fort Calgarry.

"Where's Fort Calgarry?" he asked. "Has the company established a new post that I haven't heard of?"

"The company has just established a new trading-post there, as a matter of fact, but it's really the new name of Fort Brisebois."

"I never heard of Fort Brisebois."

"Of course not—out of the world! It's a fort of the mounted police. It was named Brisebois after one of the officers of the force, but is called Calgarry now, after the birthplace of their colonel, Macleod."

"But where is it?"

"South. About as far south of the old Mountain House as Edmonton is north of it. On the Bow River. Why?"

"This letter is from an old friend who is there now. He says that the railway will be in any day—"

"Any day! Some day, he means. Your friend is an optimist."

"It's Sam Douglas, Sam Lovat Douglas, the—"

"Oh, he wintered here some years ago. I remember him well. He's got a future, if he lives."

"He's started a business and says it is a good-going concern—a freighting business. He wants me to join him." Angus glanced at the letter, "'Unless,' says he, 'you are making a fortune at your placering.'"

"Well, if you decide to join him you can ride down with no dread of losing your scalp on the way now. The mounted police have done away with that danger."

Angus went back to his cabin to pack and depart, left it for the squirrels to play upon its roof and for the tamarack needles to drizzle down upon and the snow to fall upon these, left it as though ending a life. He went on his way to meet Sam Douglas and to discover, as it befell anon, that the past lived on and the portion of his life ahead had, indeed, indeed, close link with portions past.

CHAPTER SIXTEEN
S. D.

Douglas looked older. That was Angus's first thought on meeting him at Fort Calgarry. His second was that close on twenty years had passed since they first crossed the plains together from Fort Garry to Carlton, and ten since the second traverse and the farewell at Edmonton, Sam going on to the Cariboo country beyond the ranges.

Dismounting from his horse at the long, low, mud-roofed log cabin that squatted beside tall barns and a pole-corral, with the legend over its door S. D. Transport and Haulage, Sam hurrying out to meet him, Angus had the emotion of meeting an old friend. Here, in the moment of reunion, aware they had their disparities, were different temperamentally in many ways, he had that emotion of friendship, long friendship. Yes, Douglas looked older, despite an effervescent vitality announced in gait, brightness of eyes, and tone of voice. But, of course, he would look older, thought Angus, leading his horses to the corral, Douglas in step beside him, for the years had been flying.

"I'm glad you've come," said Sam, helping him at the unsaddling. "This is going to be the hub of the West. Thirteen lines, they tell me, the engineers have surveyed, and it's down to a choice between the Tête Janue Cache and the pass back of us here. I'm gambling on this one—because it's farther south. It's coming any day now. Next year, I believe, they will be laying the steel across the plains."

Had there been anyone at Fort Calgarry then gifted with prevision to tell Sam that ten years or so would slip away before the hoot of a locomotive sounded there he would have pshawed aside the claims to second-sight and all such occult gifts in that depressing prophet.

There, at any rate, at whatever date steel would come, was a little frontier town hard by the confluence of Elbow River with the Bow. The blast of a bugle from time to time, over at the Northwest Mounted Police post, was a fanfare, in Douglas's ears, proclaiming great things to come, as in Edinburgh once bugles at the castle had been to Angus as though making an airy flourish over his escape from the Wee Black Book.

The air of the place was like a tonic. A vision of the Rocky Mountains wavering along the verge of sky (a sky, that day, of the hue that gleams inside the river mussel-shells) somehow uplifted the heart.

"We'll ride round and look at the city later," said Sam; and later they did so, Douglas an eager, an ardent cicerone.

"There's the Roman Catholic Mission," he said. "And there's the Wesleyan. Yon's the Government post. That's the interpreter's house." They rode on. "Here's the I. G. Baker store and the I. G. Baker barns and stables." (They were much like those of the S. D. Transport and Haulage). "This is the Elbow River we're coasting now. There's the ford—and a horseman crossing it." They reined in on the bank to watch a raft drift past. "There are camps," explained Sam, "away back in the timbered hills where they are felling trees for the building of this great western metropolis."

A memory of the flat-boats on Red River came to Angus as he watched that raft drift past. As they rode back a string of wagons was rolling in from east. They reminded him of the Red River carts, which were small, each hauled by but one ox, different from these. The great wagons, to the slow-swaying trudge of many yoked bullocks that hauled them, came nearer.

"We hitch these carts three together," said Sam, "and in the three is just a fair load for twenty oxen. It's a great idea, a great scheme, simple, like many a great scheme. In the rains there's whiles muddy places between here and Fort Brenton, and when the wagons get mired—they're up to the hubs at times—the drivers just uncouple the two rear ones, haul the lead to good ground and then go back with the oxen and bring the others, one at a time, link them up again, and away they go. The Benton Trail is safe for travel now. When the Redcoats came in there the whisky peddlers just walked out, the way Riel walked out at Fort Garry, I heard, when Wolseley arrived—not that there is any comparison between Riel, with his half-breeds anxious over their future, watching all the Government surveyors poking round there since the company relinquished to the Dominion, and these whisky-traders. Yes, I've got nine wagons for that work—sixty bulls, as they call the oxen here—and I've got fifty pack horses for the transport work into the Kicking Horse Pass. They call it that because of an accident to Dr. Hector, who was in there with Palliser years ago. He got kicked over a cliff by a pony that had gotten its lines fankled up with the tail of the horse ahead, or something, and was jibbing. I'm told they thought he was a dead man when they picked him up. Aye, I have pack horses for packing into the surveyors and the miners in the mountains." He paused. "So you see I need a foreman, Angus. I'll be out and about quite a bit. The cattlemen are heading into the buffalo ranges of Montana already. I'm in touch at the moment with some folk in the old country relative to the starting up of cattle here. Talking of letter-writing: we've got a fine mail service here. The police patrol handles it. They have a box in the orderly room. It goes once a week to MacLeod, once a fortnight for the big world beyond. You have to put American stamps on the letters, for they carry them down either to Fort Benton or Fort Shaw. Think of that—a fortnightly mail service! Yes, I need a man I can leave in charge when I'm looking after other matters. I think there's going to be money in bringing cattle in here. I've a young Englishman working for me who was on a ranch in Montana. I gather he was a scamp and was thrown out by his father, but he's no scamp with horses is Gus. Just little more than a laddie, in his early twenties. What's your age, Angus?"

"Thirty-five."

"Godsakes! I'm five years older than you. I've lived half the span allotted, but I'm going to live long enough, by the grace of God and the air of these parts, to say to these men—d'ye mind how we discussed with them—'I'm sorry, but I have too much on my hands to act for anybody else now. I gave you your chance once. It's too late!'"

"I don't believe you will say anything of the kind to them," said Angus, laughing.

"Oh, maybe not. Well, we'll turn, I think, and ride back and have our crack in the evening. You're no' looking at the mountains."

"Oh, yes, I see them."

"Isn't it bonnie here? Look, do you know what it reminds me of?" and he did not pause for Angus to reply. "It reminds me of the Grampians as you see them from Dundee Law."

They rode in silence awhile, Angus, as his eyes roved the expanse, thinking of Edinburgh and the Ettrick shop there, the staff adread of being out in the street without a character. The horses of their own accord, being very fresh, half-broken, fell into a trot and their hoofs kept time, the riders canted a little forward in the saddles. Then Sam spoke again.

"We'll have to get up a St. Andrew's Day dinner," he said. "Colonel Macleod would be the fitting chairman by nationality and rank, him having just succeeded French out here as commander-in-chief, but the man has such a quixotic sense of probity and duty that when he saw the fluids on the table for the toasts, in these days of prohibition of liquor, he might not just say, 'Well, gentlemen, on an occasion such as this I must not inquire too closely,' but get up and officially arrest us all instead of unofficially letting it go. Yes, yes. It would be a kind of an invidious position to put the poor man in. Of course, they have their discretionary powers. He might decide to—be discreet."

"Sam, I am indeet afraid you have in you certain of the qualities of a damned humbug, whatever," said Angus.

Meeting them as they rode anyone could see they were excellent friends. There was some bond there despite their difference in many ways.

The crack in the evening was satisfactory. The men of the S. D. Transport and Haulage were introduced to their new foreman, Angus Munro, next day. They crushed his hand, looked him in the eye, took his measure: a tall man and bronzed, with no superfluous flesh on him, with a tendency, they noted, to turn a d to a t in his speech and linger on the s of Yes.

There was much for him to attend to, with bull-whackers, bullocks, horses, horse-wranglers, orders for the local traders and traders westward, and bookkeeping. He had been at that employ over a year, seeing the wagons off for Fort Brenton and the pack strings for the hills, before public and national events caught him in private and personal fashion.

Local gossip was all of a treaty—Treaty Number Seven, by name—that the Lieut.-Governor of the Northwest Territory was bringing out to the Western tribes. Anon the day was fixed for that conclave—the gathering to hear and discuss Treaty Number Seven, and perhaps sign it. Time: the moon when the plums ripen, September, and the day the 19th; place: The Ridge Under the Water—the ford of Bow River, sixty or so miles to east of Fort Calgarry—otherwise Blackfoot Crossing.

Redcoats rode off, convoying the commissioner (in his tall hat) and other white signatories—if such they were to be: officers of the force, a factor or two, priests, parsons and three ladies, one the wife of Colonel Macleod, whom the Indians called, by reason of his head and neck, Bull Head. All day long from the door of the S. D. log-cabin office Angus could see the Stoneys trooping on their way, befeathered, with dragging travois-poles. All day long there rose pennants of dust when the Sarcees passed eastward.

"It will be a grand thing for both Indians and whites to have that treaty signed," said Sam, standing with him in the doorway. "I was talking to them over at the police quarters and they say the Indians want it, with buffalo dwindling. They're to be given herds of cattle to take their place, and in return they are to go to reservations. They have great confidence in Colonel Macleod. I heard a story of him the other day. It appears a cattleman went in to see him and ask if he, or any of his cowboys, saw an Indian running off cattle could they shoot him? Macleod looks up across his table and says he 'Yes,' and the man grins, and then Macleod pins him with his eye and says he, 'But you will hang for it!' And I hear that—"

He stopped, for a Redcoat was dismounting at the door and came in with a message. The force's transport facilities were strained by this call upon them. Had Sam a matter of a dozen pack ponies, and a wrangler or two on hand to go off at once to the treaty camp at the Crossing?

Sam turned to his foreman—who suggested, because of the nature of the call, that he had better go himself.

Sam laughed.

"Aye," he said, "I can realize you would like to be in on this. Off you go."

So off went Angus and took with him that young scamp, Gus Atkins, who knew how to treat horses.

CHAPTER SEVENTEEN
Blackfoot Crossing

It was good again to be alive on the Great Plains. This was not hell he was in, thought Angus, riding east ahead of the pack string beneath capacious blue, across expansive plain. There was a time, a period but lately past, when it seemed to his fancy that even the mountains were changed by the horrors he heard of, brooded on the horizon, and that the wind in the prairie grass was lamentation. But a new era was quickening—as the factor at Rocky Mountain House had remarked when he stopped a night there, riding down to Calgarry, a year back, to meet Sam Douglas.

The outer world—or life, existence in that outer world—was again not so sombre and cruel in contrast with the world of the mind as to make his private and personal happiness seem selfish, whether in thinking so he had been just or unjust to himself. He swung round in the saddle to see how all went, and all went well. Behind him in single file the ponies quick-stepped, packs swaying just right, not more than at the end swayed Gus Atkins in the saddle, singing. The Rockies were engraved crisply on the western light, only a peak here and there creating and drawing down a feathery vapour out of space. He settled foursquare in the saddle again and looked eastward where there was no cloud at all, only that lofty blue, that ambient spaciousness.

The place chosen for that great gathering of the clans, gathering of the tribes—the Blackfeet, their septs the Bloods and Piegans, the Stoneys and Sarcees—was beautiful in Angus's eyes when, two days later it was suddenly revealed as a surprise of nature. They say on the prairies: There are no mountains here but there are valleys. From distance the winding gash of the Bow River was unremarked; the impression to the eye was but of space and space again. Flutterings of dust at great distance, as they rode upon their way, had sometimes clearly moved, progressed, and had sometimes seemed stationary. By the size of these, tiny though they were in comparison with the low circumference of the plain and the high glitter of its cupola, Angus had surmised they indicated the Piegans and the Bloods coming from the south. Drifts of dust ahead would be the last of the Sarcees or Stoneys he and Sam had watched, trooping through that bright air to the appointed place.

Hum of voices came up when the plateau split before them and they saw below the tepees of the Indians on a great prairie at the base of the bluffs and cut-banks that in the ages the twisting river had left on either side. In the bottoms the cottonwoods were turning yellow, their leaves twinkling beside the diminished autumn flow. Angus could see at once where the ford was. Rutted trails converged on it fan-wise down the slopes and, having crossed, there was great whinnying of their horses to the grazing herds of the Indians who watched their arrival. Blackfeet these were by their carriage and by the three decorative prongs on their moccasins that signified the tribe of three in one.

"Ok-yi!" he saluted them, all the Blackfoot he knew.

"Ok-yi!" they responded.

A mite of five or so was busy by one of the tepees with much labour pulling out the tent pegs—for they used pegs as well as the central tripod of poles. He looked back, laughing at its solemn assiduity, watching how peg by peg was hauled up and tossed over its shoulder. The leather wall sagged. Out came the mother in haste, saw Angus slewed in his saddle grinning, and observing the cause of his amusement laughed back to him as she grabbed up the mite and carried it off astride her ample hip.

"Ok-yi!"

"Ok-yi!"

He saw a tall Indian striding slowly toward a lodge painted with many heraldic signs. For once the chimneypot hat beloved for state occasions by the chiefs of the plains, was not ridiculous in contrast with the usual headgear of these people. The hat that man wore was only the base for a circle of choice eagle-tail feathers. His native leggings, that showed beneath a robe gathered round him (a robe covered with bead-work, white and yellow, a sun folding and unfolding in it as he moved), were bead-encrusted in geometric designs, and on heavily beaded moccasins he moved slowly by. The attire did not obliterate the man. That was a face to remember, thought Angus—strong cheek-bones, strong chin under close-set mouth, aquiline nose, eyes with puzzlement in them, the face not of a savage in the ordinary acceptance of the word but of a great man out of the Neolithic age, not without humour. He had command of himself, by the way he walked. He bowed in at the entrance of the painted lodge and—

"Who is that?" Angus signed to a lad nearby, receiving in answer the sign for head-chief.

So that was Crowfoot!

They rode on, whistling the pack horses forward, and came to where the marquee of the commissioners stood with a table on the grass before it, rode on to where the tents of the Redcoats were pitched. There a sergeant pointed out where to unpack.

"Well, are they all here?" asked Angus.

"The Blackfeet are here, and those are the Piegans putting up their tepees beside them. The Stoneys and the Sarcees have come—the Stoneys are over there, and there are the Sarcee lodges. The Bloods have not arrived. I hear they are a bit haughty about it all."

Pack saddles empty, Angus and Gus rode away. They were not wanted there. They were civilians. All might, or all might not, go well. The Bloods had not come, and the non-arrival of one of the parties to the second part, as it were, of that momentous contract might shake the others.

As the pack string took the ford, one or two of the beasts pausing insouciantly to drink on the way, sudden music broke out back at the marquee, drowning the sound of tentative muffled drummings on tomtoms—a sort of muted band-practice that had begun among the lodges. To these gay rhythms the pack string, with heads rising and falling, hoofs digging well down, mounted to the plateau.

"Are you going straight home?" Gus called from the rear.

Angus shook his head.

"No," he shouted. "We'll camp back here a bit where we saw a slough that did not look too alkaline."

Others, when they reached it, were already camped beside it, hopeful traders, hopeful for the signing of the treaty and a disbursement of some Government money to the Indians—which might come their way for tea, sugar, or a string of Birmingham beads. On the other side of the slough some Crees were putting up their tepees, come curiously there to look on at the great gathering of their one-time enemies—friends since the Redcoats had arrived.

"Have the Bloods come?" one of the traders asked Angus.

"No, not yet."

"Well, I hope they don't spill the beans," said the man, turning back to his fire of buffalo chips and a pot that hung over it.

Angus and Gus moved round that little rush-bordered lake, that was like a splinter dropped off the high blue ceiling, and there made camp. As they ate lunch some young Crees rode away to south, dwindling in distance, were suddenly swallowed by the earth, to appear again anon diminished in size, drop from sight once more, and once more appeared very small. Had Angus not been watching them it would have been hard to tell what those jogging dots were.

Gus, hugging his knees, meditatively smoked.

"It looks flat here, but it isn't," he remarked, his eyes roving round the plain. "What a lot of buffalo bones!"

There were, indeed, a lot of buffalo bones. White ribs showed like the ribs of small boats. A skull in the long grass by the water's edge regarded them with a hollow stare. There were many bones there, some glinting like ivory, some powdery and bleached to the hue of lime.

Talkative, Atkins changed his pose, lay out on the grass, head propped on an elbow, watching the horses graze and bob in their hobbles.

"They always make me think of men in a three-legged race," said he.

Angus replied with a little laugh at the simile.

"I like to see the Redcoats at Fort Calgarry," Gus continued, "training their horses to stand what they may have to get when going into an Indian village to make an arrest—one or two mounted and others whooping and waving blankets at them. First time I saw that, and heard the shouts, I thought it was a mutiny—

and then I noticed they were all laughing, and tumbled to it. I sometimes think I would like to join the force." He sat up. "Here are some of these Crees back. You know their lingo, I suppose, living up in their country so long?"

"Oh, yes."

"Ask them if the Bloods have come." The young Indians, on the last lap home, rode wildly to make a spectacular return, all ki-yi-ing together. A fancy took them to swoop round the slough past the traders' horses and Angus's. They were in high spirits, and though they laughed as they circled the little lake, yelling, there was something of challenge in their eyes.

Angus noted it, but considered that there were rowdies everywhere. In Edinburgh there were street gamins, in Glasgow there were the keelies who would, feeling lively, jostle one of their number against a passerby and impudently await results.

He stood up. Some of the quirting hobbledehoys grinned, others glowered at him. Was the white man annoyed at the risk of a stampede of his hobbled horses? How would he take their fun?

He called to them in Cree: "Have the Kainu come?"

At once their manner changed. They reined in. To talk sign language is an aid; to talk the language of the Indian with whom one would converse is a stronger tie.

No. The Bloods had not arrived.

Angus's gaze was sharp on the rein-hand of the one who spoke, a stripling in his early teens. There was a collet ring upon it, the sight of which gave him a clutch at the heart, took his thoughts to Minota at Mountain House.

"That is a pretty ring," said he.

The lad changed the lines to the other hand, wheeled and rode away—the others at once following him with a rub-a-dub of hoofs, yelping like coyotes. They coasted the slough back to their own camp.

The abstraction of the foreman was thereafter so deep and so unremitting—with only a nod or a grunt, if that, to the chatter of his assistant—that at last Gus rose.

"I think I'll take a ride over to the cut-banks and see if the Bloods are in sight yet," said he.

Angus made no reply, watched apparently, but only apparently seeing, Gus bridle his horse, fold and smooth the blanket, and with a swing of his arms toss the saddle in place.

"See you later then, boss."

"Eh? Oh, yes, all right. All right!"

CHAPTER EIGHTEEN
A Collet Ring

Angus sat alone, remembering Minota. He heard her voice. Again, at an impulse to expel sadness and doubt from her eyes, he put on her hand the ring of his forebears and knew her fealty, a fealty so deep that the humility of it hurt.

That ring: How had the Cree boy come by it? Gruesome stories he had heard during the Great Sickness of roving parties, ignorant of the contagious quality of the disease, looting, ghoul-like, in tattered camps of the dead. So, no doubt, it was when the lesser sickness—that was almost as virulent to these people—passed through the land.

Of course, he told himself, there are many collet rings. Yet that one, he could all but have sworn, was of his people—his, Minota's. He must see it again, and if it was the one he suspected he might hear more of the end of Red Shield's band than anyone at Fort Edmonton or the Rocky Mountain House had been able to tell him. He must see that ring again for closer scrutiny. If it was the one he could all but swear it was he would offer to trade for it.

He rose, and with a manner as of casual visitor, to hide the determination that was urgent in him, he strolled round the rush-edged slough to the Indian camp. Dogs, as he drew near, came snarling to meet him. He walked slowly among them with a wary eye over his shoulder on those that sneaked behind him, beadily considering his heels. As he passed the first lodge there came a hiss from its entrance (white men hiss dogs on; Indians hiss them off) and an old squaw emerged, stick in hand. The dogs retired, and Angus nodded his gratitude.

Some youths playing Follow-My-Leader through the camp saw him. The leader dashed forward, made a motion with a wand he carried—the motion of counting coup—against his shoulder. He smiled amiably to a succession of taps from the followers. But an old man sitting at a tepee door further on rose and peremptorily shouted to the boys, telling them to treat a visitor more civilly. Clearly he was one having authority. Those at the end of the string did not administer the flick with the wands they carried. "They are young," said Angus in Cree. Hearing his own tongue the patriarch told his caller to be seated, moving a little sideways on a robe by the tepee where he was sunning his aged bones. Where had Angus come from? Where had he learnt to talk Cree? What was his age? So went the questions. Always they wanted to know one's age! Angus wondered why. And you? he asked in return. Seventy snows. Munro made the usual reply, "You do not look it," and received the wonted little laugh.

The approach would have been slower, strategic, had it not happened that hardly was he seated when the wearer of the ring rode to the lodge, dismounted, dropping the reins to the earth, and passed inside.

"That is a good-looking lad," said Angus.

"My son."

His son, and he was seventy! He must have a young wife.

"That is a pretty ring he has on."

"I will ask him to show it to you," and the old man called to the boy, "All Alone—come! Show this white man the ring you have."

"He has seen it already," replied All Alone, dipping out of the tepee.

"I want to see it close," Angus explained. Diffidently the youth took it off, doubtfully renounced it to the extended palm and watched, somewhat glum, while Angus turned it over and looked within its hoop. Yes, it was the ring he had given Minota. To offer to trade for it, however, while he held it, that expression on the lad's face, would never do. There would probably be a snatching of it away. So he handed it back lightly.

"A pretty ring," he said.

All Alone put it on again and stood, Indian fashion, without a word, hip-shot, considering this white stranger who had not, after all, wanted to trade for his ring as he had feared, only to look at it. A few moments later he moved away, mounted his horse and rode off.

"What band of Crees is this?" asked Angus.

"The band of Buffalo Calf. I am Buffalo Calf."

"My name is Angus Munro."

Buffalo Calf nodded and his brows puckered as he tried to say it to himself. Then he bethought him of some appropriate English he knew and spoke it slowly.

"I am—pleased—to—met—you," said he, holding out his hand.

The salutation over, he seemed to retire into himself, elbow on thigh, hand cupped to pipe-bowl, puffing smoke deliberately.

"That is a nice boy," remarked Angus.

"What boy?" and the chief glanced left and right.

"Your son."

"Yes."

"I knew many Crees when I was at Fort Edmonton, and met

101

others sometimes when I was at the Mountain House." said Angus. "I never saw you there."

"I always traded at Fort Carlton or Fort Pitt."

Angus nodded and sat silent while the old man examined him—and liked him. He decided to have this white visitor's opinion upon a matter that puzzled him.

"Do you think," he began, coming abruptly to the point, "that there is any sign that would bring the old days back?"

Angus had not listened to Minota for nothing. He understood. This was normal, not fantastic.

"I think the past can never come back," said he.

"I wonder," said Buffalo Calf. "Sometimes I go and sit on a cliff over which our people used to drive the buffalo long ago, even before we had ears." (Before, that is to say, any definite history). "I sit there and wonder if I could find a sign to bring the past back again—the far past before the Great Sickness, before the white man came. There have always been white men in my time but too many come now. I am not happy about this. I used to think, so many buffalo they kill and take away the beef and the robes, that they must be either very poor or very many. Now so many come that I think your people cannot always be born like us, of woman. I think many of you must be born from leaves of trees. A wind blows in autumn; the leaves fall—and they rise up white men. But, perhaps, there is a medicine sign that would send them away. Too many come. I think, perhaps, some day I may find that sign," he went on, moving his hands in air, "and when I make it the buffalo will be here—many, not few—and all the white men's forts and lodges of wood will be gone."

There seemed no hatred of the white man to whom he divulged this idea, this hope. He spoke in a frank naïveté.

Angus looked at him sadly. Minota had views touched with a similar simplicity.

"Do you think it is true, what I hear?" asked the chief. "Is it true that before long all the land here will be covered with white men?"

"It may be."

"I have heard from some Assiniboines who have been far south that the white men there—the Long Knives" (cavalry sabres) "have a wagon that goes by fire and pulls other wagons full of white men, and every day they go along. I have heard that a fire-wagon is to come to these plains. Is that true?"

"Yes. I have heard that," said Angus.

"Do you think that when the white men are all over our country we shall die?" inquired Buffalo Calf. His tone, however, less suggested that he thought so than that, if Angus held such a view, he would dispute it.

"No," replied Angus, "not if you look after your cattle. Not if you plough and sow."

"We shall not die!" exclaimed the old man. "I shall tell you why. Indian blood is strong. One drop of Indian blood is stronger than a hundred drops of white man's blood. I have seen it."

"You have seen it?"

"Yes. I have seen children of a white man and an Indian woman—and they were all Indian. The white man's blood was weak. More than that. I have seen white people here who were Indian to look at."

"I've seen that, too," Angus admitted, recalling some men at Fort Calgarry who were unquestionably of white parentage yet very like the Indians, "but I think it is just because they have to breathe as your people do the air of these big prairies. It shapes their noses. It makes their chests," he drew deep breaths in explanation, "like yours. They pucker their eyes to the sun on snow, and to the brightness of the summer sky, and their eyes become like yours. The sun makes their faces dark like yours."

"It may be so," said Buffalo Calf, as one considering an opinion new to him, "but I do not think it is that. I have thought it is because all this is Indian country and it turns even white men to Indians in time."

"Perhaps," said Angus, for pity's sake, feeling again as he had felt on seeing Crowfoot—as often he had felt living with Minota—that the general acceptation of the word savage is misleading. These were but folk out of an earlier epoch. They had minds. They could reason—but they were of the stone age. The age of steel, of knives bearing on their blades the legend Sheffield, England, was puzzling to them.

"I am an old man," said Buffalo Calf. "My father remembered when there were no Red River carts coming across the plains here to carry away the robes and the meat. My woman's father remembered also. She is sixty-five."

"How do you have a son of sixteen years?" Angus asked. "Have you a second, and younger, woman?"

"No. I made him my son," replied Buffalo Calf. "Sixteen snows back we came on a camp of our people where all were dead of a sickness like the Great Sickness, but that did not leave the bodies so bad. He was in a tepee beside his mother. They were all dead except that papoose. I took him. I made him my son. I called him All Alone." (Angus sat cross-legged, pipe gone out, staring at this savage—this neolithic man born too late). "I said, 'I will make this boy my son,' for my two true sons had been killed by the Blackfeet when going to steal horses from them."

"Yes?"

"I gave him to one of our women to suckle. I took the ring that was on the mother's finger and kept it till he was fifteen snows. Then I gave it to him."

Angus's hand was trembling, holding the pipe on his knee. How was he to know more? He had not expected this! The old man who talked might suddenly, with his views, being what he was, become silent.

"Do you think he is a true Indian?" he inquired in a voice he scarcely recognized as his own.

There were times when these people were to Angus more as a dark-hued peasantry, a genial, laughing peasantry, than barbarians. But at this point the face beside him changed. The expression altered so that it seemed the very contours altered also. It was as if the eyes drew closer. There was actually that effect as of a profile even in full face. Here was the savage, as the word is generally understood, his eyes glittering like a cougar's.

"Yes!" he shouted, and in his vehemence accentuated it by the affirmative sign. Then he pointed at Angus. "I took her things. I took the things in her tepee. I did not know they would carry that sickness as the Great Sickness is carried. They did. Many of our band died afterwards. The white men at Fort Pitt told me it was because I had taken these things."

"Yes, yes, no doubt. But how do you know he is all Indian?"

"Because the Indian blood is strong—though his father was a white man."

"His father was a white man!"

"Yes. There was a letter"—he made the sign for writing—"among her things. I asked the factor at Fort Pitt to speak it to me. He thought it should be burnt because it carried the little Great Sickness. I thought it good to do so—to wipe all out. It was from her white man to say that though he was far away he thought of her and would come back. They all say that."

"He may not have known she had a son. It may have come after he went away."

"Could he not have seen her belly?"

"He may have gone before it showed."

The look of rage died on the face of Buffalo Calf.

"Yes," he said, "it is possible."

Very Indian was he then, thought Angus, having had experience of their willingness to reason a matter—and condone.

"Yes, it may be so," agreed Buffalo Calf, and fluttered a hand before him in the sign for uncertainty.

"The white man wrote to her," Angus went on, still in that voice he hardly knew. "When white men leave their Indian women not to come back they do not write."

"That is true," said Buffalo Calf, knocking out the ashes of his pipe, and pulling the chokecherry stem from the bowl he put both in a deerskin sack.

"The man may not have known before he left," repeated Angus. "He may not have known."

The thought came to him: Did Minota know? Did she withhold the word from him because of his wish to go with Sam to the land of his people? His brows puckered as he tried to make a calculation of the time of his leaving her and the time of the little Great Sickness. No, she would not know till some weeks after he had gone. What would her thought be then, waiting for him with her people?

A little wind sighed in the grass and the rushes of the lake's edge tattled together. He looked up to find Buffalo Calf's eyes on him.

"You looked as if you died a little while," said the old man in their phrase for deepest reveries, a dwam, fainting. "The Indian blood is strong. That man would not know his own son if he came back."

"Have you told All Alone his father was—a white man?" Angus's voice sounded then as though he spoke in an empty room.

"He knows that he is my adopted son but I have not told him that his father was a white man. That might make him ashamed. I grow old. My true sons are dead. This son I will leave. There, he comes now. Is he not an Indian boy? Look at him again. I do not know why I have told you all this. Perhaps because of the way you give your ears. Even if I cannot make a medicine sign and bring back the buffalo of old, and put all the white men away, I think that in time all men on these Great Plains will be true Indians. He comes. You will not speak? Have pity."

"No, I will not speak."

"Swear! Touch the earth, point to the sky. You know my people. You know the oath. Swear!"

Angus rose. He lifted a hand to point to that tremendous sky but at the moment the lad came close and he changed the sign. He lifted both hands in air and slowly lowered them in the sign of blessing, and a haze was in his eyes, blinding them.

Buffalo Calf, looking on, was content. This man, he thought, was one of the good whites. All Alone might have been startled had

105

he seen the sign of taking an oath and have pestered with questions. The blessing would suffice. The white man was going, and in going made that sign—that was all.

To his camp-place Angus walked back round the slough, hardly noticing that the traders to south of it were no longer there, had moved while, over at the village, he had talked with Buffalo Calf. He sat down. How long he sat he did not know.

Out of a clear sky to west little clouds magically appeared, a row of them—as from the Arctic to Mexico, so high—white clouds that turned to red, that turned to gold, that turned to a file of tenuous flames, the sun setting behind the distant Rockies: but of these displays of Nature he was unaware.

He had a son, an Indian son, all Indian—all Indian! What could he do about this? What should he do? He started as a horse came close and Gus dismounted, whistling a snatch of a waltz that Strauss, visiting New York the year before with his orchestra, had let loose to be hummed and whistled across the continent. Angus looked up.

"The Bloods have come," said Gus.

"Oh!"

"Did you not hear them?"

"Hear them?"

"Yes, I thought you would hear them as far as this. They came singing—singing in from south. You missed something, sticking around here. I wouldn't have missed it for worlds. Came singing, all feathered, their bonnets swaying, over the edges of the cut-bank south. That was a sight."

"Oh?"

All that evening S. D.'s foreman, thought Gus, was as a man sickening for something, or one who had heard of a death. That was the only way he could describe Angus's melancholy abstraction. He could not get a word out of him.

For long Angus lay awake, thinking, thinking, under the eternal sweep of the Milky Way, the Ghost Trail. At last his eyes closed, and when he awoke in the morning the camp of the Crees to the east end of that lakelet was gone. The rushes, the border grass, and the sky-mirroring water had an aspect of entire possession of the morning's light.

CHAPTER NINETEEN
Prairie Schooner

Somewhat as Angus had noticed, when rejoining Sam at Fort Calgarry, that his old friend looked his age, did Sam in the days following his foreman's return from Blackfoot Crossing, see him as one changed. He wondered if Munro had received a letter containing ill news—perhaps from those Red River Settlement friends of his. Not that he went about his duties with the aspect of one cherishing melancholy. Not at all. In fact, the indication as of a private trouble came, partly, from a new sort of cheerfulness he dispensed, that seemed forced instead of spontaneous.

Angus did not, however, long permit his secret to be like blinds down at windows. He had mastered, so far as outward signs were concerned, save to the shrewdest eyes, that dolour which made Gus think—out yonder on the plains—that he must be sickening for something, or that the way to describe his condition was to say that one might have suspected he had had news of a death. Gus had found him cheery companion as ever, riding home. Still, such was Sam Douglas's impression.

But Sam had his own worries—of another sort. Rumour was flying that the railway was not, after all, to come their way, but to go swinging northwest from the Red River by that splashing of forts—Ellice, Pelly, Pitt, Carlton, Edmonton—and on through the Yellow Head Pass.

"Where," demanded Sam Douglas of Angus, as though he could change all that, "are the cattlemen who are coming in here to ship their steers if they slither that railroad away up there into the Arctic Circle?"

Angus chuckled at the extravagance.

"Laugh? It's no laughing matter for those like myself who have assured people that here was going to be the great cattle-shipping centre. They will have to drive them these millions of miles" (Angus restrained another chuckle) "over the border to ship. I think I'll have to go in for politics to see we get what we need here. Taking the railway up there to Hellangone! Well, we'll have a smoke."

Yet a little while—during which Douglas went about cloudy of brow—and all was well again.

"Heard the news?" he inquired, coming into the office, carrying two travelling bags, a robe flung over a shoulder. There was a twist to his grim mouth, an upward twist to one side, of gaiety.

"What?"

"The railway company that has taken over from the government has changed the route. I suppose they've been looking up the old reports of Palliser and seen that he vetoed not only this route but all—on grounds of finance, no immediate advantage commensurate with the required sacrifice of capital was what his report said. I mind the words well for I thought—"

"That he didn't jump far enough ahead?"

"Quite! And he affixed Hector's report telling that there were easy gradients this way once they got to the west slopes. Rogers now, I hear, is of the same mind as Moberly was these twenty years ago—how time flies! And I've just had a letter that says Sandford Fleming plumps for the Kicking Horse Pass. Have a cigar?"

There was the swaying yoked trudge past the door of a string of bullocks, the shadow of the wagon they hauled moving across the floor, the scliff of another span behind. Angus went out to see that all was in order for departure of the train to Benton and Sam followed, stepping into the group of bull-whackers that clustered round the foreman.

"Have a cigar, have a cigar," said he.

"Is this just a smoke or a celebration, Sam?" asked one of the men.

"The railway is coming this way," Sam told him. He struck a match on his leg, held the flame for them to light up. "I'll just get my things into one of the wagons. I'm coming with you."

"You are going to Fort Benton?" asked Angus.

"Yes—and on. You can do all I can do here till I get back."

So at last he went down the Benton trail—in safety.

It was two years before he returned, and during these two years many people came to Calgary. A second hotel was built to house the arrivals. Angus recalled Buffalo Calf's complaint, "Too many people come." Thought of Buffalo Calf cast his thoughts darkly into the past. If only he had known! If only he had followed that impulse that warred against his departure (which was of his own volition), these years ago, from Rocky Mountain House. Minota's son, his son, could have been educated as the sons of these old Company men, who took their women east with them, were educated. Too late . . .

Up from Nebraska, up from Kansas, came whole families, father, mother, daughters in the wagons, sons driving the cattle and horse herds alongside. One of these middle-aged immigrants told Angus that when he was a lad he had left his Ohio home for Kansas but—

"It's getting too danged crowded there," said he, "so we thought we'd move where there was room, and all got into this here prairie schooner."

Prairie schooner: it was a good word. He remembered his first crossing of the plains with Aloysius and Pierre, and how they spoke, on its flat stretches, of being out of sight of land. Still was the impression, on these seas of grass, of marine adventure.

The prairie schooners came rocking, lurching, over the long rolls, their canvas hoods to be seen twinkling like the sails of a ship at sea. Frequent were occasions, incidents, that made Angus think of his son. There came to Calgary a land surveyor in government service who was, he discovered, a full-blood Oneida Indian from Ontario (Upper Canada of old); a man of the most pleasing manners, quiet-spoken and full of character. True, that was an Indian of the east where for generations the natives had been in touch with the whites. But he met also a half-breed civil engineer, son of a Scots father and a Saulteaux woman, these retired in Winnipeg, who made him again abstracted in the eyes of others for awhile, he thinking of All Alone, all Indian. How old now? In his late teens. Too late . . . But some day, when Sam came back, Angus decided he would take a month off, go to the Buffalo Calf reserve, and see the chief and All Alone—though what good, he asked himself, would that do? Well, he could at least see if all went well with the lad.

The seasons toned one into the other. The Rockies were obliterated in rain. Any newcomer would have to take them on faith. The sky dropped a curtain halfway toward them, a quaking gray curtain. Dust rose no longer from pattering hoofs and rolling wheels. The hoofs squelched; the wagons laboured and sometimes slowly subsided in mud to the hubs. Snow came and then a morning when the mountains glittered in the west, utterly white save where some gable of rock was too precipitous even for the wind of blizzard to plaster its face. At evening the white changed to gold and pink, to blood-red, to purple. Runners took the place of wheels on the carts. A Chinook wind blew from west and the snow soon turned to slush. Frost came and the oozy ruts, with the hummock between, hardened. Wagons were sorely tried with joltings in and out of these rigid grooves. Spring came and mire again, mire quickly dried in the hot sun. Hoofs sputtered dust, wagons trailed dust.

Back came Sam Douglas, but not by Fort Benton as he had gone, came from railhead—which was halfway across Assiniboia. The basis of Sam's fortune had been laid while he was away, he

109

calmly buying and selling town lots in the hectically buying and selling "city" of Winnipeg, with no financial aid from any and on behalf of none (he had given them their chance long ago), merely with his own savings and for his own hand. Back in Calgary—they had dropped the Fort and were beginning to spell it with one r, accentuating the first syllable—a new sign appeared over the door of a new building, one not of logs but of whip-saw lumber: S. Lovat Douglas, Real Estate.

Sam thought not only of himself.

"If you have a sock under your bed, Angus," said he one day, "with any savings in it, say the word if you'd like me to treble it for you—and with no commission, just for auld time's sake."

Angus Munro, on the spot, however, was as timid, it seemed to Sam, as those in distance who had disappointed him years previously. To him his friend showed lack of faith, content with quick sales and then a dubious retreat. The men to whom Douglas sold for him seemed, to Angus's mind, to be saddled—at the prices they paid—with lots that never could they sell again, only pay taxes on! Yes, Angus, in Sam's mind, fell away to a mere ordinary man fit for no more than the management of a livery stable.

There came a day when Angus was thinking much of the Frasers, could not have got them out of his mind had he wanted to. He had not heard from them for a long while. In Fiona's last letter he had been told of Flora's marriage and, reading, recalled her as first he saw her, a mere tot of plump wonder. She had married a descendant of one of those Swiss that the Earl of Selkirk had brought to Red River as a protective military force for the Selkirk and Kildonan settlers. To that letter he had replied. Later he had written again; then silence.

So much were they in his mind that he dismissed the notion that a correspondence should be equally balanced, ding-dong. It was usually Fiona who wrote for the family. What, he asked himself, made him think so much of them all? He remembered the freits, the omens of his mother. He would write that very day—and had just made the resolve when Gus Atkins entered, greatly amused. He had what he thought of as rich humour to communicate, without malice. All day he had been driving for Sam a capacious rig full of landlookers. These, considered Angus as he listened, had been easier to deal with than the folk in Glasgow and Edinburgh when Douglas tried to awaken enthusiasm for western investment in the Auld Country, easier to deal with by the fact that they brought enthusiasm, even travelling ahead of steel at its urge.

It was the extent of the Great Metropolis of the West, as seen by his employer, that amused Gus Atkins.

"Does he really believe it all?" he asked, sitting on the table, hugging his knees and laughing a resumé of the prophesies of Sam Lovat Douglas.

"Oh, yes, he's genuine," said Angus.

"Well! Calgary is going to stretch, according to him, halfway south to Fort Macleod, halfway north to the Mountain House, and bang up west to the Rockies. 'Now here,'" and he imitated Sam's voice, "'here's the ideal site for a fire-hall. Here's a whole stretch of lots I have on my books but I can't let you in on that. I've a man considering the purchase of the whole caboodle for a stadium and I passed him my word I would give him two-three days to consider the matter.'—'Here's a fine site I often think for a town hall. Can't you see the grand situation?'—'We'll drive through the future residential area now, or a part of it. We can't cover it all in a day.' He's a mesmerist! I was nearly mesmerized myself. If I hadn't those peppy horses to handle I'd have been seeing mansions of the Calgary-to-be rising in porcupine meadows and prairie-dog pastures. You really think he is genuine?"

"I do, indeed, Gus."

"Why don't you buy more, then?"

"Because I'm not such an optimist, that's all."

A prairie schooner rolled past the door, another, astern, halted there with a swaying of whiffle-tree and a jingle of chain. Some pilgrim wanting a repair or a direction to the government post, no doubt, thought Angus.

As he looked, a young woman swung out from the seat in an agile movement to the hub, the ground, and stepped in at the door—a tall girl, over her dress a long buckskin coat, on her hands fringed driving gauntlets. He had risen as she entered. Gus slid from the table to attention. She advanced, drawing off a glove and revealing a shapely hand.

Angus stared at her.

"Fiona!" he cried out. "Fiona, my dear!"

"See you later," said Gus Atkins.

CHAPTER TWENTY
Fiona

Angus took her hands. He held them, incredulous, first, of this descent upon him and amazed, secondly, at the manner in which she had as it were made up on him. She let him hold her, canted back, laughing happily at his astonishment—and clear

111

admiration. She was like morning in that long low-ceilinged room to him.

How long they remained so he did not know. Thought, no doubt, was lightning-quick then: this tall girl, this woman—the child whose lessons he had hearkened, the child of "Thus spake the sheriff . . ." it seemed impossible. To that earliest memory of her—he sixteen, she not six—even more than to later ones (he twenty, she nine, or he going west again and she but a lass in her teens to his young manliness) his mind returned.

"But what does it mean?" he began.

"Come and see."

He relinquished her hands, and as they walked out there was a feeling in him as though his deepmost being strangely passed beyond the confines of the body and merged with hers. Was she aware of it, too? he wondered. The emotion was as one they must share.

Mr. Fraser was clambering down from the first tilted wagon as they came outside, and his greeting was a hearty, chesty laugh at the expression on Angus's face. Mrs. Fraser was still in the wagon from which Fiona had alighted, craning from the hooped open front of the tilt to see him and stretch a hand to him.

"But what does it mean?" he asked.

"You can see," replied Fraser. "And all the family unanimous, whatever."

"Where is Hector?"

"Back there with the horses. We brought no cattle, for it is the long-horned steers here, and—"

"You are—"

"Beginning afresh. And you needn't say I'm either crazy or too old, for I've seen others a lot older than me at the game as we crawled along here upon our way. Come and meet Mrs. Hector. She's in the wagon I'm driving."

"Mrs. Hector?"

"Yes, Mrs. Hector Fraser. Hector decided to get married before we started."

But the horses that Hector was guarding chose that moment to come milling towards them. Angus hauled away the bars of the big pole-corral.

"Herd them in here," he shouted.

The quality of a dream remained, was indeed accentuated when, an hour later, they all sat down together in one of the three (there were three by that time) hotels of hammering Calgary.

"It's like a dream," Angus told them.

"It has been like a dream," said Fiona. "I'll never forget the dawns on the prairie," and then suddenly was shy by her own remark.

"We saw lots of antelope," remarked Hector. "Didn't we, Mohra?" to his young wife. "It must have been a sight when there were buffalo also. We saw their wallows all the way across, and their trails—and, their bones. We saw a prairie fire far off, and the wind was not coming our way by good luck."

"A mounted policeman," said Mrs. Fraser, "told us that these fires are mostly started by bottles, broken bottles and the sun shining through them making them like burning glasses."

"He said," added Ian, "that the chief export of this country might be broken bottles for awhile to come."

Sitting there at meat with them, Angus had a memory of St. Cloud close on twenty-four years earlier, wondered why, and then realized. It was the waitresses who rolled back time for him—these four reigning queens among the tables. There were no written bills-of-fare. They stood stately beside the diners and, with heads erect and eyelids supercilious, recited the menu. The hush in the room was as in deference to them. Dido and Helen, Semiramis and Cleopatra condescended to the muted guests, setting plates before them and icily demanding, "What do you drink—tea or coffee?" St. Cloud, Minnesota, his father and mother and he waiting for the stage to start out for Abercrombie on the Red River, and his mother with a little dip of her head, an elevation of her brows, whispering, "Are we not the grand hussies, whatever?" a twinkle in her eyes.

There followed on that memory a sense of having other kindred in the world still as well as that son lost to him, all Indian. True the Frasers were but forty-second cousins, but they were his and he was theirs, whatever! Sentiment was alive in him, if not indeed sentimentality. Let it go as sensibility as still, in those days, the word was used.

He sat back and looked at Fiona and had a thought he could tell to none: Some drops of the same blood that coursed in his veins was in hers, and so thinking he had again that emotion of strange contact with her that he had experienced when stepping out of the office to greet the others. Fiona met his eyes and first a haze was in the pools of hers, then through that haze she smiled.

One of the great queens of that room bent over Mrs. Fraser in a descent from her high estate.

"Well, folks," she inquired, "was everything all right?"

The Frasers were all startled by the change.

"Just splendid," replied Mrs. Fraser, and, as the lady

lingered: "This is the first time we have been in a hotel since we left home."

"Where do you come from?"

"Red River Settlement—near Winnipeg."

But at that moment another party arrived and the queen who had called them folks departed, taking on regality again. The Frasers passed out of that hotel in Calgary—and Angus from the hotel in St. Cloud! He carried them off to visit Sam Douglas in the real estate office.

"The best move you could ever have made," declared Sam. Here were people—here was a family—to his mind, folk of wisdom and faith. "Aye, we'll get you a location. We'll take them in hand, Angus."

He explained that he could easily spare the time off to make an unhurried, leisurely search for the right spot. He deserved, he considered, some little celebration of rest and recreation.

"I have the very place for you in my mind," he said. "Spitsee Country, ye ken, Angus," he threw out the aside and turned again to the Frasers. "I've ridden that way once or twice and always I've thought, There's the place for the perfect ranch house. There's a creek trotting along round the bases of the low hills, a real wee burn. There's timber handy for the building. You are right in the lush range country, too. Angus, we'll both knock off a few days and see to this."

They saw many locations during the next weeks but in the end the one the Frasers chose was the one that Sam spoke of on first hearing of their intention to settle in that west. It was a vast land—and there were no motor cars in those days to whirl them on their way. The best part of a month was gone when the decision was made.

The rolling hills that day were of the tone of coyote pelts. As they dipped through coulees they saw the yellow tufts of sagebrush against blue. As they crested the rolls they saw the higher ones beyond crowned with stands of trees so that each mound looked like a great bristling porcupine. Backward there were vistas up long retiring valleys, from the edges of which the mountains rose abruptly. The trotting of the little brooks—the wee burns—round and about the bases of the tawny hummocks was very pleasing to eyes and ears.

They began to talk of the railway, Sam, no doubt, setting the theme. While they were on their way west, they told him, the railway had already passed Medicine Hat where, said legend, a Blackfoot chief saw the headgear of a medicine man rise from the waters, and then the head a moment—in some omen, perhaps, such as Mrs. Munro might have been able to comprehend. There they had talked to Mr. Ross—Mr. James Ross—a Highland engineer and, further on, to an enormous man who was overseeing the actual track-laying, one Donald Grant by name, from Glengarry—in Scotland. He had beaten the thrusting record, at eight miles a day, and hoped to beat his own record again.

They were actually in the midst of that talk when they came to a crest, on the shoulder of which the Spitsee trail dipped aslant toward the big coulee near Calgary. From there they had a vision of the plain as from a coast range one looks out to sea. There was a flash yonder, a flash, a gleam, drawing their attention. There was more: two silver wires lay on the prairie tapering away to one in perspective. The railway, in their absence, had come closer.

Sam led Ian Fraser to the government post to introduce him (as "an old friend o' mine") to the government agent and recorder. Hector, Mrs. Hector and Mrs. Fraser had been dropped at the hotel. Fiona and Angus remained outside. They could see from there the S. D. Transport and Haulage stables.

"There's a whole string of pack ponies," said Fiona suddenly, "gone loping into your barn and no rider with them. There must have been an accident!"

"That's all right," Angus replied, having observed them also. "There would be no rider with them. People hire them to pack stuff out to their places and they come back alone to the stables."

"I love it! I love this country!" she exclaimed impetuously.

It came to his mind that he had intended, some day, to take a month off and go to the reservation of Buffalo Calf and see how all went with his son—Minota's son. All Alone. When he was seventeen and Fiona but six, little did he dream of this day, she a woman grown, moving him to the deeps of his being by her mere presence beside him, by the tones of her voice—as at that moment.

CHAPTER TWENTY-ONE
VOILA LES BOEUFS!

The Frasers were building their new home at the chosen location in the Spitsee River country—as the whites pronounced Is-pit-si, which, being interpreted, means High Woods. A little later it would be called Highwood River; a little later still, High River, and few would be curious to ask and only a few old men would be able to tell whence the name.

Angus was back at work.

"This place goes jumping ahead," said Sam, "and the railway hasn't spoilt the transport and haulage business as some blind prophets foretold. Quite the reverse. All the pack strings out on the tote-road, the wagons rolling down the Benton road—if no further, sometimes, than to Macleod—and up to Edmonton. I see another kirk-steeple rising, though the Anglicans are still holding their services in the mounted police orderly room; and there's a wheen red lights of the Scarlet Women in their shacks down by the railway. Yes, we will let the natives see what civilization means," and he chuckled in his chest.

It was at that time, when Angus was still busy over arrears of bookkeeping, that there came to Calgary one who was to—well, there came to Calgary the Western Commissioner for the Department of the Interior (Indian Affairs) at Ottawa. He wanted somebody to drive him out to the Sareee and Stoney reserves, on a tour of inspection. Angus would have liked to go but his month of land-looking with the Frasers had left a clutter of arrears. So the Commissioner was driven away by one who figured on the payroll as Milk River Mike. (They had names like that on the payrolls in those days.)

Sam had expected that his foreman would go with the Commissioner, knowing as he did what he called Angus's Indian kink and recalling, no doubt, that when the police force wanted a pack string to supplement their transportation facilities at the time of the great gathering at Blackfoot Crossing, Angus had considered it expedient to go.

"I thought you'd be off with that Indian Department man," he remarked.

"Too busy," replied Angus.

That answer set Douglas pondering.

"If I lost him," he considered to himself, "I would be hard pressed to find one to take his place. I hope he doesn't get that malady they call the itching foot some day—and up and off." He drummed a tattoo on his desk, frowning over the thought that it might be as well to take Angus into partnership. "No, I would not like to lose him," he mused, but dismissed that for the moment—and was to lose him before long.

For on the return of the Commissioner to Calgary he and Angus had a long talk, the result of which was that six weeks later Sam, looking up from his desk over at the real estate office to see who came in, saw it was Angus who had ridden across from the stables. Everybody rode then in Calgary if it was to go no further than a hundred yards, hitching rails, or rings in posts, before the doors, though many of the horses were trained to stand with but dropped lines, tied to the ground. In Angus's hand, as Sam noted on his entrance, was a letter, governmental-looking.

"So you are leaving me," said he.

"How did you hear?" asked Angus, astonished—and in a way relieved, for how to broach his errand had troubled him.

"I didn't hear. I jaloused. It's written on your forehead. Sit down and tell me. Have a cigar—and tell me."

"I've an appointment as Indian Agent on the High Butte reservation. The chief's name is Running Antelope."

"High Butte?"

"Do you remember it?"

"Do I remember it?" echoed Sam. "Do you think that though it's the future I chiefly consider, I've no memory at all? Fine I remember it and you riding up the slope for a last look at the mountains. How many years ago is that?"

"It must be around twenty," said Angus. "The reservation doesn't include the butte, but it's so called because that's the nearest landmark."

"When do you want to go?"

"As soon as convenient. I'm to take over from a man there who has been appointed to another reservation, in Assiniboia."

"Oh, well—you'll no doubt be Minister of the Department yet, sitting in a braw office in Ottawa," Sam prophesied, and then he lay back in his chair and laughed—laughed at the expression on his foreman's face. "Oh, man Angus!" he exclaimed. "I can read that on you, too. 'No thanks,' says you, 'I'd rather bide out here.' By the way, that fellow Gus Atkins is leaving me, too. He'll be over for his time from you. He's joining the mounted police. Sojers' buttons, sojers' buttons—and the clink of the spurs! There's no future in that for him I doubt, just a wee pension if he lives to get it and isn't filled full of lead by some whisky smuggler or cattle-stealing Indian. Sojers' buttons, a Redcoat, and a hat like a pill-box on the side of the head giving nae protection from the summer sun—a ridiculous headpiece. They should have hats like the cowboys. Romance? There is more romance in my life sitting here buying and selling Canada—though I wear no red coat." He drummed his fingers on the desk. "The Frasers will miss you," he said.

"I'll miss having them fairly close," said Angus.

"There was something else I was going to ask you—oh, yes: have you two-three wagons not being used?"

"Yes."

"That's fine. I'm giving a job to some of your Indian friends. I have often, out on the plains, looked at that graveyard of buffalo

117

bones and wondered if there was no money in them. I've discovered that there is. Not much. A little. I'm in touch with a big sugar refinery business and it seems they buy bones."

"What on earth for?"

"I have no idea and it's not for me to inquire. They have use for bones and will pay for them: that's all that interests me. It's a mere side issue so far as the profits go. Och—it's a charity! I've been talking to some Sarcees about it. You let them have half a dozen wagons, they will provide the teams, and they'll go out and shovel the bones up. I'll ship them away to the sugar refinery. I'll send them over to you."

He sat back in his chair and played a tattoo again on his desk, staring moodily at Angus, pondering some thought a long while, then he seemed to dismiss whatever had been in his mind.

"Ye ken yer ain ken best, ye ken, " said he. "After all, you'll be more happy with yon Crees than you were with the Ettrick brothers. Yon was a comic interlude in your life! Godsakes, it's a funny thing, life! I sometimes think we live several lives, some of us, not just one."

It was a thought not unfamiliar to Angus, a thought that again he toyed with riding out on the Spitsee trail a week or two later. For some distance he went by the Benton road, a broad series of parallel ruts like a widely ploughed ribbon for border of prairie and foothills. He met one of the S. D. bullock trains rolling in and turned aside to avoid, as they used to say, eating its dust. He made up on a wolfer journeying to some sod-cabin of the plains, revolver on hip, rifle under the rope of his diamond-hitched pack—one of those who made their living on the sale of wolf pelts, with a bonus (cattlemen then in the land) of bounty on each one slain.

"No more poisoning a carcase," the wolfer told him, "to get them. The poison kills more than the wolves. Straight shooting and trapping now. It was the Indians kicked first about the poisoning game and I don't blame them."

"You get on with them?"

"Yes, siree! Now and then I'll have a little party of them come to my lonesome shack and try to throw a scare into me, for devilment, but I got friends among them now—though, believe me, I can stage a pretty good scare myself!"

He rode away to east and, perhaps in the change to lonesome riding again, under that high September sky, began to sing Red River Shore. The lilt of it stuck in Angus's mind. He was humming it to himself when he came to the rise from which the new Fraser home showed.

Ian and Hector, small figures, were making movements that Munro knew to be of men digging post-holes. He saw Fiona and Hector's wife appear beyond the house and begin to hang up clothes on empty air—an odd effect of distance. A row of bunting fluttered anon and the little figures were eclipsed by the building.

There was a feeling among all that he had come on a special errand. Sam Douglas was not the only thought-reader, or observer of facial expression. Almost did Ian ask what brought him to them that day, but to have done so would have suggested that Angus might not come there except on a special errand. When he did announce to them that he was leaving Sam to go into the service of the Department of the Interior, Ian cried out: "I knew there was something!" and felt self-gratulation on his perceptivity.

Deeper was the perceptivity of Mrs. Fraser. She suspected that he had come for more than to tell them that. This man, she mused, worships the ground Fiona treads on! What, she wondered, had kept him single so long? The lack, no doubt, of white women in the land till but recently. What age was he? He was over forty. "I'm a believer," she communed with herself, "in the man being a bit older than the woman. Well, you never know how things will go with the young. There was Flora, the baby, married years ago—and by the last news soon to make me a grandmother; and here is Fiona, single still, though she is a lass any man might worship—whatever."

After the evening meal was finished, the dishes washed, they went outside to the gable and sat there on a bench, all save Hector, who preferred the top bar of the new pole-corral, the high heels of his cowboy's shoes hooked to a lower one, he humped up there in the fair and proper attitude of all good men of the cattle ranges. They talked of this and that, of the news from Flora, of the river-boat that had been built down at Coalbanks on the Belly River for a Mr. Lethbridge, an Englishman, president of the Northwest Coal and Navigation Company.

"A hundred and seventy-one feet long," Hector said, "thirty-one feet broad, and with a draft of but a couple of feet."

"I heard two and a half," said Ian.

"I heard two!"

They talked of the mine at Coalbanks and how Sir Alexander Galt had had the idea to use the coal there to supply the Canadian Pacific Railway.

"Mr. Douglas never went ahead with his notion of getting coal out of the far nor'-west?" asked Ian.

"No. His interest is all town lots now, apart from the transport business."

"It's a wonder nothing came of that other idea. Of course, it needs capital. Perhaps he'll go ahead with it after all when the country up there opens. I hear some folks have applied for leave to build a railway from Coalbanks to Medicine Hat—"

"Narrow gauge," Hector stated from his lofty perch.

"Yes, narrow gauge. The boat is not very satisfactory at low water."

"Douglas was speaking about that the other day," said Angus. "It's Sir Alexander Galt, he tells me, who's at the back of that, president of the steamship company. He's applying for a charter for that line instead—narrow gauge," and he nodded up to Hector, who grinned down at him. "You know who he is?"

"High Commissioner for Canada in Great Britain now, or something like that they call him, isn't it?" replied Fraser.

"Yes, but I should have said, Do you know who his father was? He's a son of the Galt of Irvine, you know, who wrote Annals of the Parish."

"I've read that," said Fiona. "So that's who he is!"

"I wonder if Mr. Douglas will ever get a title. Sir Samuel Lovat Douglas would sound fine," observed Mrs. Fraser.

"I don't think they should have titles in this country," said Hector.

"Nor do I," said Mohra.

"His father was a Sir, wasn't he?" asked the mother.

"Yes, a knight, not a baronet, so—"

"So Samuel Lovat Douglas will have to win instead of inherit it. Well, that's the only kind of title there should ever be," Hector declared. "The Indians know what they are doing when they have chiefs by character instead of by birth."

Mr. Fraser rose.

"I've got one or two chores to do yet," said he, "as the English folk out here call them—a good old English word I have no doubt. I'll away and finish them."

He departed toward the stables and Hector, leaping to the ground, followed him.

"I'll just step in and see to the stove," said Mrs. Fraser. "These autumn nights are a wee bit cool, though the days are hot."

"I'll go," Fiona offered.

"No, no, I'll see to it."

"I'll come with you. I'll go and see if there's anything I can do," said Mrs. Hector.

"You like it here?" asked Angus, when he and Fiona were alone.

"I love it," she told him.

She stooped, running a hand up a stalk of sage, and shucked off a palm-full of the little flowers. Then she crushed them in her hand and held it open, setting free on the air the heavy aromatic scent.

"I love that smell," said she.

She closed her hand, opened it again, and he bent to whiff the fragrance of these crushed yellow blossoms. And it was once more as it had been on that day when he walked out of the office with her to greet the others—the day of their arrival. His being went out beyond the confines of the body and hers, surely, he thought, also knew that strange overflowing, because of an emotion he had of meeting, mingling, of being one with her. He took her hand, he drew her to him, and she leant to him in a great content. In that embrace they shared ecstatic culmination, a rich beginning.

When Ian heard the news what he said was, "Aye—aye! When I come to think of it I had an idea." Mrs. Fraser said, "Well, it took me by surprise. I never expected it, but I am real, real pleased, my dears, nevertheless and whatever!" Hector's wife looked from her father-in-law to her mother-in-law and smiled a cryptic smile. Hector, being Hector, had to sing:

". . . the lady I adore,
The one I would marry on the Red River shore!"

Riding back to Calgary next day Angus sang also, with the changing of a word:

". . . the lady I adore,
The one I would marry from the Red River shore."

In the midst of his singing he ceased suddenly. He asked himself if he should have told Fiona of Minota; and more, should he have told her of a neglected son somewhere out on the Great Plains? But that was past, far off. It was of a life even before the comic interlude (in Sam's phrase) of the Ettrick brothers. What could he do, he asked himself, about All Alone? Should he do anything? Could he do anything? What would Fiona think he should do were she to know of the lad's existence, Chief Buffalo Calf's adopted son—all Indian?

Riding into Calgary he saw busy movements by the track side. A string of wagons was backed up beside a row of railway trucks. Men were bending and rising at some labour there, and even from a distance he knew by their motions they were not

121

white. Drawing closer he saw Sam Douglas on a horse, watching. There were wagon-loads of bones, bones bleached like ivory, bones weathered to a hue of lime. Indians in white men's clothes were shovelling them into the trucks, their braids, as they stooped, swaying pendulum-like. There was a great rasping of shovels as they worked, and over everything hung a powdery white haze. Beyond the newly laid track was a row of white stacks—more bones.

"Hullo, Angus! Back from seeing your forty-second cousins?" hailed Sam. "And how are our guid friends?"

"Fine."

"That's grand. Well, I just came over to see to the loading of those trucks." He had a sudden inspiration and with a histrionic gesture, a sweeping wave of a hand to the consignment of buffalo bones—"Voila les boeufs!" he chanted as in valediction on a life that was past.

CHAPTER TWENTY-TWO
Mr. Hodges Advises

Mr. Hodges, from whom Angus was to take over control of the Running Antelope Reservation, otherwise the High Butte Reservation, a short, rotund man formed after the manner of a bladder of lard, welcomed them with a vulgar and sincere bonhomie. Angus was glad to have had the little man's name in writing from Ottawa, for—

"I'm sorry Mrs. 'Odges is not here to greet you, Mrs. Munro," Hodges said to Fiona—careless but not consistently careless with his aspirates. "She could not stand the isolation, nobody of her own sex and colour to speak to bar the visiting missionary's wife, and not often did she come with 'er husband. The poor woman has her nose so tilted in the air, all because the reverend wears a collar wrong way round, that she was no great cheer to my missus when she did come. It's for the sake of Mrs. 'Odges I applied for a change when the Western Commissioner came here last. 'Eart to 'eart talk I had with him, man to man. I asked for a transfer if possible to one of the reserves close to the new railway, and I got it. My wife hasn't seen a train since she got off the St. Paul, Minneapolis and Manitoba cars at Emerson. No railway there when I came in. Boat down the Red River all the way from Abercrombie, and you got to Abercrombie from St. Cloud on a stage-coach. I suppose you've been out that long?"

"Oh, yes," said Angus.

"And you?" Mr. Hodges turned to Fiona.

"I was born by Red River—"

"Well, well, a Red River Shore lady!"

"Yes. My people came in by Hudson's Bay and Nelson River."

"Hey Presto!" exploded Mr. Hodges. They took it to be his substitute for other expletive when a lady was present. "I wish you could 'ave seen Mrs. 'Odges to tell her that. I like this country myself and I wrote her that I did. But sometimes, after she came out and couldn't get used to it, always pining to be at 'ome, I got so I felt I got her out here under false pretences. And then came a time her dislike affected me by a kind of sympathy, perhaps, and I found myself calling it a hell of a country. I beg your pardon, Mrs. Munro."

"That's all right," said Fiona, laughing, and feeling what can, perhaps, best be described as a merciful liking for the man.

"Changes, changes!" Mr. Hodges continued. "I 'ear a rumour that as like as not, after the railway is completed through the mountains to the Pacific, they'll build a sideline from Calgary to Fort Edmonton. When I tried to cheer my missus with that it made her worse. 'We'll all be bones, like the buffalo, by then,' she sez. Oh, yes, this is no plice for a woman what has been accustomed to seeing lots of people and 'aving a full social life. Well, she's gone off ahead of me, with all our sticks. I'm boarding with Chantelaine, the clerk here. It will be great for her at the new plice. The agency buildings are near the railway and she'll be able, from the top window any'ow, to see the trains go by—two a day, they tell me, one east and one west. Then there'll be freight trains, and work trains, ballasting on the new line and filling in culverts with gravel."

Fiona expressed her regret that Mrs. Hodges had been lonely there and agreed that it would be nice for her, feeling as she did, to see the trains go by.

"I used to tell her," said Mr. Hodges, "that with a little imagination she could change the Indians in their battered buggies and buckboards, and with their piebald ponies, into gipsies by the 'edges of England; but she could never care for the Indians, even pictorially. And it is 'ard for an English lady to make friends with an Indian woman, even a chief's squaw—Mrs. Running Antelope or the like. No, she just fretted 'ere. I don't dislike the Indians myself, but I don't know as I'll stay in the service," he prattled on, loquacious, as though glad himself of someone new to speak to. "I've been dabblin' in buying and selling town lots and I'm thinking of going in for politics. Politics and the real estate game—'and in

123

'and—has somethink in it, I think. I'm fond of public speakin'. These Indians, by the way, they are great speech-makers. We have an interpreter here and he ruins the speeches. I've just learnt enough Cree to reckonize that. Florid they are, you know, talkin' about the clouds and the grass and all that—like the Psalms of David. The interpreter cuts it all down to 'E says 'e don't fancy that, or 'E says 'e agrees with you. It's all lost. Do you speak Cree, Mr. Munro?"

"Yes."

"Well, you can use the interpreter if you like and keep mum about knowing Cree, not let them know. You might 'ear a lot that way. That's for you to decide." He paused. "You're a Sandy—I can 'ear that in your talk," and he stretched up to lay a podgy hand on Angus's shoulder, showing he was entirely friendly. "Ah, I know. Quick hear I 'ave!" He dropped his hand, advanced it in air toward Fiona and ingratiatingly beaming upon her, said he, "But he 'asn't said whatever yet, has he?" and exploded genial chuckles.

Fiona laughed pleasantly in response.

"No, he hasn't said whatever yet," she agreed.

"I think," said Hodges, turning again to Angus, "that if your good lady will excuse us we'll step across to the office and I'll introduce you to Chantelaine and Macpherson. Chantelaine is the clerk. Macpherson is the instructor. There is another clerk—Mr. Peters, comes from near Bristol. He's away on leave of absence, but he'll be back—let me see?—not till after I've gone. Chantelaine will introduce him. Fine fellah. You'll like him."

He laid a hand on his paunch, bowing to Fiona, and taking Angus's arm walked away.

"We've got some of them started farming," he went on as they passed out. "I don't say they are doing it with enthusiasm, but—well, what can you expect?"

They left the agent's house, scliffed through a golden pool of crisp leaves that lay under the upended besoms of a clump of cotton poplars, and walked on toward the office. Hodges still talking, Angus listening though raking the prospect with admiring eyes. Winter, in the sense of flying snow, had not yet come when they and their effects had been deposited at the Running Antelope Reservation by the Calgary-Fort Edmonton road some distance, and then along two ruts the twenty or thirty miles to the place of their new life. To northwest the knob of High Butte showed purple above quiet tones of frosted green. Westward, though not nearly as clear as seen from Calgary on such a day, the Rockies were fragmentarily declared by the loftier peaks—yonder and yonder—already silvered by their altitude and gleaming in the sun, or by

124

some jutting of a promontory into the foothills. South was but sky, blue sky. The agency buildings crouched near the rim of a long coulee (just where it glided away into prairie), a coulee in the bottom of which a riband of yellow twined, indicating a creek's course there, and at every gust of wind that dipped so far a streamer of gold would flutter and another creekside tree turn from a jet of quaking leaves to a stable-broom.

"Summer here is all right," remarked Hodges; "not too many mosquitoes. The fall is great. I like the fall. Even my poor missus loves the fall. Winter varies. I've seen the first snow—to lie and stay, I mean—not till Christmas week. I've known a winter we never used runners, wheels all the time on the wagons. But I've also known a winter from November to May—real winter, cold I mean. There was one Feb'uary I had to have a rope from the 'ouse to the office else I might have lost my way in a blizzard. I 'ope your good lady won't feel lonesome," he ended as they passed under the rippling and sagging of a Union Jack atop a white pole before the office.

Hodges flung open the door and swept a hand behind Angus's back with a "Step in, step in. Ah, 'ere we are. I want to introduce Mr. Munro—Mr. Chantelaine. Mr. Macpherson."

Nigel Chantelaine showed his race in more than name, in vivacious dark eyes and quick movements, and Donald Macpherson (from Bruce County, Ontario) announced or pronounced his in feesh for fish in the little chat they had on meeting, and in speerit for spirit—which was to receive such general sanction in the land that even those prone to somethinks and nothinks would speak of the speerit of a man.

Angus admired the system, the method, the trigness of that office. Mr. Hodges was clearly a man with a turn for business. He had inventories ready for his successor to visé. Stores, account books and even the medicine chest must be examined. That took all day and half of the next in the store-room and outer office, and then they filled their pipes in the agent's own room.

"You'll like Running Antelope," said Hodges. "I do get fat," he grunted, stooping for a dropped pencil that his sleeve had brushed from the desk. "Even if I eat nothink I get fat. The Indians call me Big Belly—quite friendly, you know. Yes, you'll like Running Antelope. He's shrewd, a diplomatist. I think you'll get on better with him than you'd have done with his predecessor, who just didn't like whites being in the country. There's no doubt about that. He had no personal animus against me, mind you, but there it was—old Buffalo Calf merely tolerated us."

"Buffalo Calf?" said Angus in a tone that might have been of inquiry to be sure he had the name aright, or of amazement for some reason.

"Yes. He died three years ago. Why do you ask like that?"

"I met him once—when the Blackfeet, the Stoneys, and Sarcees gathered at Blackfoot Crossing for the signing of Treaty Number Seven."

"Yes, I remember—he went down there then. I had just come here. Well, he's gone now, he's a shadow now, as they say. Then there are two sub-chiefs. There's Tall Whirlwind, a remarkable man, though an old warrior with scalps galore I should think. He's farming now, ploughing, not just with cattle. A good example. Then there's one I can't help thinking has some white blood in him, though his father and mother are both Indian. After all, white persons have been through here for a hundred years and some of them left traces. Throw-back. Big Beaver is his name. He's a bit sly. He knows nothing about it when the police come to look for evidence of cattle having been raided off and killed by the Indians, but I've an idea he knows a lot about these little games. He looks too deeply astonished at the inquiries."

"Buffalo Calf had a son, hadn't he?" Angus asked, refilling his pipe.

"Oh, yes, but the chiefs are elected. The chieftainship ain't 'ereditary with these people."

"No. No, quite. I just recalled when I saw the old chap in '77 he told me he had a son. I saw the boy, as a matter of fact."

Hodges frowned, with a vague feeling of something of indirectness in that last remark.

"He had two sons," he said, "two of his own—killed in raids on the Blackfeet long ago, I believe, so he adopted another. The fellah wears a ring he's very proud of. I think he prizes it like a scalp-lock. Buffalo Calf gave it to him and he may have got it off some brave south, who perhaps got it in his turn when attacking one of the old emigrant trains down there. A nice ring. It's queer the things they have. I was told that the Blackfeet have an old cuirass—you know, a metal breastplate that they brought home donkeys' years ago from a long trip south. It must have belonged to one of the Cortez soldiers. They either got it in a fight with the Spaniards or in a fight with other Indians down there that stole it from the Spaniards. Interestin', isn't it?"

"Yes," said Angus, and disappointed Hodges by his seeming failure to care for the subject. "What about this young Indian?"

"The lad with the collet ring?"

"Yes."

"Well, he's all Indian from the heels up."

126

"Good Injun?" inquired Angus in casual tone.

Hodges grinned.

"He gets drunk when he can. It's difficult to nab all the whisky smugglers," he said. "You can't be everywhere watching, and there's such a thing as night—and there are dark nights. I don't know what's happening all over the dark miles when I'm in bed. Yah, it's a problem. He's all right in many ways, but when he gets drunk he beats his squaw."

"He does, does he?" said Angus, and felt a sudden paternal rage.

"Yes. This is his second—the woman he has now."

"Did he beat the first to death?"

"Lord, no. I understand he never beat her at all. She died from the kick of a horse. He married this one a few months later. The beating business seems to be a recent development. It's booze that's at the back of it with him."

"We'll cure him of that!" said Angus in such a grim tone that Hodges stared. No one with Munro blood in him was going to beat a woman!

"You can't drive them, you know, Mr. Munro," said Hodges urgently, alarmed at the new agent's vehemence. "You can't kick an Indian in the pants. Raise your fist to them and they'll never forgive you—unless you have a gun or a knife in it. They might overlook that, bury the hatchet. Take the fists to them and you're a dead man. It's an indignity they can't live down."

"I know. I know."

Hodges sucked in his belly to extricate his watch and glancing at it—

"It's time we were going back to your good lady," said he, "to help her get her house in order, moving any of the heavier things she don't like in the first positions. Oh, I know the ladies!"

Half that night Angus lay awake. He pondered telling Fiona of Minota, of how he had left her, not aware she was with a child, of how he knew nothing of that till by accident he encountered Buffalo Calf—and the boy in his teens then. No, no, he could not tell her now. She would wonder why he had not done so before. Minota, he was sure, she would accept kindly, she being dead, a dear shadow; but she might think he ought to have done something for All Alone—despite Buffalo Calf's claim on the lad. "What could I have done?" he asked of the dark night in reply to that postulated censure. Here was All Alone turned twenty—and beating his wife. He did not sleep till the dreadful quiet light of dawn was in the room.

Four days later Indians came riding and driving

to the agency to meet the new agent and say good-bye to the old.

From a window Angus watched them arrive, a window in the office. There was evidently no mock sentiment in him regarding the natives, despite his Indian kink, for he remarked to himself that there were some tough faces among them. Yes, they were clearly not people who could be kicked in the pants. Had he not known that already he would have realized it then. Some of the men had a mercilessness in their bearing. Some of the women looked of the sort who would cry coward to their sons and husbands if they did not demand a tooth for a tooth and an eye for an eye. All kinds were there. There were sonsy girls, squaws shining like new-minted pennies from ablution with the bar-soap of the agency store, laughing and chatting one to another as they congregated. His view of the arrival of these folk, somewhat (yes, somewhat) like the gipsies of the 'edges of England, was only from the end window of Hodges' own room in the office building. Frontwards was the waiting-room. The smell of kinick-kinick and tobacco blent came sweeping in at the keyhole and at the door's edges, a door made too soon of unseasoned wood. From where he sat he could see a slit of light under it and occasional gray shadows drifting there—people moving about in the waiting-room, quiet, being in moccasins.

That smell of kinick-kinick stirred him, stirred the living past and he was back at Rocky Mountain House when the Stoneys and the Sarcees came to trade, back in the log-cabin beyond Jasper with the blue jays when, tobacco at ebb, he had smoked that mixture. A burst of laughter sounded without—and he was in the Ettricks' shop, John Hill Burton conferring with him over a sentence quoted by De Quincey from the travel book of a Mr. Weld. It was not many lives he lived after all: it was one. A sound, an odour, and the seemingly separate became unified. He lived not many lives but the linked chapters of one.

"They are here," said Hodges at that burst of laughter, rising and opening the door. "Come in, come in! You there, too, Jo? Come in, Chief!"

The chiefs had dressed with care for the occasion. Their braids were wrapped in otter skin; they wore their bravest blankets over buckskins. Shell-rings were in their ears. As they trooped in and stood awaiting presentation, Angus recalled the Ioways in Princes Street.

"Well, here's your new white father," Hodges purled. "Chief Running Antelope," and he waved a hand at that six feet of savage like Julius Caesar on a copper coin (a blend of humour, tolerance, sorrow, cynicism in the aspect of his hatchet-face), with two eagle-tail feathers erect in his twisted scalp-lock.

Running Antelope gave the grunt, the little bow, holding out a long lean hand that pressed Angus's lightly.

"I—am—pleased—to—meet—you," said he.

"And this," continued Hodges, laying a hand on the shoulder of the next, whose cheeks were of the texture and hue of smoked leather, profusely pitted with old pockmarks, "is Tall Whirlwind—a good man. Heap good farmer. Plough, sow, harvest, show the white man how, eh?"

A deprecating, perhaps a commiserating smile just twisted the lips of Tall Whirlwind as he shook Angus's hand and bowed.

"And this—" Hodges slapped the last on the back—"is Big Beaver."

Big Beaver's lips were thick yet close-set, his nose aquiline though spread at the base in a distension of nostrils as by deep-breathing. Two small upright puckers in the midst of his forehead gave him an air of puzzlement in the manner of a Great Dane or a lion, and the breadth of his cheek-bones was such as to make the brow seem constricted, narrow in comparison. He, too, was pitted with these gouges from the Great Sickness. Angus could not detect in him evidence of the white man a generation or two back surmised by Mr. Hodges, but did note a little light disc under the pupils of his eyes, a whitish filmy sickle on the iris, such as he had noted in the eyes of other Indians of advancing years and seen in no white men.

"Only got drunk, to my knowledge, once in three years," said Hodges, by way of completing his boisterous introductions. "Drink no more, eh?"

Big Beaver looked aslant at him, shrugged his shoulders, and with the little bow and the close-lipped grunt took the new agent's hand as gently as had the others, but met his eyes not with their studying, directness of gaze. Perhaps, thought Angus, that was due to the little film that was forming there. The word trachoma he did not know.

"Sit down, sit down! Be seated, Chiefs," said Hodges, brightly. "Oh, this is our interpreter. You haven't met him yet, Mr. Munro—Jo Two Guns."

The interpreter wore a white man's shirt with its ends not tucked into but hanging down over wide blanket-trousers (in the manner of the buckskin tunics then worn), a cowboy's hat on his head, thick plaits pendant on either side. He was not sure if he would receive the attention bestowed on the others, but Angus held out his hand, the eyes of the three chiefs observant.

"Well, would you like to speak, Mr. Munro?" suggested Hodges.

The interpreter stood out in the middle of the floor, waiting.

"I 'ave some cigars over here," Hodges broke out.

"We'll all 'ave one," and he took the box round, bobbing from one to another with it, then bobbing again to hold matches for them. That over—there they all sat, dumb.

"Have you anything to say?" asked Hodges, looking at Angus, the interpreter still standing in the middle of the room, waiting.

Angus rose and began to speak in Cree. The three chiefs stared rigidly at him, then in Indian fashion sat forward, heads lowered a little to one side, giving ear, as he told them he had seen his first Cree when sixteen snows, and that he had gone to the Mountain House and there had—he hesitated. The three heads were raised a little and the three pairs of eyes probed into his pause. There, he said, he had met other Crees as well as Stoneys and Sarcees. After that he explained that he went across the big lake that is salt, to east, and there when he heard wind in the grass it was in his ears the wind in the grass of the prairies, and if he heard a river its voice was the voice of the prairie rivers. There he met three Indians. Their tribal name in Cree he did not know, but their sign was so—and the three heads, aslant and bowed, rose and the sign was observed. On seeing them, Angus continued, with all their feathers (Running Antelope and Tall Whirlwind chuckled) he could stay no longer, and came back, and here he was and his heart was glad.

"I have finished," he ended, according to the ritual.

Running Antelope rose. Hodges sat back and folded his hands on his paunch to await a florid speech. He was getting ready to nod to Jo to interpret it for his sake, but there was none.

"Good. Friend. Good," said Running Antelope, and shook Munro's hand again. He seemed to be tremendously impressed.

The other two stood up then, shook hands with Angus, then stepping back glanced pointedly at the head chief. He turned to Hodges, who bobbed up, disappointed that there was to be no eloquence. There were three solemn handshakes, three grunts, and then Running Antelope conjured from under his vivid blanket a bundle—a deerskin bundle bound round with strips of rawhide much knotted. Having put that on Hodges' desk he wheeled and stalked out, the others following, shutting the door behind them quietly.

"What's this?" said Hodges, and began to undo the knots.

Having removed the wrapping there was disclosed only

another below it, in its turn, bound with knotted rawhide thongs. Wrapping after wrapping he removed, each similarly tied.

"It's a practical joke!" he exclaimed, but continued, as one takes out basket after basket from a Japanese nest of them.

At last he came to an end and held up a calumet, its bowl of lustrous red stone, its polished stem protected with a covering of otter skin.

"Hey Presto!" he cried out. "Well, I'll be damned! Do you know what this is?"

"A calumet, and a fine one."

"Yes, a beaut', but I must tell you about it. I wanted to trade for it, from Running Antelope, but No, not for sell, not for buy. And now—stop him, Jo, like a good fellah, so that I can thank him."

"He's a mile off by now," said Angus. "It's what they call a free gift. That's why it was wrapped up that way—to let him get well away."

"Well, I'm damned," said Hodges again. He took out a handkerchief and mopped his forehead. "Now you know whether they liked me or not. Damned if I'm not sorry to go. And yet there's no doubt this is no plice for a woman, no plice for a woman," he repeated, holding up the pipe this way and that.

Jo Two Guns, though no doubt knowing his errand in vain, had stepped out through the waiting-room to see if the chief was in sight. Returning, he said: "They're gone. There's just some people hanging around, I guess to say good-bye to you."

"Well, bring 'em in. No, we'll go out and see them."

Yes, Big Belly was liked, thought Angus—at least by some. They went out in front of the building where little groups clustered. They moved from one to another, Hodges keeping up a running fire of chatter.

"Good-bye, good-bye," he chanted. "Good man. Pretty woman. Heap sorry to go. This is Mr. Munro, new agent, new white father. He speaks Cree good. You say something in Cree to them, Mr. Munro."

But everybody seemed self-conscious. There they were to say good-bye and all like shy children who had forgotten the little piece they were to recite and could only smile, nod, laugh and—as for the women—clap a hand to their mouths to hide the laugh.

"Well," said Hodges a few minutes later, "that's that. I think we'll move on now. I've just remembered you haven't inspected the slaughter-house, the beef-issue house. Come on. We'll step over there."

The groups thinned away. Horses that had been standing with drooping heads, as though weary of life, suddenly turned to fiery steeds when mounted, caracoled sharply and rub-a-dubbed away. Democrat wagons, buggies and battered buckboards received their load and departed as the old and the new agent walked along to the beef-issue buildings.

"This door should have had the pin dropped in the staple instead of just left hanging," remarked the methodical Hodges. He opened the door, then abruptly slammed it shut.

"What is it?" asked Angus.

"Coyotes in there. Didn't you see all the eyes shine to the light? Hie!" He cupped his hands to his mouth and shouted to some young men who were riding away. They looked over their shoulders, wheeled, rode back. "Some of you boys get down here like good fellahs," said Hodges, "and shoot up the coyotes inside. The door must have been left open at night and slammed shut in a wind."

They knew sufficient English amongst them, without need of any pidgin-Cree from Hodges or fluent Cree from Angus, to understand that. Hilariously they slipped from the saddles, on near-side or off-side, no matter which, their horses trained so. Two had rifles. They opened the door again and then crash went shot after shot into the slaughterhouse at the targets of these eyes that glinted to the outer daylight from its gloom.

On one of those who shot Angus's gaze had been keen, direct, appraising.

"Do you remember me?" he asked.

The young man turned as the others went inside to drag out the slain coyotes.

"Yes, I remember you," he replied. "I saw you when the Blackfeet went to the Ridge under the Water to sign the treaty."

Angus looked his son directly in the eyes. Both were of a height, about six feet.

"I am the new agent here." said Angus, and held out his hand.

"You are our new white father, then," said All Alone, laughing.

"I am your new father," responded Angus; and had Sam Douglas seen him then he would have thought that Angus Munro looked his years.

Hodges, standing by waiting for the others to drag out the carcasses, was puzzled.

"Somethink odd," he mused, "in this Sandy's manner."

Enlightenment came to him. He thought he understood: the

new agent was remembering, no doubt, what he had heard of All Alone beating his squaw when he got drunk; so, after he had carefully dropped the wooden peg in place to secure the door, falling in step with Angus to walk to the agency, Hodges said:

"You can't kick an Indian in the pants, Mr. Munro—nor a half-breed, for that matter."

"I know, I know."

CHAPTER TWENTY-THREE
Photograph

Chantelaine was an eager and interested aide with no faintest peevishness (even before he discovered that Angus did assuredly know something of Indians) that one new to the service had been set in authority over him. Peters, the clerk who had been on vacation, soon came also to admire the new chief's management. Both lauded to themselves, and took lessons from his restraint, his capacity for calm discussion without ever a flame of even suppressed anger in his eyes, his manner with his wards, when they were difficult, as of having studied in the school of Solomon. Neither had seen him wring the neck of a small jay at a sudden fierce impulse! Perhaps in his immediate regret for that he had learnt the control they admired.

He had a slightly different attitude to the Indians from that of Hodges. Hodges had seen himself as the guardian and dispenser of charity. Angus saw himself as the representative of a government that had made treaty with these people, arranging, in return for surrender of lands, for certain payments, attentions and offices.

He organized a native police force for the reserve. He set apart one day a week for the chiefs to come and see him, whether there was any tribal matter to discuss or not, and on that day others who had domestic affairs in which they wanted advice would come and confer with him.

All winter he had been very busy and had occasionally seen All Alone at the agency. It was not till the late spring that he had either occasion or opportunity to look into what may be called his private affairs—private family affairs.

One visiting day the chiefs had chatted, smoked, and gone. In the outer waiting-room a young squaw, who had been watching for their departure, rose and came diffidently into the private office.

"I'm Tannisse All Alone," she said.

Angus swallowed suddenly. She was a little creature with eyes like those of a deer, very clean in person and apparel (which all were not), her hair in lustrous plaits—and there was a great weal across her forehead. Imagine beating that, thought he, swallowing again.

"Sit down. You want to speak to me about something?"

"Just to you," she replied. "They tell me that our new white father is a wise man."

"Well?"

"I have had enough," she said. She put a hand to the wound on her forehead. She drew back her blanket and showed another on her arm. "My man has beaten me too much. The other agent told me to stay with him and that he would speak to him, but I can stand no more. I am going back to my father now. I want you to know. I have had enough. I have told you. It is finished."

She rose then, turning away, opened the door and went out.

Yes, an Indian agent has to study in the school of Solomon, thought Angus. He went outside. One of those he had appointed to police the reserve was sitting on the steps.

"I think it would be good," said Angus (never did he begin, I want you to do . . . It is hardly in the Indian speech), "I think it would be good to ride every day near the lodge of the father of Tannisse All Alone."

"I will ride myself every day near that lodge," replied the man.

Fiona wondered what might be the cause of her husband's quiet that evening.

"Anything wrong?" she asked. "Any troubling matters today?"

He seemed startled by the inquiry.

"Oh, it's only one of the men has been beating his squaw—and she is such a little thing!" he said.

"It's dreadful!"

"It's dreadful."

"Are you doing anything about it?"

"I'm thinking what to do."

He waited to hear further news. Two days later the policeman to whom he had spoken came in.

"There is nothing to report," he said.

"Not about the lodge of Tannisse All Alone's father?"

"There is no trouble there. She is living with her father. I see. I stopped to talk and smoke."

"That is good."

The policeman went away. Just before noon the door opened and All Alone entered. He had dressed himself for the visit. He had ochre paint on his face; he had little brass rings round the braids that hung below the shoulders.

"Sit down," said Angus.

All Alone sat down and there was silence. Angus looked at him. All Indian, eh? Indian from the heels up? He sat like an effigy. By the way the light fell a hint of gray was discernible in the dark eyes, but that did not necessarily indicate white blood in him. Chief Crowfoot of the Blackfeet had gray in his eyes and one could go back a long way in his ancestry and find only Indian blood, and no rumour of any cuckolding by, or obliging of, any white explorer. The Blackfeet cut the noses of unfaithful squaws and the unfaithful husband was scourged. The Bannacks, by the way, made the man pay damages—or killed him and let the woman go. Gray eyes could be seen in tribes that had never had touch with white men. Gray in the iris did not mean that one was not Indian from, the heels up.

There was something of Minota in the young man's face, much of Minota. Angus looked at the hand that held the blanket in place, at the ring on it.

"I have come to see if you will get my woman back to me," said All Alone. "She has left you?"

"She has left me."

"Why did she go?"

"Because I beat her."

"Why did you beat her? What had she done?"

"Nothing. I was drunk."

"Are you going to get drunk again?"

"I may. I do not know. I never know."

"What do you want me to do?"

"Get her back to me."

"Do you think I will get her back for you to beat again next time you are drunk?"

No answer.

Angus studied that face. Yes, there was a strong resemblance to Minota there. The eyes were like hers then in their wide innocence: innocence seemed to be the right word.

"I like her," said All Alone at last. "I am lonely without her."

"Lonely without her," Angus echoed. "Have you asked her to come back?"

"Yes."

"And she will not come," said Angus with a note of triumph.

"No. That is why I am here. She says no. It is the last time, she says. I am fond of her."

135

"You want me to ask her to go back to you for you to beat her again?"

All Alone made no reply, but produced from under his blanket a small packet. He opened it and held forth a photograph. Angus took it from him. It showed him very erect with his hand on the back of a chair, and in the chair sat an Indian girl. To one side of her was a small round table with a book and a vase on it. Her elbow rested on the table's edge.

"Who is this woman?" Angus asked, puzzled.

"That is my first woman," All Alone answered.

"Your first?"

"Yes."

Then All Alone produced another photograph.

"This," he explained, "is my second woman, the one who has left me. It is of her alone. I wonder if you could get a man who makes these pictures to take out my first woman and put this woman in her place. If you could get a man to do that—take out the first woman and put this one in—perhaps she would come back."

"Leave it to me," said Angus. He was about to put the photographs in his pocket, but All Alone handed him the deerskin wrapping. He folded that round them, and said he, "I shall see what I can do."

Meditation on the matter sent him with Fiona to Calgary next day—close upon a week's drive, but with two new way-houses with a roof for travellers when they came to the Calgary-Edmonton road. The Rockies were a white frozen wave westward, but snow was all gone from the prairie and among the rolling hills lingered only in those creases that, by their position, received no more than a few hours' sunshine. On all the sloughs ducks were talking.

Two nights under a roof and two under stars: they would look back on that little journey before long and think, remembering, that they should feel old. Hardly could they recognize Calgary, so rapidly were the houses going up.

Their first visit was to Sam's office, and there they found him in high spirits. The original townsite had been on the east bank of Elbow River. Douglas had believed that the west would be the chosen one (or perhaps "friends at court" had whispered to him) and there had bought land and held it. Therefore, with the ultimate survey of the townsite on the west side he had been gaily reaping. Was there a photographer in Calgary? Angus wanted to know.

"Yes. Everything is here now! Mark my words, you won't know the place if you come back in another six months."

The photographer was found.

"I wonder," said Angus, "if it would be possible to make some sort of composite picture—to take this figure and put it in place of that—or even the face alone, in exchange."

"Whatever for?"

"Well, it's an idea of one of my Indians. I'm an Indian agent and they come to me with lots of odd requests. This is his first wife and he wants to put this one, his second wife, in her place—"

The photographer cast back his head and bayed to the ceiling—but he guessed he would have a stab at it.

"Ain't they queer people?" he cried out. "Leave the two with me and I'll have a stab at it. Yep, I guess I can make a nice picture of his second wife in his first wife's place—good enough to satisfy an Injun, anyhow."

"I would like to get back as soon as possible," said Angus.

"I'll get busy on it right away. Come in tomorrow."

To be so far on the way to Highwood River—two-thirds of the distance, or so—and not go on to surprise them there was tantalizing, but they promised themselves a visit to the ranch later in the year.

Well, it was cleverly done. Angus laughed when he held the result in his hand. A week later, back on the reserve, he saw the agency policeman—the one who had kept an eye for a day or two on the lodge of Tannisse's father.

"I think it would be good." he told him, "to go out and bring in All Alone."

"Do I bring him with my gun?"

"No. He will come without a gun."

"Good."

All Alone was keeping close to home. He arrived speedily, though again he had taken pains with his toilette for the visit.

"There you are!" said Angus.

All Alone studied the new picture and smiled.

"Perhaps that will bring her back," he said. "Now I will send it to her. I will not go myself." He wrapped up all three prints carefully together. "I will send it to her—and wait."

Three days later he returned, very gloomy over the waiting.

"She will not come back," he said. "I went to see her today because I was lonely for her. I thought, perhaps, the one I gave the picture to, to take to her, had not given it to her. But he had. She said it made no difference. It is not that she thinks I think more of the first woman. She said I have beaten her once too often. Will you go and see her and ask her to come back?"

Angus pointed a finger at his son.

137

"I will," he said. "I will—if you promise me this: that you will not get drunk again."

"I cannot promise that because I do not know, and if I make a promise I always keep it. It is not well to break a promise."

"Make this one and keep it."

"I do not know if I can. That is why I will not promise."

"I see."

They sat silent a while.

"This I will promise," said All Alone after profound thought, "I will not beat her again."

Angus shrugged his shoulders.

"How do you know?" he demanded. "If you get drunk you may."

"No. I will be very strong even if I am drunk and remember I have promised."

"Leave it to me, then," said Angus. "I'll see what I can do."

All Alone rose and left him. That afternoon Angus saddled a horse and rode to the lodge of the father of Tannisse All Alone.

"No," said Tannisse, when he spoke to her, "I have told him. This is the last time."

Angus had the impression that he could, by his influence, renew and retain marital felicity in the home of his Indian son.

"Then you will not mind," said this disciple of Solomon, "if All Alone takes another woman, seeing that you won't go back?"

A look of startlement passed in Tannisse's eyes at that suggestion. Then she was grim again.

"No," she said, stubbornly.

"That's all right," replied Angus easily. "You will not go back?"

"No."

"So he can take another woman?"

"Yes."

"Good."

He rode back to the agency and left it so for the time being.

In the evening he told Fiona all he had done and as he told her, so deeply interested was she, there came a moment when it was but as the breadth of a hair between his retention of his secret and his revelation of it to her. "I want to tell you something . . ." He did not say that: he thought it. "I want to tell you, Fiona, about the days when I was at Rocky Mountain House and . . ." No, he could not speak. He was intensely happy with his wife—and did not wish to cloud that happiness. He did not realize that were she to know of Minota and Minota's son, closer might she have come to him.

Next day he happened to be looking out of the window in

the main office, thinking his own thoughts—of Fiona and his past, Minota, All Alone, Tannisse, Fiona—when there came two riding together, an Indian and a squaw.

All Alone and Tannisse!

Angus passed into his room and sat down at his table to await them. The door opened. They came in, both smiling.

"I have come to let you know," said All Alone, "that she has come back to me."

"Good!" exclaimed Angus. He put a hand on his son's shoulder. "Now will you repeat that promise with Tannisse to hear?"

"What promise?"

"Will you promise to us both not to beat her again?"

"Oh, that! I will not beat her again. I have promised her. I promise you. Even when I get drunk I will not beat her again. I will try not to get drunk, but about that I cannot promise. I will not beat her again."

Angus walked out with them, saw them ride away. As he turned back, the snapping of the Union Jack atop its pole, as it flicked to a plucking wind, and the thrashing of the halyard, sounded like faint applause, perhaps not ironic.

CHAPTER TWENTY-FOUR
Birth

Time seemed to fly that spring for Fiona and Angus, happy together, happy with the weather, even with the gummy-sheathed buds of the cottonwoods in the coulee, the rattling of catkin clusters, the burnished tone of red-willow stems.

At this season occasional homesickness often came to him such as his mother was never without. The link, the hint that led his mind to Scotland, might be vague, in a scent or a word, or obvious—on hearing, for example, some song of the land that had been his forebears'. A party of glee-singers coming west once on tour, Fiona and he went to Calgary to hear them. For an encore they gave Over the Sea to Skye and sang him back to the country from which his people had been cast out. He saw a stream, little more than a foot broad—not so broad as an irrigation ditch in this west—with miniature cut-banks, and miniature falls rumbling into little whirls of water-beads, and was a boy again guddling for trout, a boy again shouting to the shout of the flowing tide among the Black Rocks by Loch Brendan. A sudden hate came to him for landlords and factors who had exiled his folk; then—for he hated hate—he dismissed it from his mind: he told himself that like Sam (remembering what Sam had said to him once on the International as they came down Red River) he was, after all, unfitted to live over there again. The land of exile was also the land of adoption; but still, even while so thinking, he was humming:

"Mull was astern, Rum on the port,
Eigg on the starboard bow . . ."

In his work Angus was very happy. The agency police had been a great help to him—and to the Redcoats—in keeping fire-water from the reservation. The sole temptation, so far, for them to disappoint the trust in them had been in that fire-water, but they had—so far—been incorruptible. Macpherson was happy. He had several new pupils to instruct in the white man's road, behind a plough, though still the preference of those whom he called our progressives was for cattle-raising. Peters, observing good cheer as part of Fiona, thought the west was a place for a woman and mused much of a girl in Toronto. He must tell her of the settlement—it was called, obviously, High Butte—only twenty miles to northwest. He had been long enough in that land of accepted distances to have other measure of proximity than obtained in urban centres. Chantelaine, habitually happy, was devoted to the new agent and the new agent's wife.

As for All Alone—shortly after the return of Angus and Fiona from Calgary, he arrived at the office to talk about a man he had heard of at Medicine Hat who made pictures. He showed some specimens. They gave the impression of being good portraits, though the sitters, in each one, were taken against what appeared to be but a sheet tacked to a wall and the poses were stereotyped: elbow inevitably on table where inevitably reposed the family Bible atop a clasped album, and beside which was a vase of dogwood leaves.

All Alone wanted to go down to Medicine Hat with his woman to have their portraits taken together—the genuine article. Despite the surrender of thousands of square miles of their original lands the Indians were not confined by the precincts of their reserves. They were not relentlessly immured. The treaties allowed of their passing beyond the borders to hunt, while game lasted—or to have their photographs taken.

Well, they went; and Tannisse came back alone, very sad.

"There is something wrong," observed Angus as soon as she entered his room.

140

"Yes."

"Sit down," said he, "sit down," and then—"He is not dead, is he?"

"No."

"What is the trouble?"

"He did not beat me."

"I don't understand."

"It was in Medicine Hat. We had the picture made. Then he went into the village alone from our tepee and a white man sold him whisky. But he did not come back and beat me. He stabbed a policeman."

"Stabbed a policeman!"

"Yes."

"Killed him?"

"Oh, no. Not bad. The policeman hit him over the head with the handle of his quirt. They open the handles and melt a white stone and pour it in. It hardens inside and is covered over again. That makes the handle like a war club. He sent a message. He said I was to tell you he had got drunk but had not beaten me. I went to see him in the—" she could find no Cree word for jail, so raised a hand before her with spread fingers, looking between them to convey the bars in a cell's door.

"How long will he be there?" asked Angus.

"Three moons."

The three months passed quickly, at least for Angus if not for Tannisse. Chantelaine went on vacation to visit his people in Winnipeg. Macpherson, the red-headed Canadian Highlander from Ontario, the sowing over and the spring round-up (that was more to the taste of his pupils than shambling and stumbling behind a kicking plough), went for a holiday to Bruce County. Peters, after Chantelaine came back, departed to Toronto; and on his return Angus and Fiona drove down to Calgary again, had a glimpse of Sam Douglas there, and went on to the Highwood River ranch, finding no visible alteration in Mr. and Mrs. Fraser, they still at that span of life when there seems to be a halt physically, no facial change, whatever mind and spirit may be experiencing.

On the way home they looked in on Sam again and he had disturbing news. Riel—they would remember Louis Riel—was back in the country from his exile in Montana to lead, so said rumour, a rising of the Métis.

"The situation is serious," Douglas opined. "It is a time for tact instead of for ignoring. They have, I think, their grievances more or less—and assuredly their fears. It's the old trouble, intensified. They fear the loss of their lands. They have the impression that the white men engaged on survey work are a collection of rogues in league with the land-grabbers."

When they reached the agency the blue gentians were streamers and pools for Fiona's delight—and the time for the return of All Alone was due. Angus prepared carefully a little talk in the nature of temperance homily, that he called to himself his fatted calf.

Tannisse, who had been counting the days, arrived at the agency with a led-horse one afternoon and sat there till sundown—and no All Alone. She went home dejected and was sitting on the office steps, smoking a little pipe for solace, when Angus went across the next morning, two horses with drooping heads beside her under a limp Union Jack.

About noon there was the rattle of a patrol wagon, its horses briskened up for a final dash to the gate. A Redcoat looped the lines over the brake-handle and climbed down to deliver All Alone—who leapt out after him—and get the receipt.

Angus, in his office, cleared his throat in preparation to say his little sermon. He could not but admire the build and carriage of his Indian son. All Alone had bought a new hat (of the kind called ten gallon) that had a devil-may-care and saucy flaunt of brim. As he entered he swept it off.

"Good afternoon," said he, chanted he, in fact. "Good afternoon! Just back from college."

"Well, I'll be damned!" exclaimed the policeman.

Angus said nothing at all, his homily, his little lecture gone.

Tannisse, sitting there awaiting the return, was all admiration and devotion. Father and unacknowledged son looked at each other. Then an ingratiating smile lit All Alone's face and, his woman rising, she and he walked happily away. From the window Angus watched them ride off.

"Pretty good Injun all the same," remarked the policeman, who remained to eat a meal with them.

Over that meal he gave them more news of that brewing rebellion of which Sam Douglas has spoken. There had been a meeting of the Métis at St. Laurent at which a speaker had stated that the Northwest Territory belonged to the Indian and to the half-breeds, not to the Dominion government for it to dispose of as it pleased. A new police-post was to be established at Fort Carlton and the force was being increased specially for the patrolling of that sweep of country from Carlton and Prince Albert to Ellice.

"It's clear that Trouble is expected in that quarter," the Redcoat told them.

That was in September. The year was flying. Soon the wild

asters (that Fiona loved to have in the house in great clusters) bloomed again, as usual, and the fleabane was in flower to tell the season whatever the conspiracies or tribulations of men across these leagues.

It was then that Big Beaver came to the office, inviting the agent to accompany him on a fall hunt. Fiona was pregnant—near to five months gone—and thought it better that she should remain at home, though asked to accompany them. Resolutely she contested Angus's view that, for her sake, he should not leave her. She pointed out that to have such an invitation from Big Beaver was evidence of how Angus was making good in the reserve. She pointed out, further, that Big Beaver would feel hurt, perhaps offended, if he did not accept. Only when she said, "Well, then, I shall just have to go also, though I think I shouldn't," did he submit to going and leaving her.

The Indians, for the fall hunt, went in small parties through the hills and often, in the following days, he was reminded, by the scent, sight and sound—smell of red-willow smoke, shadow on bole of tree, tom-tomming of creeks—of his first meeting with Minota. He felt, too, that he was not living many lives but living a double life, because of Fiona knowing nothing of Minota—and because he grew more and more devoted to Fiona.

"I have had a very happy time in the hills with you," he said to Big Beaver on the way back. "The hunting has been good. You have good venison, good moose-meat, and good hides for making many moccasins. I hope we may go hunting again next year."

Big Beaver turned his head and looked at him pensively a moment.

"I am growing old," he replied solemnly. "I may be dead by then; but if I am not here next year I hope your hunting will be good."

And Herbert Hodges had thought that Big Beaver had white blood in him!

"I hope you will be here," said Angus as calmly, but with a catch in his voice—for he had that Indian kink, as Sam Douglas said, and these people often moved him suddenly, poignantly, with a word.

There seemed to be little amiss with the old man save that his sight was not as good as it had been. He had a way of lowering his head and peering as though to see under some barrier or through a haze. In aiming his rifle, stock held tightly to shoulder and cheek, his face would pucker in a multitude of wrinkles as he strained for a clear view along the sights. But that little failing of vision seemed to be all that was wrong with him; yet they had not been back a month when he was gathered to his fathers, slipped away in his sleep one night to join the procession on the Ghost Trail that is thronged beyond counting. Mrs. Beaver knew that where his shadow went there would be buffalo aplenty and good water, but she grieved over her loss, put ashes in her hair, and cut off a finger, which she cast into the blanket and deerskin in which he was wrapped and sewed. She keened and cried all night under the tree in the forks of which his body was elevated.

A new sub-chief had to be chosen to take his place in the council of the band. Angus had an idea: As the bad boy of the class is made monitor he thought of using what influence he might have toward the appointment of All Alone. A responsible position might be the making of him. He discussed the matter with Running Antelope, being frank with him, up to a certain point, regarding his reason, but asking that it might be their secret. The chief chuckled over that motive and, holding his left hand out before him, slightly arched, slipped the right below it and held it there a moment—in the sign for secrecy. It was better than a wink!

The friends of All Alone were mostly of those impetuous youths who would fain live up to the stories of the old days as told by their grandfathers round the winter fires. He had already been spoken of by them, young though he was, as one who might be voted for. Into the agency he came one day for a chat, a day when idle odd flakes of snow, no larger than a pin-head, trembled down and vanished, and the horses that waited before the office looked disconsolate. To west was no hint of the mountains on the horizon, there being no horizon there, only gray space. All Alone had heard gossip that the agent was hopeful that those who wished to elect him as a sub-chief would have their way.

"Why do you want me to be a chief?" he demanded.

Angus did not reply, Because you are my son and because I want to do my best for you. Nor did he say, Because I think if you were in a position of trust you would stop drinking firewater at every opportunity. All Alone, thinking over that gossip he had heard of the agent being for him, had recalled how Angus, on their first meeting—or their first parting, rather—in some inexplicable emotion had raised his hands aloft, lowering them toward him in blessing.

"Because I think you are at heart a good man and would make a good chief," said Angus.

By a large majority the young man was, in the event, elected.

On the day the first snow came, one of the agency policemen had a duty diffidently to perform. By his diffidence Angus realized that the band was divided in the question of joining Riel's rebels or remaining aloof—neutral. There was a half-breed on the reservation, he said, who was calling meetings and addressing the people. Angus did not ask if Running Antelope was party to it. It was understood that his police were not spies upon the chiefs.

"It will be good if you bring him to me," suggested Angus.

"If I bring him with a gun there may be trouble. And I do not think he will come without one. Many of the people give ears to his words."

"Then do nothing," said Angus. "I shall speak to the chiefs. Tomorrow is the day they all come to smoke with me."

But before the morrow—that very afternoon—there arrived three Redcoats (one of these by the way, a son of Charles Dickens, the novelist) who had received information that emissaries of Riel were in the vicinity drumming for recruits. Yes, said Angus, he had heard only that morning of one who had arrived. The three policemen rode away, directed to where the half-breed was camped, and Angus watching for their return, saw the snow turn from starch-blue to gold and red, then suddenly fade to desolation in twilight.

There they came. The half-breed had evidently been warned of their proximity and had fled. They stayed the night and there was much talk again of what was afoot in the land—volunteer forces being raised at Winnipeg, and at the other end of the plains, cowboys being sworn in to patrol the Benton-Calgary road and neighbourhood. Militia were coming from the east. Cloud was over man's affairs from the Red River to the Belly. Angus now and then, as he listened, looked at Fiona, worried lest she might be agitated, because of her condition.

Frequent patrols came their way. On Christmas Day there sat down to dinner in the agent's house (Angus and Chantelaine—who was a remarkable cook—helping Fiona to prepare the feast) not only the staff but a mounted policeman—none other than Gus Atkins, who had been caught, according to Sam, by the sojers' buttons and the clink of spurs. All through the winter patrols came to the reserve, though the Running Antelope band was not among those distrusted. Further east the Big Bear Band, the Ermine Skin and the Bobtail—were sullen and suspect. There was much rain instead of snow, dismal sleet adding somewhat to a sense (or, indeed, more than a sense, a consciousness, in view of all that was known) of calamity impending.

Fear was in the land, the mounted police told them. A panic suddenly seized many in Calgary, the restless Blackfeet so near them, and messages were sent to those Redcoats who had been despatched through the mountain passes to keep order among the

145

railway construction gangs, imploring them to return. From Red River to the Rockies people recalled stories of early massacres, such as one that occurred in the beginning of the century near where Qu'Appelle flows into Assiniboine: a fur party was set upon there and even a six-months' old child was a target for the arrows. The Minnesota massacre, of which Jessie Grant had talked at Lasswade, they remembered. Though they did not freely speak of it they knew that whites had as mercilessly and barbarously slain Indians. They dreaded a revenge for such exploits as the Baker Massacre and the massacre in the Cypress Hills.

One day early in March (Angus with his own anxiety because of intermittent pains having begun for Fiona), Running Antelope came to confer with him. Peters sent him over from the office, knowing that Angus wished to stay close to his wife that day. The agent was amazed, during that talk, to discover how much his Indians knew of the whole country's affairs. This head-chief seemed to know more than the mounted police, telling him that Chief Crowfoot of the Blackfeet had ridden down to discuss with Red Crow of the Bloods the advisability of joining the half-breeds, but Red Crow had refused to join, would have nothing to do with the rising. The Redcoats had not known of that, apparently, though they had told him that Père Lacombe (of whom he had first heard from Minota years before), and Père Doucét, had gone to advise the Blackfeet against participation. Evidently Running Antelope was aware of all that was afoot from the Red River to the Belly, from the North Saskatchewan to the border—and beyond. The half-breeds of Riel were among the Lakotah or Dakotah Indians—the Sioux—and some of them might come north to help the insurgents.

"What would you advise us to do?" he asked.

"It would be better to take no part," said Angus.

"My people are divided," replied Running Antelope. "I come to you now to ask because you think much for us. If Riel won would that be the end? Would the Indians again own all the land? Big Belly, he who was here before you came, was a good man. His heart was not hard, his tongue was straight, but he thought as a white man. You think for us as well as for the white man. You think with us"—and he laid the first finger of his right hand against the palm of his left, "with us."

"You want me to speak now not just as the agent here but as your friend?"

"Yes."

"If I was not the agent, if I was only your friend and you came and asked me what to do, I would say, Keep still. Eight snows back I talked with Chief Buffalo Calf when he went to look on at the gathering at Blackfoot Crossing. He told me he thought, perhaps, he might find some medicine-sign that would bring back the buffalo and send the white men away. There is no such sign to be found."

"There is no sign to do that?"

"No. And all the half-breeds and all the Indians could only make blood flow for no good end."

"More white men would come?"

"More would come."

"Good. It is as I thought." He was silent a minute or two and Angus did not speak. Then, "This land is my mother," said Running Antelope.

Angus did not smile, even inwardly. He had met Englishmen at Calgary who were forever speaking of the Mother Country; Germans he had met, years back, in Minnesota, who were forever talking, and singing, of Fatherland.

After another pause Running Antelope spoke again.

"I do not want to see it red with blood for no good in the end," he said.

He rose then. As he went out of the door something in his back, blanket gathered round him, erect though he walked, stabbed Angus with pity as, at times, a mere word of these people could poignantly surprise him. "People of the stone age, born too late," thought he.

He was thus thinking when the chief turned back. He had come to the agency with much in his mind and had discussed it. He turned back.

"Your heart is heavy," said he.

"I am troubled because of my woman," replied Angus. "The pains are on her."

"I have seen that she is big with child. It will soon be over."

"I have sent Mr. Chantelaine to High Butte," Angus said, "to see if the doctor is there. With all this trouble he may be away. She has no woman with her."

"Is her time due?"

"Yes."

"I will bring my woman," said Running Antelope. "She has had three of her own. If the child comes before my woman can get here there is Red Head" (Macpherson). "He could help. I have seen him with a cow and calf."

"O God!" exclaimed Angus.

It was dark when Running Antelope arrived in the buck-board of which he was inordinately proud, his squaw with him smelling strongly of agency soap and shining with cleanliness and midwifely importance. Mr. Herbert Hodges had wished that his homesick spouse might see the Indians as much like the gipsies by the 'edges of England. Mrs. Running Antelope, surely to any eyes, was somewhat like the midwives of Scotland!

She was all midwife. She took possession.

"I will stay here," said she, "until the child comes. It is good for a man to let woman do all."

She went tremendously upstairs while the chief, with eyes upon his horses at the door, aired his English.

"Mr. Macpherson," he said, "says I am to go to his tepee" (he always called the agency houses tepees) "to sleep after I have put buckboard and horse in stable. I think we will play black-jack before we sleep. Maybe I skin him five, maybe ten, dollars, ain't it?"

His wife came downstairs to say that hot water should be ready on the stove. The odour of bar soap reassured Angus again. After Running Antelope had made his offer to bring her and had ridden away, he had remembered a sick woman, suffering from an abscess, and how a medicine man had lanced it with a sharp flint—which must have been dirty, for septic poisoning followed. He had ardently hoped that if Chantelaine returned without the doctor the old Indian woman might be hygienic in her midwifery. Her clean smell and her request for constant hot water were comforting.

Having tended the stove and filled all the kettles, he stole up after her. She was sitting on a chair, by her bulk entirely hiding it, beside the bed, attempting to cheer Fiona.

"It is nothing!" she declared. "When my last one was nearly ready we were moving from one place here to one place there. We were moving when the time came. I went into a bush beside a creek and had the babee, and then followed my people with it. The tepees were all up and the fires were lit, but I was in time for supper."

Fiona began to laugh. She seemed slightly hysterical. Mrs. Running Antelope looked at her in surprise, then supposed she was laughing with delight at the ease of it all, and her look of astonishment or affront turned to one of satisfaction at having so thoroughly encouraged her.

Suddenly the pains took Fiona again so that she moaned. Just then there was a sound without and Chantelaine's voice. Angus dashed from the room and downstairs. Another voice! Doctor Tulloch of High Butte had arrived.

He took immediate control. He ordered Angus to keep out, young though he was, very masterful and authoritative when assuming a case. On the bottom step of the stairs the distraught husband sat in agony, saying, "O God, O God!" Fiona screamed and he rushed upstairs again, colliding with Mrs. Running Antelope. As she bumped into him she demanded hot water, and together they hurried down to the kitchen. Angus filled a jug for her, then as she went away he attended to the kettle, saying again, "O God, O God!" Back and forth he paced, listening. At last, hearing sounds inexplicable, he went out to the foot of the stairs once more. Mrs. Running Antelope appeared, tremendous on the landing.

"It's a boy," she said.

Angus crept into the room. There lay Fiona, it seemed to him dead; but she opened her eyes and smiled at him, not only pain showing on her face but a light of ecstasy. What had happened to her had not been all unmitigated agony. At the bottom of the bed lay a small exotic monkey, wrapped in flannel. He stared at it. He gaped at the doctor. He tried to make private signs—elevating his brows, then looking at that object, then back to Tulloch again—mutely asking him what manner of creature had been born to them.

"A fine, healthy boy!" said Tulloch, drying his hands carefully. "I must go soon. I'm wanted back at High Butte quickly. You have a great midwife here."

He turned to the Indian woman. He had a breezy manner of self-confidence, or over-confidence, as one saw it. His comportment gave some full assurance in his ability and made others doubt it.

"What you don't know about obstetrics and gynecology," said he, with a twinkle, "is hardly worth knowing."

She conceded him a small embarrassed laugh, and making hazard that, "Oh—yesss!" would be satisfactory reply to give, gave it. He chuckled, slapped her on her ample shoulder, wheeled for one more look at Fiona and the armful of new life, then chucking his chest as though he had done the whole thing, the stork of all storks, marched from the room, Angus following him.

"You must have something to eat, Doc," he said.

"I will go over to Chantelaine," replied Tulloch, "and he will drive me back. How are you feeling? Relieved, eh?"

"Yes, indeed."

"Had pains in your tummy?"

"Yes, I did—now you mention it."

"Ho-ho!" the young medico shouted; and away he went, ho-hoing with laughter over to Chantelaine's.

Angus went upstairs again. Fiona had the fine healthy boy (on the doctor's word) in the crook of her arm.

"Kiss me," she said.

He stooped and kissed her and then sat beside the bed holding her hand.

"Isn't he lovely?" she sighed.

Mrs. Running Antelope, coming and going, was beaming with midwifely content.

"I go to tell my man at Red Head's tepee," she said anon, "and come back."

She left them alone. Fiona's eyes closed and she fell asleep with that light of ecstasy on her face. Still Angus sat there. Suddenly he heard a high, shrill ki-yi-ing of Indian voices. He listened. They were drawing nearer. Over his loins cold ran. The yells broke out again, high and shrill, as though learnt from ululating coyotes in full chase. He loosened hold of his wife's hand and, rising, went to the window.

A rub-a-dub of hoofs drummed outside. There came the riders, befeathered and armed. Fiona, pale and staring, had wakened and was calling him.

"I'm here, I'm here," he said. "It's all right. I'll go down and see them."

There was a volley of firing.

"They have joined the rebels!" she moaned. "And after all you have done for them, Angus. It may be dreadful. Where can we hide baby?"

He ran downstairs, opened the door and stepped outside. The house was encircled by Indians. Angus raised his face, imploring to them. He would throw himself on their mercy. He would get in a word. He would tell them he had once had a Cree woman (daughter of a Cree chief and Stoney mother), he would tell them he had a Cree son. He would tell them—

There was All Alone confronting him. He was evidently the leader of this party. In answer to Angus's imploring gestures the firing stopped, the circling of the painted horses was ended. They joggled this way and that. The young chief dropped from the saddle and, advancing to the agent, held out his hand. Angus stared, then held out his.

"We have just heard your woman has a child. We have come to say it makes our hearts glad," said All Alone.

Holding the hand of Minota's son, Angus looked at the half-circle of braves before his door. The other half-circle from the back came surging round the corner of the house to join their fellows. All yelled again. At that moment Running Antelope appeared, followed by his squaw thrusting a way between the horses, Julius Caesar afoot to the rescue. "This is bad, this," he shouted. "It must be stopped. It may frighten the white woman."

"I will go and tell her," said Angus. "This will put the day into her heart."

He passed indoors and ran upstairs to Fiona's bedside. Cold sweat was on her forehead.

"They came to congratulate you," he explained.

"To congratulate—oh!" and she burst into tears.

As he sat beside her, consoling her, he wished she knew all—but the time was past, he considered, for telling her. He could only hold her hand, linking his fingers with hers, as in assurance of eternal unity.

His Indian son had come to congratulate him on the birth of his white son: he was hurt that he could not share that secret with Fiona. He looked down on her with adoration while outside were the squelching sounds of horses' hoofs, and the little tinkling of the small, round Hudson's Bay Company bells that some had tied to the manes—a tinkling, a squelching, and occasional subdued voices in the musical Cree as the painted braves, headed by All Alone, rode away with little explosions of receding laughter.

CHAPTER TWENTY-FIVE
Changes

The miserable business was over, Riel hanged, the snow of another winter quaking down over the land, and Macpherson's chief concern in life was whether it should be wheels or runners to carry the wheat of those he called our progressives to the grain elevators that had been erected by the side of the railway. Those who drove the sledges, or wagons, as the case might be, were proud of their duty. In an odd Indian fashion even the ones who would not follow the example of the progressives—stumble through the furrows at the plough-tail, sweat in the sun stooking—watched these go with a sort of tribal pride. There, they could raise wheat as well as the invaders!

From the gable window of the room in which Dan had been born a year past, Angus watched the departure because, up there, could be had a view over the coulee rim to south. The sky was emptied; the sun was on the snow. A vision of the great northwest had once come to him, a vision of a sea of grass (with scattered islands of poplars and pines here and there), and, as though splashed by a giant's hand across the leagues, the forts of Ellice and Pelly, Pitt and Carlton, and a final sprinkling of Edmonton, St. Ann's, Jasper, Rocky Mountain House. Another vision he had as he watched the departure of the wheat sleighs from that window: from as far north as Prince Albert the settlers would be making up their parties to sledge the grain, putting on their fur-lined Mackinaw coats, adjusting their fur caps for the trek. Parallel lines, so went his fancy, were being streaked down the land, slowly moving on to Brandon, Regina, Moose Jaw, Swift Current, Maple Creek, Medicine Hat, to the tune of the jingling bells.

A movement to right caught his eye. The High Butte contingent had evidently been of the same mind regarding the weather as Macpherson. There they went, drawing their indigo trail through the snow, small and distant puppets. He wondered by what belt of sheltering woods they would call it a day, halt for the night under the quaking plumes and shifting beams of the Aurora Borealis.

Soon even that—the jingling trudge of the wheat sledges—or at least over such distances, would be of the past, far sooner than Peters, for instance, had imagined. For Peters had quit the service. His girl could not marry the prairies, the wild west, she wrote, and had found him a job in Toronto that they might wed. By the time his successor, Norman Murray, arrived, all the talk of the neighbourhood was of the new railway to be built from Calgary to Edmonton.

Two missions, of different sects, were granted permission, by Ottawa, to tend the souls of his people; and, out of the Indians' private funds, with their entire approval, Angus had a hospital built and a trained nurse installed. Soon one or two of the young girls, on leaving the mission schools, went into training there. Dr. Tulloch (who had brought Daniel into the world—with the assistance of Mrs. Running Antelope) came over, appointed by government to do so, every Sunday, and treated these neck sores that were beginning to appear.

It was about this time that Angus became a secret grandfather: a son, Peter, was born to All Alone and Tannisse. The custom of taking a white man's, or white woman's, Christian name, and using the name of the Indian father as surname was well established by then. Thus it was Peter All Alone. In after years (granting the survival of the race), interested genealogists would know that the family surnames had originated in the middle and late years of the nineteenth century. Only the mentally deficient among the conquerors would giggle at them more than over many names of their own people—Buffalo no more odd than Lamb,

Sagebrush no funnier than Greenwood, Duck no more to be derided than Swan!

Five years later, on one of the first trains to run on the Calgary-Edmonton branch line, Fiona and Angus went south to Calgary for the fun of it, like children with a new toy.

"All aboard!" the conductor intoned. Still a marine implication! Out of sight of land, prairie schooners, all aboard! On their last visit to the ranch in the High River country it had seemed to them both that there was no physical change in Mr. and Mrs. Fraser, the years light upon them. On this visit they saw change. It was, as a matter of fact, a mellowing of Ian that made them realize how the years fly. Genial he had been all his life, live-and-let-live but, even so, in this mellowness there was a suggestion of age. In Fiona's mother they noted a new frailty, a manner as of handing over the world to any who had the physical vivacity to be eager about it. They had enlarged the original house since the addition by Hector and his wife of two young people, a boy and a girl. Financially all went well with them, their herds dotting the hills.

On the Munros' return they were driven out to the reserve in a buggy hired at the High Butte Livery Stables. In tall letters the name was painted on a false front over the doorway, the wooden building standing with gable to the street in the authentic manner of a frontier town of that period. High Butte! It seemed to Angus that he must be ageing also as he looked at the butte sharply outlined, seen at close range there, against a golden sky. How many years ago was it that he had ridden, parabola-fashion, along its shoulder for a last look—like Lot's wife—at the west he was leaving of his own volition and yet without pleasure?

"What are you dreaming of?" asked Fiona.

"Of the day I rode along there, coming east with Sam Douglas, to see at Kildonan a wee lass but nine years old."

To her eyes came a tender light that hurt him because he had been thinking also of Minota—and wished he had told her all that, long since, he had decided she had better not know.

On the way they passed prairie schooner after prairie schooner, many of them apparently at journey's end. They gave good day, as the way was then, to the folk in these, once or twice halting for a talk, hailed by a cry of: "How-do, strangers! What's the hurry? Stop and have a cup of coffee." Angus divided these immigrants in his mind (with his Indian kink) into two classes. Sooner or later in the chats there would be inquiry as to what he was about, driving through the land.

"Indian agent? Well, I got no use for the varmints. I left six

153

good Indians down on my place in Nebrasky. Yes. sir, good Indians—down in the bottom of an old well there."

"Indian agent? There's a reservation near here, then, is there? Well, sir, that's good news. I don't know why it is but I like them folks. Danged if I don't even like the smell of them—wood-smoke, and the way they tan their deer-skins, and maybe a whiff of sweet-grass in their tepees, or some of the squaws with kind of sachets of herbs stuck inside their clothes. Yes, sir, I'm darned if I don't like to see an Indian or two around."

Already a community of Mennonites had come up from southern Manitoba and settled to east of the reserve.

"Do you realize," said Angus to his wife, "that we are almost an island now—the Mennonites to east, these Minnesota and Nebraska farmers to west, cattlemen to south? It's no-man's land only to north of us now."

The year young Dan started to ride to and from the settlement school, five miles west of the reserve, the year Peter All Alone went to the mission school, the No-Man's Land was suddenly Doukhobour land in a possessive communal influx. The reserve was islanded. Many people had come, indeed. By the following winter there was no hauling of the wheat to the main line: by the side of the track at High Butte station, on the Calgary-Edmonton line, the tall grain elevators stood waiting.

"You must come down to the Burns' Nicht," Sam had said when last he saw them, and he had written:

"You must come out once in the winter anyhow to join us—either at the Burns' Night or for the Bonspiel. We have a grand Curling Rink now and a growing club, international, irrespective of race, age, or religion! Our latest member is a Cockney, a real-estate man, one Odges as he calls himself. He said he had always thought that Curling was a Scotch game but begins to think it is Scotch and Soda! Well, Burns' Night or Bonspiel, but it must be one or the other . . ."

For Fiona's sake Angus voted for Burns' Night if the weather allowed passage.

Early in the month it looked as though it would be wheels to go to High Butte station. There had been snow, and then cold, the thermometer at twenty below zero, when suddenly it rose to fifty above before a chinook wind that came roaring out of the west, whipping over the trees in the coulee bottoms like fishing-rods and melting the snow. That was three days before the one on which they would be starting out, weather permitting.

Then came snow again, but crisped to a point or two of frost. So it was runners. In a two-horse sleigh, with hood and windows, plenty of hay at their feet to keep them warm, they set out. Angus looked up at the sky.

"I hae ma doots," said he, and asked one of the Indians what the weather was going to do.

"Snow," was the reply.

There was a quiescence in the air, a feeling as of a lull before some great occurrence. The horses were eager, but Angus would not let them tire themselves, for they had far to go.

Sledges were part of the happiness of life to Fiona. To travel when the snow was packed, travel behind rhythmic patter of hoofs and jingle of bells, made her eyes sparkle as at seventeen. She sat forward and looked down through the side window at a frill of snow folding back from the runner like the scroll of foam at a ship's bow, then tucked herself again in her rug.

Under gray sky they swung from the agency road to the road that twined from that settlement where Dan had his first schooling (in a one-room shack, presided over by a "school-marm" to High Butte). Angus was glad to have got so far without trouble of any kind. The quiescence was ominous. Suddenly the snow foretold came, thicker, thicker. He had to unlatch and drop the window before him to see, the driven flakes being like a white plaster there. At once the whirling storm came into the sleigh.

"Tuck yourself up," said he.

The horses went more slowly, labouring instead of restrained. They reached a place where, from earlier falls, there had been drifts. There the team dragged strenuously, puffing white gusts of breath into the rising blizzard.

"I'm glad we got here before this started," remarked Angus.

"Where's the road?"

"They'll have to find it," replied Angus. "That's why I'm glad we got this length. Off the road nearer home, and given their heads, they'd just turn and go back. They know now where we are going."

The snow increased in volume. He could hardly see the horses' ears. They picked up speed again, straining into the collars, the muscles of their haunches sliding under the skin in unison so violently that they dislodged the coat of snow on them. It slipped off in layers.

"They want to get to the end," observed Fiona.

She had hardly spoken when they halted.

"Giddap!"

They refused.

"Hullo, there!" a voice hailed.

"Hullo!" shouted Angus, opening the door beside him.

"Where do you think you are going?" the voice called.

"High Butte. Why?"

"You're there!"

The horses wheeled so abruptly that the sledge canted like a careening boat, wheeled, charged through drifts ahead, and there was the gray loom of the High Butte livery stable.

In relief Fiona laughed.

"We'll never forget these days," she said. "Great life!"

No, they would never forget them. In the morning a snow-plough cleared the track, its rotating nozzle throwing fountains to either side, fountains that twinkled with rainbow colours in the sun.

The weather had permitted, changeable though it was, and there they were in the private "banquet room" of the Alberta Hotel, reading the place-cards on the table, each with a verse of Burns on it. Soon a parson was saying grace:

> "Some hae meat and canna eat,
> And some would eat that want it;
> But we hae meat and we can eat,
> Sae let the Lord be thankit."

Two pipers came in marching, swaying, piping, and behind them was a beaming Chinaman—Sam's own "butler" as he called him—keeping step with them and holding high in air the platter of haggis. Sam called on Tam Somebody (neither Angus nor Fiona caught the name) to give the haggis its address. Up rose Tam, with a wave of his hand to the dish.

"'Wee, sleekit, cow'rin', tim'rous beastie . . .'" he began.

A roar of laughter sounded and Mrs. Tam—there was no doubt about it being she—looked embarrassed round her and sadly at her husband.

He cleared his throat and started again:

> "'Fair fa' your honest, sonsie face,
> Great chieftain o' the puddin'-race . . .'"

Later, all the toasts drunk, the trestle tables were carried away and the evening progressed to the part Fiona liked. Round the sides of the long room while the tables were being removed the groups clustered in a buzz of talk. Then, from a throne at the end, came the sound of fiddles tuning up, little premonitory scrapes and pluckings. It was old Red River days again for Fiona.

First lady and first gentleman, balance; first lady and first gentleman, take hands; first couple down the line, and wildly went the fiddles; next, follow suit, and merrily went the fiddles. Gaily they danced in the old Alberta Hotel the dances of an earlier home whence some had themselves come, or whence their parents or grandparents had come: strathspeys, reels (and Red River jig), Highland flings, schottische, lancers, petronella. And Hooch! Hooch! they cried as the night wore on.

Going bedwards in the wee sma' hours along a corridor, Fiona paused and raised a finger to Angus in a sign for him to listen. Through an open transom they heard a man speaking.

"I'm as fou as I can haud," he announced, "and I can haud nae mair."

"I ken fine," a woman's voice replied. "And early ye began. Ye was addressing the wee mouse instead of the haggis."

"I only did that tae enliven the proceedings."

"Oh, Tam!"

"Weel, ye are no going to be hypocreetical, are ye? Burns wouldna hae minded!"

They moved on to their own door, that discussion following them.

Before going home next morning, while Fiona was doing some shopping, Angus called in at the office of Herbert Hodges, real-estate agent.

"Yes, I 'ad to come back," said Hodges. "Even the missus got that way. We went 'ome, you know. I quit the service. That new reserve wasn't to her mind. But she got 'omesick to come back and I can assure you Barkis was willing. If we had just waited out here what we might have been! Millionaires!"

At that moment entered Mrs. Hodges, to whom Angus was at once introduced. She, too, was shopping and had just come in for some more money.

"Delighted to meet you, Mr. Munro," she said. "I've heard of you from my 'usband. Oh, that was a lonely plice up there but I like it here now we are back. Somethink in the old life I couldn't abide when we went 'ome. We held it down awhile and then just had to come out again. Funny thing, you know. Our young people like it here, too. In summer we drive up to the mountains and, d'you know, Mr. Munro, there are forests there just put you in mind of Epping Forest. Have you ever been in the mountains?"

"Yes—yes, indeed," replied Angus.

"You've seen them?"

"Oh, yes."

"The young people," remarked Hodges, laughing, "tell her she'd know if it was Epping Forest if she got a slap from a bear—to teach her respect."

She smiled pleasantly at that.

"Oh, I see it all from the 'otel veranda," she explained. "You can see everythink from there without having to go walking and climbing. I'm not greatly impressed by mountaineering. But I like living here now. Jack's as good as 'is master 'ere."

"Quite. Yes," said Angus, "and the master as good as Jack. It's a man's own character that counts."

"Well, er—oh, yes, I see what you mean," but she looked somewhat combatively at him, with a flash in her eyes. Then, drooping her eyelids, she examined him, up and down, became a little frigid, almost condescending. "Well, I'm pleased to have met you, I'm sure, Mr. Munro. My 'usband often talked of you and wondered how you were getting on in that outlandish place, and if your poor wife could put up with it. Of course, being newly married in those days, she might for her husband's sake, as I said to 'Erbert when he told me about you. And the dreadful Indians! I suppose it's all according. Some people don't mind. Some people are brought up to it, raised, as they say 'ere. I do so 'ate to 'ear slang. But this is a real city, and we could never go back 'ome but on a visit. You 'ardly ever see an Indian here now except on special occasions when they come in dressed up in their old rubbish. I must be going. De-lighted to 'ave met you, Mr. Munro."

"Yes," said Hodges, after she had gone back to her shopping, and after a series of nervous little throat clearings, "it's good to be back. But if we had never gone we might have been millionaires now. Look at Mr. Douglas. He believed in the country and he's the wealthiest man 'ere—and no side to him. Calls me 'Erbert and I call him Sam."

"Yes, Sam Douglas is very—"

"You know him?"

"Yes. I've known him some years."

"Well, fancy you knowing Sam Douglas! 'Ow did you get to know him?"

Angus made no reply and Mr. Hodges hurried on.

"It was kind of you to look me up, Mr. Munro," he said. "Good luck to you, good luck to you! Any time you have any money to invest in real estate, delighted to advise," and he waved a hand in cordial farewell.

CHAPTER TWENTY-SIX
Descendants

As the years passed, Daniel's progress was gratifying to both mother and father. Before his settlement school days were over, despite his outdoor enthusiasms, his handling of horses, Angus and Fiona decided he would not end his education when he passed out of High School. Munro himself had always been a reader. Two walls of the sitting-room were book-shelves from floor to ceiling, and always there was a space in them somewhere that signified Dan had a book out.

A second child was added to All Alone and his wife Tannisse, a daughter this time, christened Louise. Peter, the elder child, Angus was told, was one of the ninety per cent who (in an old phrase of the land) go back to the blanket. But, at least, having learnt English at the mission, he did not refuse to speak it. It was not always, by the way, stubbornness, Angus suspected, that caused an Indian who knew English not to talk it. Diffidence, shyness, he believed, as often—perhaps more often—was the cause. Nor did Peter spend his time, school over, in riding aimlessly about the reserve, like some of the boys. He worked with his father in the fields. Macpherson reported him keen on cattle and not averse to a plough, which was much to be thankful for.

When Dan went to High School in Calgary, living there with a family advised by Lovat Douglas, school reports and reference to him in letters from Sam (who had, as he wrote, an eye on the lad) were very pleasing. Home for the holidays at the end of his first term, he inquired, "Do you know what I'd like to be, Dad?"

"No."

"A doctor."

"A doctor?"

"Yes. There's a first-aid class I've joined. I can't understand why everyone doesn't learn it. One ought to have that knowledge anyhow—never know where you'll be. Suppose there was an accident and you couldn't do a thing, or somebody was sick and you knew no more than the lily-white hand on the fevered brow. It's fascinating, too."

Angus became more and more business advisor for the band. The cattlemen to south, because of the barbed-wire having come into use, were in jeopardy. Their steers, drifting in winter before blizzards, were held by the wire and "frozen on the hoof," as a rancher who called at the office put it.

"It's a darned queer thing to think of," said he. "When I

started here we had our spring round-up that carried us plumb down into Montana and not a strand of that Goddamned barbed-wire all the way. We got back home with the branded calves, had a little smoke and a rest, and it was time then for the beef round-up and drive. When we got through that there was another year shot. But no barbed-wire. How's the chances, Mr. Agent, for a deal for grazing rights on some of the reserve land? They ain't using it all."

"'I think," replied Angus, "the chances are good if we can arrange terms."

Many of his Indians were already self-supporting. Here was opportunity toward fruition of a dream he had of a larger tribal fund. With Running Antelope (who, in the passing years, had come to look more like Rameses II, mummified, than Julius Caesar, though straight as ever in the spine), with Tall Whirlwind and All Alone he discussed the matter. Ottawa was willing. It was at his discretion in his knowledge of conditions. Yes, they were willing also. They were eager, indeed. They would leave the matter of price to him, for he thought with them.

Changes, changes! The steers of the cattlemen grazed on the spare part of the reserve unmolested, no more the Redcoats coming to look for evidence of Grand Larceny of Live Stock by Angus's wards, and sub-chief Big Beaver (gone these years) the picture of unbelief that a Cree could pilfer so much as a hair of a steer.

All Alone's first son was but a year younger than Dan. The little girl, Louise, would soon be going to school. It looked as if there were but to be the two from that union but after a lapse of some years came another boy.

Few of the women could brook a doctor interfering at a delivery, but All Alone was proudly progressive, all Indian though he believed himself to be. What a white woman had, his woman would have; and so he drove Tannisse to the hospital, then went off to High Butte for Dr. Tulloch.

"Well," reported the doctor to Angus, "Mrs. All Alone had an easy time—just like shelling peas."

"Healthy?"

"Yes. No tuberculosis in that family, but I must say the small son who has arrived does have a sort of white cast. No imputation suggested on the lady! Probably each generation, getting more civilized, will display an increasingly European and decreasingly Amerindian cranium."

That view seemed as much and as little authoritative as that of Buffalo Calf on the subject of race, but Angus had other considerations apart from the reasonableness or unreasonableness of it.

"Peter should be rechristened Beginning," remarked Chantelaine, hearing the news, "and this last one End."

Not only the changes in the land told of the flight of time. The arrival of this third (secret) grandchild—for whom he might be able to do something—gave Angus thoughts to that tune. The child was named after him by the proud parents. Fiona was delighted by the compliment. To Angus it increased the burden of his secret life.

The growth of Dan—physical and mental—was the chief cause for his considerations that the years were flying. His wife seemed to him as youthful-looking as when they married—which was absurd, no doubt, but his view. Only the other day, it seemed to him, All Alone had come to the agency with a gift for little boy that Tannisse had been busy upon—a play-tepee not five feet high. It had been set up beside the house; and here was Dan long since grown beyond it and off to his second term in Calgary.

Sam Douglas, coming up in the autumn to the agency house for the duck-shooting, was full of sincere if slightly oratorical admiration for young Dan. The sight of High Butte took his mind also back to old days. All his dreams had come true except the first of which Angus had heard. No, he had not bothered about coal.

"Man, man," said he, "coal! That takes me back a way, back to the Missouri where I heard of the burning rocks and thought I was on to something wonderful."

He had taken a jump ahead of that. Natural gas was his latest and more profitable interest. There was a reservoir of it under Medicine Hat and he was sure others would be found elsewhere. But still he was prophesying. He believed there was petroleum somewhere under that earth that had for æons been only buffalo pasture. He was chairman of this, chairman of that, director, or president, of this, that and the other—such as Great Northwest Hail Insurance and the S. D. Wheat Pool. The Transport and Haulage business he had sold.

To Angus he did not seem to be happy. There was the sound of a flaw when one tapped: he did not ring true. There was disappointment lurking in him, as of a man who had got to the rainbow's end and found the holding of the crock in his hands less elating than the quest for it. Still he must quest.

"Petroleum! Aye, I believe in petroleum!" he exclaimed, and nudged Angus in the midriff with an elbow, sitting under the cotton poplars by the house gable, cleaning his shot-gun. But even that note of elation, and the nudge, were as of one playing a part. He went away laden with ducks and saying, "Grand to have seen you again, Angus. It's wonderful to see old faces, old friends again."

Fiona felt a vague sense of pity for him when he was gone.

"Why I should feel it," she said, "I have no foggiest idea. He has everything."

They saw him again—and Dan—sooner than they expected.

For fun they had taken their first trip out of the country on the new railway-spur years ago. For this, that and the other cause—Burns Nights, holiday visits, they had, since then, often travelled on that line. At a sudden call from Ian they went again to High River in anxiety. Mrs. Fraser had been taken suddenly ill, the telegram said, and the doctor thought that any relatives should be advised. All the way they had the wonder, in common, if she was already gone—Angus conjecturing that perhaps she was dead when the wire was sent to them, and Fiona feeling (foolishly, no doubt, as life goes, yet this was her emotion at the time) that she had been selfish ever to leave her mother, and thanking God that her father, Hector, and Hector's wife, were with her.

Mrs. Fraser was gone by the time they arrived, had indeed been gone when the telegram was despatched to them, as later they heard, it being couched as it was on the advice of the doctor who, out of experience and pity, would temper shock. That sense of touching some other life not understood in this one was in all their hearts at High River, so that even the sound of the running stream by the door was different for awhile, and the sighing of the little winds trooping through the pines that topped the gray-green hummocks there was as a sigh out of eternity into time. All were old enough to know it had to come to them some day and she had not died in pain. For that they were grateful. After the funeral Fiona stayed at the ranch, arranging to follow Angus later.

Stopping on the way back at Calgary to do some duties for his father-in-law, Angus found that there was talk of nothing but the Boer War. Nobody seemed to have a clear idea of what it was all about—nor to care. Britain was at war: that sufficed—and that war, anyhow, is good adventure was the froth atop the crowd-emotion there.

His morning offices seen to, Munro lunched with Sam Lovat Douglas, having arranged to see Dan in the afternoon when school was over. Sam expressed himself very sorry to hear the news of Mrs. Fraser, but repeated several times, consolatory. "All got to come to it." After a decent pause he mentioned that he had been over in the old country for some months and was engaged to be married—me, man, confirmed bachelor!—to an old friend, of place and property, Angus gathered.

"Will you be going back there to live?" he asked.

"No, no. At least, she's coming to see how she likes it here."
He glanced at a leaflet on the wall. "Look at that," he said.
"Paderewski is coming to play in Calgary on his tour. She'll be all
right. And look at the grand library they are making here now.
Man, it's wonderful. Aye, it's time for me to marry and settle."

Lunch over, they sat in the hotel rotunda, where the easy
chairs stood in files facing the street, like a grandstand to view the
passersby. As they smoked and chatted round them were excited
and boisterous young men, discussing the war and recruiting. A
hilarious group surged in, and others sitting there hailed them.
They had been, they announced—everybody listening, as the
conversation seemed common property—to a test for recruits for
Strathcona's Horse.

Colonel Steele said to one of the fellows, 'Where have I seen
you before?' and he answered, 'I don't know.' But Steele looked at
him awhile and then said, 'I've got it!' It was a fellow who had been
convicted some time back for horse-stealing. Some of those who
were standing near heard the colonel remark, 'Well, we'll not lack
for horses if we have you along!'

Into the hotel came an urgent, red-faced young man who
dashed up to the group.

"Here," he began, telescoping his words. "I can ride
anything with hair on it. When they put down the rows of saddles
in front of the horses today, and we all lined up, and they told us
When the bugle blows, saddle and mount, I was one of the first at
my horse. And there was no bluidy bookle on the belly-band, and
the belly-band was split in two!"

Those he addressed shouted with joy at that description of
the cinch.

"Where do you come from?" inquired one, a six-footer with
bright eyes, full of fight and bonhomie—an odd blend.

"From all over the place, and wanting to see more of it,"
replied the newcomer. "Born in Yorkshire, been in New Zealand
and Australia—Queensland. Worked my passage to British
Columbia. It's all the same—work everywhere, hard, bluidy work.
Goom trees and your swag in Queensland, pine trees and your
blanket-roll in B.C. And here's a chance for me to see South Africa
if it wasn't for the lack of that bluidy bookle!"

"Say, you come along with me," said the six-footer, "and I'll
elucidate for you the mystery of cinch and latigo while you wait.
Then you pop on the train and get down to Moose Jaw. I hear they
haven't got all their number there yet."

"That's the speerit, that's the speerit!" exclaimed Sam. "I'll tell that little story in my speech tonight. I'm slated to address a meeting. 'Ladies and gentlemen, in this hour when the mother calls the children answer.' I've a grand end to it: one flag, one empire. That's sure to get them. I'll tell that little story—how the young men rally."

"To see South Africa," said Angus.

Sam's head turned slowly. He looked at his friend gloomily. Then he glanced at his watch.

"Man, it's grand to have seen you—grand to have had a crack again. I'll have to be running. I have work to attend to."

CHAPTER TWENTY-SEVEN
Business

About a week after Angus's return to the agency, Fiona wrote a suggestion: Did he not think she should come back and bring her father with her? It appeared that the old man brooded at the ranch. She thought a change might do him good. So Ian Fraser—looking his years then—came home with her.

He had the manner of not wanting to give trouble, of one thinking he might be in the way rather than of one wanting to be left alone, and in his eyes was an odd dreaming dullness that gave the impression he no longer looked forward but backward. Anon, however, as with an effort at first, he began to join in their talks. Young Daniel brought him out of himself more than either Angus or Fiona.

"And what are you going to be, son?" he asked him once.

Dan told him of his ambition, and he seemed to approve of it. When the lad went back to high school the old man thought it perhaps time for him to be returning to the ranch.

"Better stay a bit now that Dan is gone again," suggested Angus. "Fiona is always lonely without him."

"Yes, the house is quiet without the boy."

"Why not make your home here?" said Angus. "Don't you like the place?"

"Oh, I like it fine. I like it fine. I can see the mountains from here and I can see the plains. I have all I want—all I want," and a sadness came to his eyes as though, truly, he had not. He sat back in his chair and began that gentle humming, characteristic of him.

Thus it was that he made his home there, though on the next summer they all visited the High River ranch together,

164

picking up Dan on the way. In the Autumn of that year Fraser had a slight stroke, but soon recovered.

"It's nothing very serious," Dr. Tullock told them. "He's of an age for it. He's just got to go easy, that's all."

He went easy. All the evidence, facially, of his stroke was a slight muscular constriction of one jaw, not noticeable except to intimates who knew him of old, when the face was in repose. When he laughed the two sides did not equally participate, but strangers might have thought it was but a mannerism of his—a lop-sided smile. A dullness in one of his legs troubled him more and made him take to using a stick—a cane, as all walking-sticks were called. In summer he sat much on the veranda, where he could see the play of the shadows of the cluster of poplars that stood by the gable and hear their rustling. Indoors, Fiona would hear him lilting to himself and the tap-tap of his stick keeping time. He had a second stroke in the following winter and slipped away. As long after as the next summer Fiona, in absent mood, would sometimes hear the tap of his stick keeping time to his singing, and then come back to the present. That year an offer regarding his wards came to Angus, an offer that a few years earlier he might have listened to but at that time rejected.

Into the office one day came the three chiefs for a conference. A white man had been on the reserve talking to them, they said, wanting them to sell a parcel of land, a strip at the east side. They filled their pipes. The blent odour of tobacco and kinick-kinick was in the room.

"Well," said Angus, taking from a drawer his black book—larger and of a larger content than the black book of the Ettrick brothers', "a few years ago it might have been different. You know it yourselves: it looked as if you were dying out. But you have steadied. And you've got to think of your children's children. One must think of one's children." Three grunts came in response to that. "Suppose," Angus continued, "that in another generation or two you increased in numbers and wanted more land—you'd have to buy then if you sell now. With whites all round you that would divide the band. You'd have to buy somewhere else. Now that you've steadied you may increase." The chiefs smoked quietly, hunched forward, eyes on the floor in the Indian manner when listening.

"No, I certainly would not advise you to sell," said Angus, and he threw down on the table a paper-cutter he had taken up.

The three Indians raised their heads. They knew that little mannerism. It was his way of saying, I have finished. They rose. The business was over. They moved to the door with a faint scliff of moccasined feet. There was no good day, but he, rising with them and standing at the door, laid a hand for a moment on the shoulder of the last to go out—All Alone—who looked back at him with a smile. He had come to love this agent. He remembered his first meeting with him, and how he had lifted his hands in the sign of blessing.

There was a swish of saddle leather, the creak of buggy wheels, Running Antelope, stiffening with rheumatism, preferring driving to riding.

Angus stepped back into his office, dense with the smoke they had left, and opened the window wider. The blue haze whirled about in the room in ribands and fluttered into the open air.

"All the same," said he to himself, "the man had no right to go jinking over the reserve and sounding them before coming to me."

Three days later the jinker arrived. In the morning one of the missionaries had called at nine to lodge a complaint against the other. At ten the other had called to make a report against the one—"I think this comes within your province, Mr. Munro." Angus was learning. He said to the second, as to the first, "Well, that's too bad. I'll see what I can do," and thought no more about it. He spent much time trying to make brotherly love continue between these two. When the second, in his turn, had departed, there was a sound in the room, faint but insistent in the office corners.

Angus opened the door again. Yes, it was the unremitting pulse of drums. Mennonites to east of them, Doukhobours to north, all sorts and agnostics to south, and the same to west—well, why not the drums also in some ritual of their own observance?

Thus, right or wrong, he mused, and stood there with folded arms, his body rising and falling lightly in time with the distant, far-carried thud, thud, thud. As he was standing so there whirled up to the steps a buggy from the High Butte Livery Stable and a personage—surely a personage he would have been in the eyes of William Ettrick—stepped down, the vehicle oscillating on its springs, relieved of him.

"Is the agent around?" asked this stranger, removing a large cigar from a large mouth.

"I am the agent," answered Angus.

"Could I have a word with you?"

"Surely. Come right in."

Angus, pointing to a seat before the desk, watched his large visitor subside.

"I am Walter Crank Barlow," began the personage.

"How do you do? Munro is my name."

166

"Well, I've been talking to some of your Indians here," said Mr. Barlow, "about a purchase I want to make of a piece of land at the east side of their reserve."

"Oh, it was you."

"It was I? What do you mean?" and Mr. Barlow flicked ash onto the floor.

"Pardon me," murmured Angus, setting an ash-tray before his caller.

"What do you mean 'It was I?'"

"They mentioned to me that a white man had come to the reserve and talked to them about that," explained Angus.

"They did."

"Yes. I could not understand why he had not come to me first. I am glad to see you here now."

"Well, here I am, Mr.—ah—Munro. I hope we may be able to fix up the matter. The Indians said they would think it over."

"Quite. I have discussed it with them and I have advised against it,"

"Against it!" ejaculated Mr. Barlow.

"Yes."

"Why that?"

"I can give you the reason," replied Angus. "There is a steadying of their numbers now. They may increase. We are now almost surrounded by white settlers. They may need, for themselves, all that land."

"I doubt it, I doubt it! I think it is a short-sighted policy on your part. You can afford to rent some of the reserve as grazing lands, I believe."

"Yes, I do. If a strip was sold it would mean having to lose that income. The Indians might need all for their own stock eventually. And I think, for the time being, the rentals are better for them."

"I think the heads of your department would not agree with you," said Barlow.

"If you have an offer to make," replied Angus, "I can communicate it to the department."

"Along with your advice against it—heh?"

"Precisely."

"Well, personally I think they are a vanishing race, and it should be your part on their behalf to do the best for them—on their behalf, I repeat, instead of just leasing to the cattlemen," and he gave a look at once shrewd and insolent.

Angus did not like it. Though with no guilty conscience (needless to say) that look was to him of a man who would suggest

167

that he got what was called a rake-off from the ranchers. A sudden rage took him and he wanted to wring this person's neck.

"If you have an offer to make you might make it in writing," he said, quietly, "and I shall forward it to the department, although personally I advise—whatever the price—no surrender."

"What do you mean, 'No surrender'?"

"It is the department word for a sale of land by the Indians," Angus replied.

"Oh, I see. Well, of course, seeing how you feel I'm willing to meet you. You are not, I suppose, in the service for your health!"

Angus frowned, produced his pipe slowly, and filled it. Mr. Barlow misread the scrutiny.

"I am willing," said he, "to put the matter on a business basis between ourselves. I am willing to do it—let's say—on a commission basis. If you can use your influence to get the Indians to agree and the department to agree, I'd be willing to arrange a commission basis for you."

Angus drew a deep breath. He rose, and then suddenly had a quaint memory. He was for a moment in his old cabin in the forests beyond Jasper House, and in his hand was a blue jay dead. Having risen to kill the man he did not sit down again.

"I have already told you, sir," he said, stepping to the door, "I am entirely against any surrender of lands on the reserve."

Deep, thought Mr. Barlow, deep.

"But you would, perhaps, see your way," he suggested, telescoping the words in his anxiety, "to reconsider that opinion for a sound commission—a worthwhile commission, say twenty-five per cent of the price agreed upon?"

"Mr. Barlow," said Angus, "will you get to hell out of here!"

There! He wanted to be civilized—but that was how it ended.

Mr. Barlow rose, ash from his cigar falling all over his clothes.

"You will hear more of this," he vowed. "I have influence. I can pull wires. I have political pull. I can fix you!"

"I'll fix you," replied Angus, "so that you will be carried out of here if you don't walk out quickly."

Mr. Barlow did not step to the door by which he had entered, the handle of which was between the agent's fingers. He stepped out into the main office, the door of which was just ajar—either, despite his weight, in dread of coming close to Angus or, in the flurry of the moment, hardly aware of his steps and thinking that there was another exit. Seeing Chantelaine and Murray hooked there over their ledgers—

"I have witnesses!" he exclaimed. "I call these men to witness. You hear that, sir?" and he addressed himself to Chantelaine. "I call you to witness I was threatened!"

Nigel paid no heed, left hand running down the columns of an account-book on his desk, right hand holding a pen poised in air. He made an entry, then looked round.

"Do you hear me?" shouted Mr. Barlow.

"Pardon," said Chantelaine. "I am a little deaf."

"A little deaf!"

"Yes. Dull of hearing. When a voice is pitched very high," he went on with charming amiability, pivoting slightly on his stool to face Mr. Barlow, "I miss it—as some people can't catch the highest notes of a bat."

"Oh! So the staff takes after the chief, heh? Well, we'll see."

Murray, at his desk, was quaking with mirth. Barlow shot a look at that heaving back, and tramping across the office stepped outside.

"Don't slam the door," called Murray.

The door slammed and through a window they saw the personage drag the well-sprung buggy to one side as he climbed aboard, almost as though he would upset it. He took his seat violently beside the driver.

"Too bad," said Chantelaine, with that slight French accent that he had inherited, "too bad. There's only our Union Jack to wave him good-bye."

"He called us to witness, indeet!" snorted Murray. "We are witnesses also to his venal and immoral suggestions. Wires or no wires, he dare not pull them. We can witness more than that you threatened him! He has the voice of a bull and I think the soul of a worrm!"

CHAPTER TWENTY-EIGHT
Two Sons

They saw then All Alone and Tannisse drive to the door. The canvas of a tepee showed behind the seat, and to the side of the rig lodge-poles had been lashed, their ends thrusting out behind. All Alone handed the lines to his wife and alighted.

The three in the office continued to discuss the recent visitor. They heard All Alone go into Angus's private room.

"Shall I tell him to come in here?" asked Murray.

"Yes."

"This way, Chief!" hailed Murray in the connecting doorway, then stepped back to lean against his high desk again.

All Alone entered, wrapped in a gorgeous blanket. On his feet were heavily beaded moccasins; an eagle feather stood upright behind his head from the braided scalp-lock. He carried a pair of polished buffalo horns.

"Oh, look at the Indian!" exclaimed Chantelaine.

They were good friends, these two. Chantelaine had some Cree—more than pidgin-Cree—but Murray had none, so in the outer office All Alone always spoke English.

"Heap good Injun," he replied, and laughed.

"Where are we off to?" asked Angus.

"Medicine Hat," said All Alone. "I have brought you this pair of buffalo horns, Mr. Munro."

"They are beauties. That's nice of you, All Alone," and Angus took them in his hand. "Where did you get them?"

"Oh, lying around, lying around."

"You polished them?"

"No, no. The big chief does the hunting. The squaw does the polishing—and the chief helps her a bit," and he laughed again. "I've got some more out there. You-all should come out and see them. Got over a dozen."

"What for?" asked Chantelaine.

"Tourists," said All Alone.

At that Murray bellowed with mirth, slapping his leg, and Chantelaine pivoted on his high stool chuckling gaily. Angus considered his son thoughtfully.

"Yeah," said All Alone. "When the train stops at Medicine Hat the people have time to get out and walk up and down a little. They see me with buffalo horns. They say Oh, look at the Indian I do nothing. They come along and say Buffalo horns? I grunt. They say, How much, you sell? I hold up three fingers. Sometimes they give three dollars, sometimes they say too much! I give you two, and they hold up two fingers to me. I grunt, and give them the horns. Two dollars."

Chantelaine, humped on his stool, grinned admiringly. Murray, leaning against his desk, jerked his head back and laughed afresh. Angus gave a tight-lipped smile, holding the horns in his hand.

"Sometimes they say, Oh, give him three—the poor people used once to hunt the buffalo. Then I go to my woman and get another pair out of the basket she sits on. If they see too many all at once they think not so much of them."

It was Angus who laughed deep in his chest at that. It was a stratagem of Rocky Mountain House when the Indians came into the trade-room. As a party entered only a small stock was visible. When the trade was done those who went out had to show the curious ones what they had got. To display much stock might create the impression of superfluity. Scarce and of value: that was the scheme of limiting the display.

"These horns should go up over the door," said Murray. He dragged a stool to the entrance to the private office and climbed on it. "Let me hold them up here for you, Mr. Munro, to see how they look."

Angus renounced them.

"There—how about that?" asked Murray.

"Little lower," advised Chantelaine.

"There eh?"

"Yes. They'd be all right there," said Angus, half-heartedly.

"Maybe where you can see when you sit in your room," suggested All Alone.

"Yes, in your own room," agreed Murray, jumping down.

"Maybe in your room where you sit in house," said All Alone.

"I'll take them over and show them to my wife, anyhow," said Angus, and Murray gave them back to him.

"Come out and see," said All Alone.

They filed after him. Tannisse, no longer a slip of a girl, growing broad and plump, was wrapped in a bright shawl, a bandana round her head. She smiled a welcome to them.

"Where are the horns?" asked Chantelaine.

"In basket. I show you," and Tannisse leant back to raise the lid.

"Nice polish," observed Chantelaine.

"Yes, nice polish," agreed Murray.

"Yes, nice polish," said she.

All Alone took out a pair—and posed. He stood statuesque, horns in hand, expression blank, from beaded moccasins to the erect eagle feather (that added to his height) splendid for a painter's eyes. Then he held up a hand, three fingers raised.

"Oh, too much!" declared Chantelaine, entering into the spirit of the thing. "Two—"

This was humour to delight, extremely, Mrs. All Alone. She rippled a merry laugh.

"All a-board!" cried out Chantelaine.

All Alone stepped to the wagon, grinning, put the horns of his exhibition back into the basket and climbed to his seat.

Away they gritted, the fine dry summer soil pouring over the wheel-rims between the spokes. A foal of one of the mares that had been frisking nearby during the halt cavorted and went stilting along beside its dam. A dog that had been lying in the shadow below the rig, and when it started had just risen to patter between the wheels, slithered out from the dust. Foal to one side, dog to the other, away they went trailing their powdery pennant. The three white men watched the departure, somehow fascinated by the picture, often though they had seen the like, watched the rig dwindle up to the coulee-rim, show large there, All Alone and his squaw side by side against the fine beaten blue metal that was that day's sky, and then dip from sight followed by a dropping flutter of dust.

"Indian from the heels up," declared Murray as they turned indoors again.

"Yeah, all Indian," agreed Chantelaine.

The agent of the High Butte Reservation said nothing at all.

It was Dan home from Calgary the next week-end who eased Angus's mind (ingenuous though the lad's talk was) of that constantly recurring thought that he might have done more for his Indian son, done something of real value, educative, had he only known of his existence sooner—eased him also of the regret that so far he seemed unable to be of any real help to All Alone's boys.

Dan, nearing the end of his second year of high school, was at an age for seeming to some bumptious, and to others promisingly inquiring. Those who had not forgotten their own hobbledehoy awakenings would look leniently upon the tangle of his probings, no doubt, and let them go as awkward rather than as bumptious.

Angus was reminded, listening to him, how once he had felt that Fiona had made up on him. His son was making up on him. They were riding—Dan and he—over the reserve, and he could not but hear the lad's voice as a man's, and his laugh had but the slightest rumour in it of the notes that used to ring round the play-tepee only, as it were, the other day.

The boy was at an age for enthusiasms. Angus had been, to Sam Douglas, somewhat of a drifter. The son, thought Sam, seeing him in Calgary, was "a great improvement on the father."

"Angus has the Celtic dreaminess," Sam told his wife, Patricia. "He'd be happy—well, he'd be happy looking at the colours in an icicle! Daniel has ambeetion."

It was ambition that Sam, with hearty approbation, chiefly noted, but, riding over the reserve, some other quality did Dan divulge to his father. He had been saying he was more keen than ever to become a doctor.

"And when you have passed," said Angus, "where would you think to take up practice? Or have you not thought as far ahead as that?"

"It doesn't matter much where," replied Dan. "I'd like to go into the Indian service—doctor on a reserve. I mentioned that to Mr. Douglas once, and he seemed rather horrified—disappointed. He said he had hoped I would aim beyond that. In the early days the Indians didn't have the diseases they have now, and it is up to us, Dad, to get them back to the old state of health. I know some of them are still magnificent specimens. I saw one wrapped in a blanket the other day run several hundred yards to head off some straying horses, and he didn't have to drop his arms from holding the blanket round him. He came back without a puff. But we've put them into houses out of tents, and they don't know how to keep the houses clean. Nature cleans up an old camp-site and its neighbourhood. A lot of them have lost heart. They used to be far cleaner in the old days, according to what one hears, than they are now."

"We want better, more sanitary houses for them," agreed Angus, "and that calls for funds. Some of the houses are just hovels. I know it. A trapper lives alone in his one-room cabin, but a whole family in one small shack—"

"And that's why I prefer medical missionaries to the other sort," said Dan, "hygiene before hymns, sanitation before sermons."

Three Indian youths appeared on a crest, clad only in breech-clout and moccasins—running.

"They can run farther than a horse could carry them in a day," said Dan. "I wonder how long they will be like that—fit for the moccasin telegraph. I often think of the stories you've told me of the old Northwest before I was born. It's the stamina of their grandfathers they are doing it on. A man was telling me in Calgary the other day that he has seen the Blackfeet snaring gophers. When the Bloods were restless, and Colonel Macleod advised Ottawa, he got a reply to use his discretion, and his discretion was to open a sort of soup-kitchen for them at the fort. Malnutrition over a certain number of years may tell on them badly, make them susceptible to T.B. and trachoma."

So he had inherited, it would appear, his father's kink! They rode in silence some way. They saw an old man on a crest heliographing with a disc-mirror in his palm to some young men in a coulee—signalling them home to a meal perhaps—former Indian usages surviving there. The sight of a string of Mennonite wagons moving across distance turned them to the subject of the

173

right to free worship. There had been talk of trying to put a stop to ceremonial dances on the reserve as tending to keep them Indians, and Angus had pointed out, discussing that with the visiting commissioner that Doukhobours and Mennonites had religious freedom, that two different sects were represented at the missions, and (with a deep antipathy to coercion and breaking of the spirit that was no doubt implanted in the days of hopeless rage against, and broken acceptance of, the Clearances)—"we don't want to break them utterly," he had finished, to which the commissioner agreed.

He recounted that talk to Dan.

"We give them," said Dan, "a bell for a drum, poker and black-jack for their own games of chance, hard leather shoes that hurt the feet for moccasins that allow full play of the pedal muscles and a correct standing attitude—" then he raised his head and laughed, in a sudden diffidence. "You see what I'm trying to get at, Dad?"

"Yes," answered Angus, promptly.

So the boy recovered and continued:

"They have the sun, they have all this, and they love it."

"Yes, they love it," said Angus, and thought how he had come to love it also—and yet, growing older, longed again to see Brendan and the loch with the inverted mountains and the silver passage of reflected gulls in its veneered darkness and the sunlight slipping off Ben Chattan. His heart was sick sometimes with such memories, but memory of the eviction (unforgettable) and recollection of the Ettricks' minds and ways allayed homesickness. His Scotland was no place on which he could set foot and feel beneath his tread, but a country of the mind at once definite and unsubstantial—as a song, an old ballad, sung and dying on the air.

"There are slums in all cities," observed Dan, breaking into his father's reverie of a moment, "lousier than the lousiest Indian camp. We can invent steam-engines and the Indian can only call them fire-wagons, and no more than a dog wonder how they go, just say mystery. And yet—scratch the civilized man and where is he? Bang down at the level of what he imagines is the average level of depraved savages."

They were riding up the flank of a long coulee and came to the windy summit. Just below the opposite rim they saw the house of All Alone. They could see Peter—who had just come in from the range, to judge by the horse standing by—down on all fours to amuse his little brother, the small boy astride his back waving an arm in the air in a game of bucking bronchos. On the porch was a figure—not Tannisse by the size. That would be Louise, of whom

Angus had had a fine report recently. They did not think, at the mission, that when her schooldays were over she would go back to the blanket.

"Up to a certain point," said Dan, as they rode on, "this civilization business is fine. Then it passes into sophistication. Right here on this reserve you, Dad, are doing all that's worth for these people."

"Oh?"

He was doing all that was worth doing for them, was he? Yet, listening to the uncrystallized talk of his fumbling son he felt somehow eased.

"Gosh!" exclaimed Dan. "I do have an awful lot to say. And all muddled, too, I suppose."

"God bless the lad," thought Angus. "He's on the right trail, but young, young."

He, himself, was beginning to feel, and look, old.

Yet there were times when he did not feel old, rejuvenated with adventure and celebration. There was that St. Andrew's dinner and dance, for example.

There was just a drizzle of rain wetting the surface of the land. The Rockies were no longer peaks. They were a seeth of darker vapour on the horizon. Here and there, in the running gray above, a hole was punched, showing blue for a moment. It was a snell day.

The era of closed cars had not come yet, but open cars were beginning to oust the horse-hauled buggies, cutters and sledges. They had one at the agency, and for Fiona's sake Angus decided to go to the station in it, automobile being speedier than horse, though he preferred the feel of reins in his hand to a wheel.

When they reached the first slope, where the road swerved to go over the crest, the car hesitated then slowly, deliberately, slithered sideways. Fiona gave a little yelp.

"All right, all right!" soothed Angus, clinging to the wheel. "She won't go over."

She didn't. The car slid broadside to the bottom of the coulee among the glistening wet scrub there. He backed, turned, and they went like a small boat in a choppy sea over the uneven ground to the two ruts that were road, lurched into them again and purred uphill.

"Giddap! Steady! Giddap!" Angus gaily counselled.

Just at the curve the hummocks between ruts were slightly broken down. Too soon he whooped, "Made the grade! Away we go!" Away they slid sideways once more to the bottom of that greasy knoll, with a gasp from Fiona.

"I feel as if I've left my stomach behind up there!" she said.

"All right. Chains!" Angus decided.

He got out in a drizzle, pulled on overalls to protect his suit from the mire, and laid the chains on the ground. By that time Fiona, who could drive any sort of team and ride almost any sort of horse, was beginning to feel nervous. When he slacked the brake and let the car slip back a foot or so, to bring the wheels over the chains, she gasped again. Chains on, he rolled up his muddy overalls. As he slipped in behind the wheel she noticed flakes of snow on him.

"Snowing!" she exclaimed.

"Just beginning."

"And cold!"

"Away we go. All aboard for the dance!" he cried out, slamming the door.

Up the slope the motor purred, hesitated near the crest, then with increasing roar swept on and climbed the ridge. Angus speedily changed gear. That little hitch was over. But, with a hiss as out of a thousand salt-shakers, the snow was on them out of the gray.

"A cutter," remarked Angus, "a hooded cutter, with plenty of straw to put your feet in, is the thing. These gasoline buggies— huh!"

The wind shrieked round them. In a few minutes the glass shield was plastered white. He stopped to turn the screws and open it that he might see where he was going.

"Tuck yourself up," he advised. "Tuck yourself up."

His fingers, on removing his gloves, stuck to the metal handles and they were stiff. They would not budge. He had to get out pliers and turn them. Then he blew in his palms, drew on his gloves.

"All aboard!" he chanted. "All aboard for High Butte and all stations south to Calgary and the St. Andrew's dance."

Fiona glanced at him through the drive of the white gale.

"Do you think we should turn back?" she asked. "We may not be able to see any road. If we turned now we could see our own trail."

"Our trail is covered," he replied. "We have to go by feel in the ruts. I think I know the lie of the land, anyhow."

But there was no land. There was just blizzard, and through it they chirred on.

"These cars," he assured her, "can do anything."

She brightened up.

"We should have brought a compass," she said.

"Yes. Or towed the house behind on a trailer," he suggested.

"It seems to have been snowing here far more than back a bit," said she.

"Just drifts from the last fall."

She wondered if they had left the side road and were but travelling in a circle. The snow seemed to come from every side. Suddenly they went ploughing to the mudguards and stood still.

"What's that ahead?" he asked.

It was a dark bulk and it moved. A man came forward, advancing to the car.

"Where are we, stranger?" called Angus.

"At the road to High Butte—main road. Where you want to go?" It was an Indian who spoke.

"High Butte."

"I tow you for three dollars."

"Hullo!" said Angus, for the man was one of his wards, called Dick Big Beaver. He had hunted with his father.

"That you, Mr. Munro?"

"What are you doing here, Dick?"

"I come here with my brother when road going to drift. We come with wagon. We stop till car come and get in drift. We haul car out. We haul you for nothing."

"Well, get busy. It's cold."

"A bit cold. Yes, little bit."

The Indians had all ready for such emergencies, with ropes, chains, and a hook. They acted quickly and in ten minutes Angus and Fiona were being hauled on again, ahead of them the towing wagon with two dim figures in it wrapped in blankets on which the snow lay so that they were like blocks of marble on which a sculptor had but begun his chiselling. He thought of their father's hunting—and of theirs, their still-hunting for a motor car in drift. "Aye, aye," he muttered to himself.

"We'll never forget this," said Fiona, her teeth knocking together as they rolled on.

At last they came to a thing that looked like a snow man. "What's this?"

"Roadside gas-pump. We're there!" Three dollars Angus gave to Dick Big Beaver and his brother. They deserved it, he thought, sitting by the hour beside a bad drift in the road. What would their fathers have said could they have pictured such a way of turning an honest dollar?

But they almost forgot about the adventure next evening at Calgary, sitting down to dinner under the bright lights, Sam Douglas in his kilts at the head of the table and those who had no kilts wearing tartan ties of their clans or septs. After dinner they had all the old dances, strathspeys and reels, Highland fling, schottische, lancers, and Red River jigs, with the fiddles wildly playing and shouts of Hooch, Hooch! ringing to the ceiling.

The old Alberta Hotel was packed that night, and up and down the stairs, in and out the rooms, Fiona heard—with an extraordinary emotion considering that her birthplace was Red River—the Gaelic speech. Going to bed she halted and raised a finger. Through the open transom of the room next to theirs came Gaelic again.

Indeed, time was passing. While Dan was in his first term at McGill the year for Angus's superannuation arrived and Angus and Fiona talked of a visit to Scotland. But the department did not adhere strictly to the ordained age limit for retirement when the right man seemed to be in the right place and his capacities were not impaired by age. "A man is as old as he feels," the new western commissioner quoted to him on a visit of inspection.

Yes, the years were flying. The addition to population told it as well as much else. Chantelaine imported a wife. Macpherson had done likewise, and together he and his wife had produced a son. The mission schools were far off, across the reserve, but on one of them was also another woman, the missionary not considering that here was no place for her. She had not, by the grace of God, that malady of the parson's wife who had not helped homesick Mrs. Hodges. That her husband's collar was worn wrong way round did not make her a social burden.

They had a daily mail-service—a daily mail-service, there, one of the Indian lads the Rural Mail Courier. Far off were the years when Sam, at Calgary, was elated at a fortnightly postal service between east and west.

To most people, no doubt, there seems at times a sort of happy chance in life. A reconstruction of the expected, or even a seeming hitch, it may be, takes to itself the quality of a dispensation of Providence. To the sense of uncertainty of tenure Fiona and Angus became accustomed. Carry on for another year, said the visiting commissioner; and when the year expired came the same direction by letter more formally expressed. Then suddenly came conclusion: Chantelaine, it was decided, was the man for the post, to succeed Angus Munro. That delay made a happy synchronization, for the year of Angus's retirement was the year of Dan's passing at McGill.

His wards had, of course, known that sooner or later he would have to go. It was not till he was on the point of leaving that he discovered part of the cause for his retention (during the last four years) had been due to a letter—a letter dictated in collaboration by old Running Antelope, Tall Whirlwind and All Alone, and put into English by young Louise—which the department at Ottawa had received.

He drove round the reserve with Fiona before leaving, bidding good-bye. Running Antelope was stiff with age but of clear mind. He said he would come to the agency to say farewell on the day they were to leave, but Angus explained that they were calling to save him that journey.

"I am like an old horse now that lies under a tree all day," Running Antelope admitted.

His old shrivelled woman wept when they left.

Tall Whirlwind and his two wives (for two wives he had like some Old Testament gentleman, despite the missionaries' dislike of the wives and concubines idea) laughed at the parting. They asked where Angus intended to go, and he told them he was sailing across the big salt lake to east to where he had been born. For Fiona and he had decided, when retirement did come, to visit the Auld Country. Tall Whirlwind, who had learnt some English (not at the mission) spoke it then in courtesy to Fiona, who had but little Cree.

"You come back," he said. "I know. You come back. Honest to God on hell's own bible, you come back, ain't it?"

"Oh, yes, we'll come back and see you."

"This hell of a good country," he added. "All white men come back some day."

Driving home, and thinking of Tall Whirlwind's vocabulary, Angus chuckled, but Fiona wept.

"How silly of me," she said. "I feel so dreadfully moved."

They were to be moved more on the day they left when All Alone came to say good-bye. He was dressed, all Indian, for the occasion, on his face ochre paint, his braids wrapped in otter skins. The increasing infirmities of Running Antelope decreed that though he was titular chief, Tall Whirlwind and All Alone were the officiating ones.

They came together. As they were going Angus suddenly recalled the day when Hodges sat in this room with a package profoundly tied and knotted, for All Alone put a similar—though smaller—parcel into his hand and made the sign for a free gift, a prairie gift. They would be miles away by the time he had it opened and held in his palm a collet ring.

There was a note with it, written in flowing and sloping school scription, Because you have often looked at it as if you liked

it, from your friend and signed, in a preposterous scrawl, All
Alone.

CHAPTER TWENTY-NINE
Heather

In a shipping office in Glasgow, a lean, tanned elderly man,
with a slight stoop of years between his shoulders, made inquiries
across a counter (which was a sheet of gleaming glass over a map
of Scotland), regarding sailings for Loch Brendan. On a divan
under the long windows sat a woman, a decade or so his junior but
with certain lines on her neck that would be called tell-tale were
she one, which she was not, to whom ageing was subject for
secrecy. In her eyes was a girlish vivacity. Wandering round the
place, looking at the pictures that decorated its walls, was their
son—Dan.

"Grey Galloway," he read, and, looking at the poster, he saw,
in the gray-green hummocks, some resemblance to the rolling
prairies that lie between the flatness of the Great Plains and the
definite lift of the foothills. "Peebles for Pleasure," drew his
attention, a vivid representation of a castle on a knoll with a twist
of river below. He considered how this country he visited was
dotted with the ruins of history.

From studying a painting of purple Grampians beyond a
carse of yellow corn he turned and observed that the young man
who attended to his father seemed to be in difficulties.

"No, sir," he heard, drawing near, "the steamer does not go
to the loch-head, unless by special request. There is no public
landing there. It called on the last trip by special arrangements
with the gentleman who has a shooting there."

"Has a what?"

"A shooting there."

"Oh!"

"Just a minute, sir." The clerk departed for assistance,
returning from an inner room with a pleasant elderly man who
dropped his head to examine Angus over pince-nez.

"You want to go all the way by boat?" the newcomer
inquired. "You don't want to go by train to Oban and—"

"No, all the way by boat."

"If Sir Ernest Reynolds expects you—if you are expected—"

"No, I'm not expected," replied Angus, "not expected."

"Well, sir, I believe your best plan would be to get off at
Catacol Head. There is an inn there."

"Oh, there's an inn, is there?"

"Yes. It's a small place. We have no leaflets about it."

"Which side of the point is it?" asked Angus, trying to picture it.

"This side," said his informant with a finger on the glass over the map. "Just inside the sound."

"Very good. That will do."

It was a fine August. There was a golden glow on the dust-motes of Glasgow. In the parks that they visited the scent of flowers was heady and heavy. The little breezes that came to town stirred the straw at the door of warehouses, troubled young clerks and warehousemen with hints of heather hills out by.

Arran, as the Munros went down the firth, was purple, veined with zigzag burns, Goatfell lit like a beacon by the terrific sunset. When they came on deck in the morning Ireland was astern, Jura on the port, Argyll on the starboard bow, and Angus, looking at the coral-tinted peaks, the slumbering dark-blue glens, thought to himself that a man had but one life to live and that it was a pity he had not been able to live his here. He seemed to know it even from beyond his youth, as though in the corpuscles of his blood were memories of these colours and the solemn quiet broken only by the hiss of wave-tops.

"It's hard to have to go below even for meals," said Dan, "but appetite here is sharp."

When on deck again Angus saw the purser fussing between folding chairs on which people reclined wrapped in rugs, the fringes of which a wind plucked, a cold wind despite the sun.

"Oh, there you are, sir. Are you going to Sir Ernest Reynolds'?"

"No."

"We have some people on board for the head of the Sound—for Sir Ernest's place. You're for Catacol Head, then. Nice little inn there. It's not what you would call Ritzy but the good lady makes her own oatcakes and scones. It is the real thing. I'll send a steward to see about your luggage."

"That'll be fine!"

The Clansman turned a little inshore. A fresh volley of gulls came out to join those that convoyed her. Ben Chattan looked through a notch. She took the turn into the Sound. There were twinkling windows and whitewashed walls on the inner side of Catacol Head. As they surged close inshore Angus could see the twists of the loch stretching into the land and two yachts, by their polished hulls and rakish yellow funnels, at anchor.

The deck shook under his feet as the siren roared. He

listened to the echoes as they came tumbling back. She slowed down and lay there. A great boat, two men pulling at the sweeps, came alongside, and down went Angus. Fiona and Dan on the overside gangway. The men in the boat were talking Gaelic to each other; Angus wished he had not forgotten almost all of his.

There was a little strip of concrete walk, a miniature esplanade, on the inner side of Catacol Head, and a cluster of boats joggled together at a jetty, with white-painted cork fenders overside. As they stepped ashore a young lad approached.

"Are you for the inn, sir?" he asked shyly.

"Yes," said Angus.

"I'll carry your bags up."

What was that whiff in the air? What was that odour? It gave him a sickness at the heart.

"You burn peat here still, my lad," said he.

"Yes, sir, indeed."

"So that's the smell of peat!" exclaimed Dan, and then, "Say, young fellow, you can't carry all that."

The boy looked astounded as Dan grabbed two suitcases from him.

"Put them down, sir," he implored, "and I'll come back for them."

"That's all right."

The youth was highly puzzled; and puzzled, too, was the landlady as she saw them advancing. What kind of folk were these? She eyed them keenly. Aye, the right kind, she decided, though one of them was helping with the luggage.

"That's kind of you, sir, rale kind of you," she said, "helping the lad, whatever. Just put them down here."

As they entered Dan could not but notice one or two people sitting in the big front room because of the manner in which they examined them, turning their heads as if, though they were not wearing high collars, they imagined they were. Well, we have been duly examined, he considered.

Fiona looked all round, radiant. Had she told any of them that she was fifty they would have cried out, "Nonsense!" It was a quaint interior with a big fireplace at one end, and there were the authentic peat divots smouldering, a big pot hanging over them depending from a hook—chiefly for ornament, she surmised. A tall grandfather clock against one wall ticked loudly. A ship inside a bottle stood in a window embrasure. She was going to like this place.

Angus was extraordinarily quiet. He felt as a ghost and was to feel more so when in the morning they set out for a walk along a

182

gravelled road that skirted the Sound. At a bend he could see to the very end of the loch beyond the two yachts. No houses there! And, as they proceeded, there was no fail-dyke round an acre or two but, instead, a high barbed-wire fence—a very high fence—coming down the hill, crossing the road, and passing even into the water. Dan opened a gate in it and closed it again behind them.

"So this is Loch Brendan," said Fiona with a catch in her voice, thinking that here her forbears had lived, breathing this air, hearing that guttural plop of water, seeing that lift and fall of the seaweed fringe.

"This is Loch Brendan," replied Angus, a thickness in his voice. It seemed to come from far away.

Suddenly they heard the sound of the pipes. There had been pipes at Fort Garry, but these took him back to a more distant piping. It was, however, no coronach that was played that day. They were piping him home with The Cock of the North—and here, at any rate, was a birch wood on the shoulder of the hill, all its leaves dancing together.

"In a cot hereabouts the girl of my calf-love lived," said he. Jessie he could jest about. Of Minota he could never speak.

Fiona laughed.

"You must tell me about her," she said.

"Oh, indeed, indeed, that's far away," he answered. "I might not recognize her now."

As they walked on, coming beyond the wood, they saw a house upward a little way, a large house with wide windows and many gables. On a lawn before it the little figure of a piper strutted and wheeled.

"So that's the shooting-box they told me about," observed Angus. "Aye, aye."

He turned aside from the road. He went wandering here and there, looking left and right in the bracken. Something in his manner made his wife and son stop. They sat down on the heather as he tapped to and fro among the sun-scorched ferns. They saw him turn facing the loch, raise his hands before him, and spread them apart a little way.

"Yes, this was the door," he called to them, his hands elevated so.

They rose and came closer.

"What do you mean, Dad?"

"Hold up your hands—like that," said Angus. "There's the view from the door, son. That bides. Aye, that bides."

He looked round at the sound of a foot on a stone. A man about his own height, but of heavier build, in breeches, leggings,

Norfolk jacket, was standing there. He seemed uncertain how to begin, examined them, and decided that before he spoke he should touch his cap.

"Are ye aware," said he, "that ye are trespassing?"

Angus returned the half-salute.

"No, I'm not aware," he replied.

"Well, ye are. I'll have tae order ye off."

Angus was suddenly proud of an emotion that possessed him. His Scotland was perhaps chiefly a kingdom of the mind, but he had learnt something in that other country, his country of exile and adoption (in which more Gaelic was spoken than in Scotland), and he was glad.

"Very good," he said. "You have told me. You have ordered me off—" and he gave the man his back.

"I have tae order ye off," the keeper repeated.

"Well, well, you have done your duty—you have ordered me off," replied Angus. "And having ordered me, I order you go and tell your master that you have done so."

The gamekeeper looked at Fiona, looked at Dan. That young man was smiling gently, proud of his father.

"My friend," said Angus, turning, "it may interest you to know I was born here," and he swept with his stick among the heather, tapping it upon a row of half-embedded lichened stones.

"Inteet, sir?"

"Yes," said Angus, "and evicted. And I'm not going to be evicted now."

He spoke very quietly. Puzzled, the man turned away, giving another half-salute to all three, glancing again at Fiona and Dan as though for some gesture of ratification from them, as though wondering if they were in some sense keepers of a lunatic.

Angus paid no more heed to him. He dismissed him from his mind, walked on by the loch-side and left the road where it took a bend uphill. They saw him feeling there again among the bracken and heather with his stick.

"What has he found now, I wonder?" asked Dan.

Angus had told his wife much of his early days and so—

"I expect," said she, "it is the old graveyard. Everything seems to be gone. You heard what he said. The little church he described to me once is not here. I fancy it must be the gravestones he has found."

Slowly he came back toward them, did not call them over there. It was then, down the path up which the gamekeeper had gone, they saw a lean little man in a kilt approaching. When he halted beside Angus they looked away that they might not seem to be staring, and when they pried back again there were these two seated on the hillside in converse, too far off to be overheard.

"Good day," the kilted one began.

"Good day, sir."

"One of my men tells me that you say you were born here."

"Well, he's being truthful," replied Angus.

"Sit down. By the way, I'm Ernest Reynolds."

"I'm pleased to meet you. My name is Angus Munro."

"Sit down, Mr. Munro, and tell me. I'm interested to know the old history of this place."

"The old history," echoed Angus, dryly.

Fiona, glancing round again, saw that they had risen.

"Here's the best way to tell you," Angus said, and led Sir Ernest Reynolds into the bracken. He dabbed with his stick. "That's the place," he explained. "That's where I was born."

"So! Yes, I can see there are stones there."

"Aye, and there are other stones yonder, where I was when you came down the hill. I see the rains of the years have left but few of the letters on them."

"Gravestones?"

"Gravestones."

"So! Tell me about it."

"Sit down, sit down," said Angus this time, as though he were the host. "Sit down here and put your feet on the bed where my mother bore me, so to speak. We'll sit on all that's left of the wall. There was a text from Scripture used to hang just about here, where your head is—God is Love, in the Gaelic. They were distributed by some society for promulgating Christian knowledge among the savage Highlanders. Well, sir, there were worse evictions than ours. There were evictions for generations, when they burned the thatch over the people's heads and flung chairs, stools, and spinning-wheels out of the doors. That is the history you wanted to know. The whole length of the Highlands there have been even pregnant women turned out. My mother was the one that knew that old history. Yes, and when they made themselves a shelter in some ditch on the hillside with cabers across it for a roof they were driven out of that."

"But why were they evicted?" Sir Ernest interrupted.

"To make room for the sheep, and sometimes not even that, only nominally so, really to make room for the deer."

"So!"

"Yes. The landlords, their old chiefs, would never show up, left it to a factor and his menials and the law officers."

"Oh, the evictors had the law on their side! How was that?"

185

"Because they first served notices of ejectment, the way your man came down here and warned us off just now."

Sir Ernest, who had been studying Angus's face, looked away hurriedly.

"Did they never fight?" he asked of the air before him, gazing up at Ben Chattan. "Did they never offer resistance?"

"Now and again—and they went to the penitentiary for it. But often enough the evictions were made when most of the men were either at the herring fishing or in the lowlands for the hairst."

"The what?"

"The harvest. The harvest work."

"But," said Sir Ernest, "ground like this must always have been rather poor for cultivation."

"It was," agreed Angus. "They were driven onto it from better land in the glens—my own father was—and then finally driven away from even the poor soil. People would say, 'I can't think why they want to cling to that poor soil.' Another turn of the screw, always another turn of the screw. When they were forced onto an arid place like this they took to the manufacture of kelp, from seaweed, as another means of livelihood. When it was seen they were making money on that their rents were raised."

"So, so, so!" exclaimed Sir Ernest in a new tone, and turning to Angus, again he inquired: "Could not the clergy do anything—preach against it?"

Angus shrugged his shoulders.

"The clergy!" he snorted. "The lairds had the church patronage at their disposal," and he looked into Sir Ernest's eyes to see if he understood.

"Enough said—"

"Exactly! That's another reason why they did not put up a fight. The clergy told them it was foreordained by the Almighty, or as a punishment for sins, and there would be a wrath of heaven and eternal damnation in hell-fire on all those who resisted. We had our passage money and our rations on the boat, a month's sustenance allowance for when we landed in Canada, and signed a paper that we went of our own free will—to save their faces."

"Oh, well, most of them did go of their own free will in the end, I suppose?"

"The kind of free will that desperation ordains," said Angus. "I thought of it all once when I heard of a band of Sioux Indians in America finally driven to sign a treaty giving away their land. They put their crosses to it and then the chief said, 'We have signed. When do we eat?'"

"It was like that, eh? You went hungry sometimes?"

"Often," replied Angus, "even in my time. Shell-fish and potatoes was a good meal. Did you ever try stewed nettles with a pinch of oatmeal thrown in?"

"I can't say I ever did," said Sir Ernest Reynolds. At that they both raised their heads and laughed.

"They seem to be getting on pretty well," Dan remarked to his mother where they had seated themselves.

"You mentioned Indians," said Sir Ernest. "You come from—"

"From Canada."

A sound of shooting broke out. The little man glanced over his shoulder.

"Those are my guests," said he, "shooting my grouse. To hell with them," he added, gently.

Angus looked at him with surprise and curiosity. Sir Ernest—sitting there, because of the lowness of all that was left of the wall, hunched with his knees to his chin—edged himself a little closer, confidentially closer.

"I think, sir," said he, "that you are heaven-sent. I have nobody to talk to."

"With all your guests shooting your grouse—"

"So! So!" repeated Reynolds, nodding his head. "I think I envy you. I wish my father had stayed in America."

"Oh?"

"I wasn't born over there, but my people went out, tried it for awhile, came back. He was a timber merchant. We got pretty poor after our return to England. It's odd what a fellow can date his beginnings from. My beginning was one day in the dinner hour—a fifteen shillings a week junior clerk—sitting at the back of St. Paul's Cathedral eating my lunch out of a bag. I threw some crumbs to the pigeons, onto the grass, and a policeman came along. 'Can't you read?' he said, and pointed to one of the notices. It announced distinctly that pigeons must not be fed on the paths. I said that I was feeding them on the grass. He told me he didn't want what he called my sauce and walked off a little way and stood with his head slewed round glaring at me—you know that horrible look. That was the beginning of my fortune!" He tapped Angus on the knee. "I said to myself, 'My boy, you are going to get into a position in which—and always going to dress in such a way—the police will respect you.' I think lots of men have had something back in their lives that has had a tremendous influence on them, whether they know it or not. You understand me?"

"Yes."

"Mr. Munro, I'm just beginning to think, when it is almost

187

too late, that it's a pity I allowed that policeman to make me a climber!" and he laughed wryly.

So vigorous was his utterance, though his voice was low, that Angus sitting there beside him turned to scrutinize his face—a lined old face, a lean old face, parchmenty, with a grim mouth on which was marked an odd blend of arrogance and bitter humour.

"See me now," said Sir Ernest Reynolds. "I have a home in London with grounds, gardens, and the address is not Surrey or Kent, but London. So you know. Gardeners of lords come to look at it; lords themselves come to look at it. There's a little garden as big as—as small as, I should say"—his wrinkled, skinny hand moved in air before him—"this cottage you were born in, oh, half the size if that's the end over there. It's a freak thing, a Japanese freak thing. I had two gardeners—from Japan—to design it. You sit back from it and focus your eyes till you get the illusion of an immense garden, acres, with the paths through and a statue here and a statue there. Well, all right. Then there is a big garden, a replica of that miniature one, but on a large scale. You should see my house parties there. Useful people to me, and they know it, so they use me. I live in a little sitting-room at the top with a bedroom off it. Just across the landing my secretary has a room. My guests ring the bell and order tea when they want it; they ask to have the menu from the butler to see what the dinner is to be, and if there is any special dish they want that's not on it they ask for it."

"No!" ejaculated Angus.

"So!" shouted Reynolds, and brought his hand down with a slam on his new friend's knee.

That loud "So!" caused Fiona and Dan—he then lying flat upon his chest on the heather—to look toward these two again. They wondered if there was some trouble there but, by their attitudes, all seemed well.

"And for why?" asked Sir Ernest, and himself answered: "Because they know we are climbers."

"It doesn't make any excuse for them," said Angus indignantly.

"So. No. Well, my two boys have gone to Oxford, but even Oxford can't make a silk purse out of a sow's ear. Go up to Oxford a snob and you may come down an accentuated snob and bounder. One of them is a snob; the other—he's all right. And that will protect them from something I've had to suffer. I've known the ignominy of poverty—though I've never eaten nettles and oatmeal. But I've suffered another ignominy. Do you know there are people who will fire off Latin quotations when they are talking to me, with a sly kind of look in their eyes. I've learnt how to cope with them. I say, 'No spika ze language!' That finishes them! Anyhow, I don't pretend. I don't bounce about being self-made any more than I pretend to be 'varsity-bred."

He suddenly began to laugh loud as if he saw, in a flash of discovery or revelation, the fun of life.

"Pills!" he broke out.

Angus stared at him, wondering what he meant.

"The foundation of my fortune was in pills," he explained.

"Oh, yes," said Angus.

There was more shooting behind them.

"They are sitting up there in the butts on their shooting-sticks and their camp-stools, and the descendants of those who were not evicted from this land are strung out by the mile waving little flags, with dogs trained to go along and poke in the bushes, raising the grouse, and getting into trouble if they let one fly back the wrong way. There they go again. Can you understand, Mr. Munro, that I'm getting a little tired of it? Lady Reynolds doesn't quite see it as I do. Well, well, I'm afraid I'm keeping you. I shouldn't say that of her, anyhow. If that's your wife and son with you I wish you'd introduce me."

They both came stiffly to their feet and walked over to Fiona and Dan, Dan leaping up as they drew near.

"How do you do?" said Sir Ernest Reynolds. There was a suffusion of friendliness and kindliness on his face. "I'm afraid I've been very discourteous, but your husband and I have been having a great talk. You see," his mouth twisted to one side, "I don't meet many people. I hope you will make yourselves at home. I hope you'll go just where you will. I'll tell my men not to bother you—anywhere, anywhere," and he waved his skinny hand. "I would like you to come up to the house but I'm afraid it would bore you. It bores me. You know, it's very nice down at the inn. She's a nice woman."

"It's a quaint place," said Fiona.

"Yes, a quaint place," he agreed. "I like that ship in the bottle in the window. Her husband made it. You'll be staying for a little while, I suppose?"

Angus's gaze roved the mountains opposite. Beside one of the yachts lying at the Sound's end there was a sudden splash that drew their eyes. The deep darkness of the water was ringed with silver and there came winging from here, winging from there—to pounce screaming on what had been ejected from the galley-chute—watchful gulls. They swooped down over the quiet crisscrossing of their reflections.

"I think, probably," said Angus, "we will be going tomorrow."

"So? Well, sir, it has been a great pleasure to meet you. But lest you should decide to stay—it's all yours, anywhere, please." He backed away from them, bowing. "I'll tell my men."

They turned and walked slowly back to the inn.

"He's a fine old fellow," said Dan, when they were well out of earshot. "But he doesn't seem happy to me. You'd think he would be happy here. Listen to those gulls, Dad. Listen! Don't you like to hear them?"

"Yes."

CHAPTER THIRTY
Buffalo Bill

Back from Loch Brendan to Glasgow, they went to London. They motored out to Hampstead Heath, saw a clump of firs there, strolled on Parliament Hill under high kites, smoke in the valley below them and the bubble of St. Paul's protruding. They took train to Loughton to see Epping Forest and were sunk deep in melancholy on the way—as they looked from the carriage windows on unlovely streets and alleys, a desert of dismality—to think that people lived there, the uncurtained dreariness accentuated, or taunted, by what sunshine percolated through the twilight of that forenoon.

They came back uncheered by the sinister pollarded hornbeams of the forest, and next day went to Kew Gardens, where Angus recalled winter evenings at Rocky Mountain House and talks there of the days before his days because of David Douglas, sometime of Perth and of this place, who went wandering with a buffalo robe and a vasculum among the western ranges from Fort Spokane to the Babine country. They walked on Westminster Bridge, watching the blunt barges scoon below on a flowing tide, looked at St. Thomas's Hospital, and, leaning there, Angus asked Dan how he would care to take up practice of medicine in England.

"Oh, I don't know," said Dan, noncommittal.

They went to Edinburgh and admired the Grecian effect of the columns on Calton Hill, drove to Hawthornden, drove to Roslin, drove to the Forth Bridge and stared up at its high iron lace-work. For a sentiment, or a light curiosity, going to see what used to be the Ettrick shop, Angus was amazed to find it a bookshop still—with the name Ettrick over the door and windows. He entered to make a purchase. There of a certainty was the younger brother of former days, crabbed and old, and there, by facial evidence, was his son. From an anxious look in the assistants' eyes he surmised the business was carried on as usual. William, he of the Wee Black Book, was dead, no doubt.

The shadows were extraordinarily real to him that day as he stepped out onto the hot pavement again. The shadow of Hill Burton, handkerchief—pocket-napkin—protruding from the tail-pocket of his surcoat, passed by. He thought of Lasswade, wondered again where Jessie Grant was. Odd to be here and not to wish to see her, try to discover her. The Camerons would be dead by now, surely dead: she would not likely be there.

They made Edinburgh their headquarters awhile, taking trips to Melrose and to Peebles (for pleasure) on the one hand, to Stirling and to St. Andrews on the other, ever and again Fiona and Angus wondering how it would be to live here, each trying to find out just what the other felt on the matter. But always, when that subject was broached, Dan would give his noncommittal "Oh, I don't know—"

Then one day, walking on Princes Street, clearly taken for American tourists, drivers of cabs and brakes chanting to them, "Roslin, Roslin, Forth Bridge," Angus wondered if his mind had become deranged by thinking too much of the past on this visit. For, moving grandly along the street with slow steps, moccasined, and topped by enormous war-bonnets, came three North American Indians.

Something had gone wrong! He was on his way to the Ettrick bookshop again. He knew what would happen. He would halt them with the sign-talk and they would lead him to a hall hung with pictures and there introduce him to a clean-shaven man with keen and kindly eyes.

He looked at Fiona. He looked at Dan, who eased him by asking, "Do you see what I see?" The people on the pavement gave way to these three figures.

Angus halted, held up his hand, made the signs Where from? Expressionless, the three observed the gestures. They were on guard. So many marvels they were viewing that they had schooled themselves not to make ejaculation, show astonishment, over anything.

"I come," he told them with his signs, "from the land of the Blackfoot and the Cree."

One or two passing by turned their heads, puzzled as to what he was about. There was an old man, possibly drunk, making funny passes to three Indians of Buffalo Bill's Show! That is what they would think. But in Princes Street folk are more decorous

191

than in some other thoroughfares. The tallest of the three raised both hands to his head, drew them down, ran a finger across his throat, and one of the passersby, who had paused, mouth open, moved on speedily, thinking it was a sign that murder was going to be done.

Sioux! But where from? For there were Sioux in Canada. From the bad lands west of the muddy river. They were Dakota Sioux—of the generation between the unconquerable and the starved, plundered, profaned, disinherited, broken, dejectedly yet bravely dying.

"Buffalo Bill Show," said one, speaking English in the usual slow, deliberate enunciation. "You must come to our camp in the showground."

"I surely will. I surely will."

And they did, that very afternoon, and found their three there again. They talked with Kicking Bear of the glittering and steady gaze, the mouth shaped, it seemed, by misdoubt from many promises unfulfilled, a mouth of disappointment; with John Shangrau in charge of the military hostages who were with the show to see how many more people could come if they cared; and with Colonel Cody.

In the evening Fiona, Angus and Dan sat and watched a pageant of the west, saw a curtain rise at the proscenium beyond the arena, revealing an ancient forest of the Atlantic seaboard, Indians walking there (no white people come) under the trailing of lianae and moss tassels to the music, rendered softly, that Angus had first heard in '77 played by the Mounted Police band as he rode up the north bank of the Bow from Blackfoot Crossing. Strauss had been in New York in '76 with his orchestra and a year later his waltzes were played, hummed, and whistled at what was then the Back of Beyond, still, on the maps, the Great American Desert! The curtain fell and they saw Indians walking on the plains, the arena, before they had horses, meeting others there, conversing at long range by signs, gathering together, smoking a pipe in fraternal circle, dancing to the thud of their drums, passing away in groups to the strains of a Sousa march. The curtain rose to reveal some buttes and bad-lands, tufts of sage-brush, Missouri way, and a frontier fort in foreground, a sentry pacing on the walls. A rider of the Pony Express galloped by, made two leaps with the mail-bag from his horse to the one held awaiting him, and was gone. Then the Deadwood stage-coach swept in, pursued by the Indians they had met on Princes Street—and others. The shooting and the cries nearly drowned out the strains of Washington Post. There were horse races between cowboys and Indians that took

Fiona and Angus back to Red River and Dan to the reserve and fair days at High Butte. There were exhibits of rifle marksmanship and revolver shooting that recalled to Angus's mind the shotgun experts at Fort Edmonton in the days before the Redcoats arrived. A herd of buffaloes lumbered across the scene, Cody behind, riding easy as in a rocking-chair—a dozen or so of the survivors from the herds he had helped to bring to the state of relics.

Not from a land of stage-coaches being attacked by Indians, not from pastures of the buffalo, but from pastures of steers for market and wheat-fields had the Munros come; and yet, sitting there viewing an exhibition that many, possibly, considered but as a glorified three-ring circus for schoolboys, they were so moved that the dust raised was not Edinburgh dust but dust of Alberta—and as for the tufts of sage-brush in the back-drop of the fort scene, it seemed to Fiona she could whiff them as though she had run a hand up the stems, husking the flowers and crushing them in her palm.

The band played God Save the King and they went out from illusion to—well, to Angus it was illusion of another sort: From George Catlin to Colonel Cody, in the flying years, all was as a dream to him.

In the morning they sallied forth as usual to decide, after they got into the streets, what was to be the special outing of the day. To go to Lasswade and see if he could trace Jessie again was still in the back of Angus's mind. Wondering whether he should or no, he found they were passing the window display of a shipping agent's office. All halted as at the dictate of some shared nostalgia.

"Well," said Angus, "I suppose we can't stay here forever. How about going in and seeing what boat we might make reservations on?"

"I think we might as well," agreed Fiona, slipping a hand over his arm.

"How about you, Dan?"

"It suits me," replied Dan.

CHAPTER THIRTY-ONE
"A Married Man's Town"

The years that followed were Dan's years, the years of a new generation, Angus and Fiona in the slack-water.

They swithered some time between settling down at High Butte, Calgary—or Edmonton, capital of the Province, where the logs of the old Fort's gateway were but as a memorial and the ducks, still flying north and south in their seasons, looked down on a provincial university and government buildings. Angus had his private vote for High Butte but did not wish to influence Fiona, left the decision to her. The railway decided her. It was easy enough to get to Calgary and to High River, where her brother and his wife still lived. So there they had a house built on the very edge of "town," which meant, at that time, that they were far from its last building. They were on the south slope of the butte in a home not so palatial as Sam's at Calgary, but one that delighted them, its meshed sleeping-porch (meshed against mosquitoes) looking west, and a large window in the main living-room giving an outlook east, south and west.

They thought to have a girl from the reserve to help in the housework, as they had had at the agency, but the proximity to High Butte was a deterrent to that suggestion of Angus's. Indian maids in such service, Fiona reminded him, were looked upon as lawful prey by the hot young blades of town—the reserve was practically free of venereal disease and it would be good to keep it so. Therefore a Chinaman, Mah Yip, reigned in her stead.

Fiona it was who suggested, when they heard of the remarkable progress of Chief All Alone's younger son at school that, as they had money to spare, it would be nice to pay the lad's fees at High School.

"You are almost a sort of god-father to him," she pointed out. "He's named after you, and according to Nigel Chantelaine it's a shame that he should not be given a chance to get on. There have been lots of Indians in professions and—"

"I'd like to do it for him," said Angus, his face expressionless—and so it was done.

Young All Alone who, reserve school days over, had been acting as a sort of agency chauffeur, went to High School in Calgary on the opening of the next term.

On going to the Old Country the Munros had stored their belongings in an empty room of Murray's house on the reserve. During the unpacking and arranging, Angus came on a bit of the past, unaware that it had been preserved: a pamphlet, Information for Emigrants to British North America, PUBLISHED BY AUTHORITY. Price Sixpence. Yes, he was in slack-water before the fall, thought he.

Sam Douglas was then his best friend and longest in the west among those with whom he had kept in touch, and ever and again they exchanged visits. They liked Sam's wife. The gossip was that there was quite a romance there. She was a widow, rumour said, and Douglas had been in love with her as a young man but she would not have him—which had set him wandering. To be sure Angus did recall that when he was in Scotland with Sam in the sixties there had been various private absences, and considered that these might not always have been for visits to his guardian. People came to the Munro house in High Butte to talk about other matters and then to pump him about Douglas. "I really don't know," he would say; and they would go away remarking that they believed he knew all about it! Some declared that Sam married her for her money. Others argued he had no need to do that, being rich himself, much as they said of the politicians of their own colour when peculation was hinted of them, "He has no need to—he has enough!" Sam was a man to gossip about.

Fiona and Angus believed that these two, the old bachelor and the elderly widow, had married for affection and companionship: that was the inference on their visits. Mrs. Sam was better preserved than Fiona, whose face began to have the little lines of prairie winds and hard water on it. Patricia, a year or two younger than her husband, had still the colour of climates less trying on the skin. Fiona had an elderly beauty to the eye of many; Mrs. Sam was still what's called pretty, though when Fiona once admired her complexion she replied, "I got it in a drugstore on Eighth Avenue in a little box."

Sam liked to show people round his house. "If I had built it bigger—and more as I fancied," he told Angus, "it would have had a hint of an old castle, but I didn't want to have them dubbing it Douglas's Folly. You remember seeing the house built by James Rowan, the old factor of the twenties at Fort Edmonton—yon edifice that they called Rowan's Folly?"

There they were off in talk of the old days, their days, that had followed the days that they had arrived but to see the end of, when the factors from Fort William to the mountains—yes, and to the coast, through the ranges—would don the full dress of their clans for anniversaries and celebration and, if possible, have a piper playing.

That was a charming house of the Douglases to Fiona and Angus. It had a great hallway in which hung pictures by Charles Russell, who was called "the Cowboy Artist," and carved woodwork of bears, prowling and rampant, of mountain-goat on a shelf of cliff, and such-like, by a half-breed Blackfoot Indian south of the line—carvings very different from those made in Switzerland that began to appear for tourists in the curio shops of Eighth Avenue.

"And here's something to interest you," said Sam, holding

195

up a photograph. "I got that from Sir John Macdonald. It's of himself and old Chief Crowfoot sitting on the steps of the Parliament Building at Ottawa. It's extraordinary how the two are alike in type and character. I believe Sir John realized that when he arranged the picture."

"I have a portrait of Crowfoot," said Angus, "showing the life-pass that the railway company gave him and his two wives, hanging by a chain round his neck. It was taken by Harry Pollard years ago. Harry gave me a copy."

"I've seen it. I've always wondered what the thing was that Crowfoot had hanging there in a little frame. Well Sir John gave me that one. I suppose you'd think that second-best to getting it from Crowfoot!" Sam chuckled and prodded Angus in the side with his elbow, moving on.

There were pictures that came from another quarter of the world. There was a Raeburn that had been in Sam's family, and there was old furniture from Mrs. Sam's home. Douglas, in these days, lost for them that manner that had suggested disappointment in life. Tapped, he rang true.

That night there was an odd little talk over the dinner-table. Sam had been saying that Patricia and he would soon be going to the Old Country, and that he was worried about leaving that house for long. He was interested in oil then and had floated a company, the head office of which was in Shaftesbury Avenue, London. They might be gone some time—even years.

"Aye," said he, "the future of this country—indeed of the world—is in what they call petrol over there, gasoline here, or gas, though I don't like the abbreviation. It's confusing when you consider the natural gas of the land."

"I'm always afraid," observed Mrs. Sam, "when I think of all the natural gas under Medicine Hat, that some day that natural gasometer will blow up!"

They all laughed.

"Aye, times are changed," Sam went on. "I remember when folks used to say This is no place for a woman. I was down at the station the other day, the depot, and saw some young fellows getting their tickets, and heard one say 'This burg is worse than a married man's town. It's a damned metropolis. I'm off to the Athabasca.' No place for a woman, and then a married man's town. Sic transit gloria mundi, eh? Gasoline and rubber: that's the future. We can't grow rubber here, but we have shares in rubber plantations in South America. That's all we can do with rubber. Oil we have under our feet, just as they have natural gas under their feet Medicine Hat way. Where was I?"

196

"I thought you had strayed," remarked his wife. "You were at a married man's town—"

"Oh, yes. That's long ago."

"Well, some of the factors and early men married Indian women," said Patricia. "When I see some of them I wonder how they could. Poof!"

"Oh, but there are bonny ones and as clean as clean. Eh. Eh, Angus?" Douglas had no sooner come out with that than he was urgently saying, "Ye are not finished, Mrs. Munro? Have some fruit! Have an orange! Have some grapes!"

His wife followed the cue of grapes with a private thought, and when they were alone that evening, her guests gone to bed, she revived the subject.

"I know what I want to ask you," she said. "Did Angus Munro have an Indian woman in the early days?"

"Not that I ever heard of," answered Sam, who thought he had nearly put his foot in it, spilt the beans, and was going to be sure of not doing so again.

Patricia knew him very well, and to herself thought she, "He did!" She knew when her husband was lying and accepted him as he was.

Up in their room Fiona turned to Angus.

"I know something I want to ask you," she said.

"Yes?"

He guessed what was coming and, if it came, he thought he would tell her all. She would understand then why he was specially interested in All Alone, in Peter, in Louise (who was then in the reserve hospital, training as a nurse), and in young Angus, who continued to come out top of the class in high school. But he had guessed wrong.

"Did Sam Douglas have an Indian woman in the early days?" she asked.

"No," said he. "No. Not that I ever heard of. No!"

"Not that I would blame a man who did," she declared, after a few moments' pause. "There were no others practically. And—well, you know what a lot of men in the Service say: 'The more I see of white men the more I like Indians!'"

In that pause he had thought it was perhaps better that his secret remained his secret after all these years, was not shared. He could not vacillate between to speak and not to speak. So it slipped into Limbo again.

It was shortly after this visit that the Douglases left Calgary, and the next they heard of Sam—apart from letters that he or

Patricia wrote—the next public news they had of him was that he had been knighted. Knighted!

With the departure of the Douglases, and the death of old Running Antelope, which occurred about the same time, it seemed the West changed. A new breed came there. A little while ago at Calgary they saw a blackboard in the station entrance with the words Eastbound, Arrive, Depart; Westbound, Arrive, Depart. To that there had been added notices of the arrival and departure of trains to north and south—south-east, south-west, north-east, north-west. The land was webbed with railway lines.

Angus came into a period of crankiness, not with Fiona but with others. He could not suffer fools gladly. Here was a generation that knew not Joseph, and members of it exasperated him. One day in town, detained there, he lunched in the High Butte Hotel, and overheard at another table two men talking, one a local real-estate agent, the other evidently a visitor.

"Have you any Indians round you where you are?" asked the realtor.

"No," replied the visitor. "We have hardly any foreigners at all."

Angus wanted to rise and hit the man over the head with a carafe that stood on the table. Little things like that infuriated him.

"The damned fool!" he rumbled. "Foreigners!"

The stranger glanced in his direction, uncertain if he had heard aright, then looked round the room and saw the covert smiles of other diners. When Angus rose and departed he looked after him.

"Did that old fellow say something?" he inquired.

The real-estate man laughed.

"Yes. He said 'The damned fool! Foreigners!' You needn't bother about him. He's not a bad old guy. Straight-shooter. Gets kind of cranky sometimes. Retired too soon. It's a mistake. A man is as old as he feels. They kept him beyond his time, anyhow."

"What was he, then?"

"Indian agent, and keen on his wards."

"Oh, I see!"

A character—that's what Angus would be if he was not careful.

Dan's progress was then Fiona's main interest in life. He did hospital work in Winnipeg, remained there some time and later, the West calling him, moved to Calgary. He bought a small car and they saw him often, very full of vigour, tireless it would appear. He found life amusing as well as splashed with troubles. He was in partnership with another young man and jocundly explained the position.

"It's politics," he said.

"Politics?"

"Yes. There must always be two on the job. You never know when an emergency call may come, and it's good to have two. You never know, either, when you will have a case in which you want another opinion and don't fancy calling in a stranger."

"But that's not politics?" said Fiona in an inquiring voice.

"No, I'm coming to that, Mother. One of us is Conservative, the other Liberal. When the Conservative Party is in power the Conservative partner gets the Government jobs. When it goes out, and he goes out, the Liberal partner steps in till the Liberals are flung out. You keep it in the family, you see," and he laughed gleefully.

"The country has gone to hell!" exclaimed Angus.

"Oh, no, Dad, oh, no. We temporize. We humour 'em."

The idea of departmental service—service with the Department of the Interior, Indian Affairs—Dan had not discarded, but he wanted to have more general practice, experience. He had not been long in Calgary, however, when the Archduke Francis Ferdinand was slain at Sarejevo and the beans were spilt in Europe. That's what everyone said as they read the papers, or, "It looks as if there was going to be scrapping in Europe."

People parroted what they read. With great force one would explain that international finance made a war impossible there, and another pronounce that if conflict did come about it would be short in those days—"Look at the arms countries have now!" Knowing ones declared there was more in it than met the eye, political secrets, secret treaties. They did not like the look of things. Then came the invasion of Belgium, that little nation. The whole thing had been planned, apparently; Germany had been building her railways up to the frontier and then, all ready, awaited the moment to pick a quarrel. Anything would serve. But, whatever lay behind, here was a little country pounced on by a big one contrary to promises. And then came the recruiting news that Britain had agreed to assist Belgium in precisely such a pass.

There were still horsemen in the West, many of them despite the motor car, but soon came information that this was a pedestrian's war. The war correspondent of a certain London newspaper—that had, for some reason, a large overseas circulation—happened to mention, in his account of watching the first British troops land in France, what was the song they had marched away to the slaughter singing, so all over the land recruits marched and marched in the mud or dust, singing that it was a long, long way to Tipperary—and farewell Leicester Square. Even at High Butte they marched, singing that. They could be seen and heard from the big window of the Munro house as they trudged and sang.

In Calgary, Dan was a civilian attached to examine recruits—and then one day home he came. Angus, reading a paper on the veranda, looked up at the sound of a step. The train had just gone through. He was expecting no one. There was Dan, and as he put down the paper and gazed at his boy, he knew. Dan exuded it. It was, as they say, writ large on him. It was in the swing of his shoulders, in the light of his eyes. A promise was a promise. He had come home to tell them he was going to enlist. He could not stand it any more—examining men for the army and sitting there at ease. He had to be out with them, he had to be there with them.

At the sound of his voice Fiona promptly emerged from the house, got the drift of what had been said on his arrival, and stood listening to the rest, making unconscious puckerings of her lips.

"Well, I suppose what is to be will be," said Angus. "Ye ken yer ain ken best, ye ken."

"We can't go back on it. It's impossible," said Dan. "We promised Belgium. They are going to need doctors in this war."

"Oh, you'd go as a doctor," said Fiona.

"Sure."

She was on the point of remarking it would be safer, but there was that about her son, a light as of the ecstasy of service, that caused her to leave the words unspoken, with a dread—a foolish dread, perhaps—that he would whip off and enlist as a soldier instead.

Angus put a hand upon his shoulder.

"I remember during the Boer War," said he, "being glad that you were too young. Now, man, I wish you were too old. But, as you say, we are committed."

"And even if we were not," replied Dan, "even if we were not, it's a dirty business—the invasion of Belgium. I'm not sorry I was too young for the Transvaal. Most people don't look back on that with any intense pride. But, honest, I'm glad I can be of use in this."

CHAPTER THIRTY-TWO
Sacrifice

Angus was glad, a little later, that they had decided to settle at High Butte, handy to the reserve. A telephone had been installed and there was a call from the agency one morning.

"Can you come over at once, Mr. Munro?" said Chantelaine. "I'd like to see you here."

"What is it?"

"Well—"

"Anybody dead?"

"Good gracious, no. It's nothing serious—exactly; but I want your help. A little trouble."

"Trouble!"

"Nothing serious," Chantelaine repeated, "though I'd like you to come at once if you can. Don't ride. Get a car."

Angus 'phoned to the High Butte garage and in five minutes a taxi was at the door. In three-quarters of an hour he was at the agency. He liked being here. The old West lingered round the place. Women in bright shawls were sitting smoking their little pipes, and groups of men wearing big hats (the leather band replaced by one of beads, yellow and blue) were waiting, with all time at disposal, to confer with Chantelaine. Arrived at the office he saw a mounted-police car at the door; and when he entered the private room there sat Chantelaine, a Redcoat whom he knew, and Peter All Alone, silent and sullen in khaki.

"Well, Angus," began the policeman, "Chant' wanted you to be in on this, so I waited."

"What's the trouble?"

"He'll tell you," and the Redcoat nodded to Peter.

Peter told.

"Hell!" he said. "I enlist for war, and I drill and form four, and two deep, and single file, and say Yes sir, No sir, and I drill more, and I dig trench like Bohunk and Dago—and walk and walk! All right. I think maybe by and by I go to war. I go with company to east. We stop in east, at Valcartier, and dig trench, and do form four, and bayonet practice on sacks, and walk every day. No fighting. So I come home."

"There you are," exclaimed Chantelaine. "Q.E.D!"

"There you are!" said the policeman. "He's a deserter. He wants to fight. He doesn't want to walk. He's liable to be shot."

Angus frowned at that. Peter was clearly, even in khaki, very Indian still, and he might take his own life rather than let that

201

befall if he thought the Redcoat spoke the truth. There had already, in the Northwest, been a small war of the force with an Indian and his relatives due to a jest of that sort not understood by the man who was under arrest for some minor misdemeanour.

"Oh, they won't do that," said Angus sharply. "What do you want me for?"

"Well, you have friends. You might get Sir Sam Douglas to put in a word for him. He's all in the public eye over the Canadian contingents."

"I'll write a letter to the O.C.," Angus said, "and I'll write to the Deputy-Minister of Indian Affairs, Duncan Campbell Scott, in Ottawa, to see what his department can do."

"He's got to go back," announced the policeman. "They are sending an escort for him. I had only to find out if he was here."

"I see. Well, Peter, you can't do this. If they say dig, you've got to dig. If they say form fours, you've got to form fours."

"I wanna go to fight."

"Yes. That's all right—"

"If you say I should go back, Mr. Munro, I'll go, but I'd a never enlisted if I had a known I was going to dig and dig and walk and walk and never fight."

The policeman whooped with joy, though he had heard it all before Angus came.

Well; that was successful. Away they went, Peter carrying an explanatory letter from Munro, who also wrote to the department in Ottawa and direct to the O.C. He would keep Sam, in these days Sir Samuel Lovat-Douglas, in reserve. Two weeks later he received a very friendly and understanding reply from the O.C. about Peter—who was appeased soon, by the departure for England at least. On Salisbury Plain he became embittered again, digging and drilling and walking. He wrote about it all to Angus, a letter in caligraphy and expression scholastically far below the powers of his young brother, but a gem of human expression.

It was on the day that Dan received this half-querulous, half-hopeful epistle that Dan came home again. He was in his uniform with the doctor's tabs. A man grown, he was; and yet here he was suddenly, for some cause, as a child. He was wanting help: they knew that and wondered for what distress. Would he go overseas without broaching it? He did, indeed, himself so wonder, for it was difficult to broach. Was he nervous? his father asked himself, and then—no, he decided, he was not that.

"He's feeling badly about going," Fiona thought. "He doesn't want to break down."

In his eyes was an expression that reminded her at times of

when, a very small boy, he came to have a cut knee bandaged. He tried to speak to them when they were both together. He tried to speak to Angus when alone with him, but in the end it was to his mother, alone with her, that he spoke—suddenly, to get to the matter that vexed him. He was of a height with her, she a tall woman, and she was tremendously moved when this son of hers, a man grown, abruptly put a hand on either shoulder.

"Mother, I want to ask you something," he said.

"Yes, Dan?" There was a light of love on her face. Tears were very close.

"I've never told you," he said. "There's a girl I'm in love with. She's a nurse in Calgary. I met her when I was at McGill."

"I thought there was a girl," she replied.

"How?" he asked, dropping his hands to his side.

"I don't know, dear. Sit down and tell me. What is it?"

"Well," he said, "we had an understanding. We were going to wait till I got on a certain length, but here's this damned war and our duty. It makes a difference. I think I should wait and see if I come back. I've put it to her that way. We've talked it over this way and that. Do you think we should be married before I go?"

"Oh, my dear boy!" Fiona cried out. "I don't know what to say. I'll have to ask your father."

"No," he said. "Leave it. You know now, anyhow. We're not going overseas at once. I'll discuss it with Marjory again."

"What is she like?"

"I'll bring her over next time—you'll meet her."

After he had gone back to Calgary, said Fiona to Angus: "Dan's got a girl. He's going to bring her next time he comes home."

"Oh," said Angus in a quiet voice, and again, "Oh."

When Marjory came they were entirely satisfied with her. Fiona took her upstairs to show her the spare-room, father and son looking at the backs of these two as they ascended. They were chattering gaily together but—neither of the men could have explained how—something in their shoulders, in their movements, suggested that up there the door would be shut and there would be a long talk. And there was.

On the veranda Angus sat staring at the distant mountains, unconsciously humming to himself and tapping the time with finger on the chair-arm. Yes, he was getting old. An observer who knew the story of all there, watching him then, might have recalled Ian Fraser tapping and humming on the veranda out at the agency. Dan paced to and fro. Finally he vaulted over the rail and stood on the lawn looking up at the spare-room window.

"What's keeping you up there?" he called. He came back. "They don't seem to hear," he complained.

"They're having a crack," answered Angus.

When at last the two women came downstairs—

"Where are you? Ah, there you are—out on the veranda," came Fiona's voice, very cheery, but they could see by her eyes that she had been crying. She had an arm round Marjory. "Sit down, my dear," she said, and went indoors as the girl and Angus began to talk.

Dan rose and followed her. She suddenly turned, gathered him into her arms, then thrust him away.

"It's for you two to decide," she told him, and passed into the kitchen.

They decided. They were married, and what a genial man, what a gay man was old Angus Munro, in whom some had seen crankiness of late (though never Fiona), a genial old man at a wedding—for one must go bravely.

It was a great send-off for the contingent a week later, with a band playing. When its music ceased, voices began to sing about it being a long, long way to Tipperary, and others surged up to drown that out with "O Can-ada, O Can-ada . . . We stand on guard, We stand on guard for thee!" The coaches rolled out.

A group of officers stood upon the rear platform of the last, above a placard on which was inscribed To Berlin. Just visible between the shoulders of those in front, Fiona could see her son. The rail joints clicked—click, click, click—and there were more cheers, more tears, as the train dwindled in size, diminished to a little toy and went from sight.

It was a relief to her to hear later that Dan had been detained (like Peter) in Eastern Canada. She had a wild impulse to go and see him there, say good-bye again, an impulse to which she did not give way. There was relief again for all of them to learn that he was further detained in England, with his battalion, on Salisbury Plains.

"About all I do," he wrote, "is to attend to bad feet, and to men who have a leg or a collar-bone broken in a sack-race. This place is very much like Southern Alberta. There are long, slow, rolling hills, and we've brought over our own wagons with the wide whiffle-trees, making it look more so. If there were only the Rockies at the end of these plains to complete the illusion, I'd be absentmindedly jumping in a flivver and coming up to High Butte to see you. The railway company here has given up trying to keep the boys from walking on the track. I was in the little town the other day, at the station, when a lot of them came in, and the agent—I mean the station-master—gave them a lecture, told them that some of them would be killed one day. It made me laugh—the puzzled expression on his face when one of them said, 'You should worry! We're accustomed to hitting the ties.'"

Then they heard from him again, Somewhere in France, "Very busy. Received your letters."

"Very busy, he says," and Fiona handed the card to Angus.

"Aye."

"I wonder what that means?"

"Well, there's a war on," he replied.

They had many notes, and now and then long letters that said little about the war. He had seen a bird like a western meadow-lark; he had seen a place that reminded him of the road turning off to High Butte, "—where, by the way the brush has grown, it is like a hedge;" he had made a friend of a doctor with a battalion of "Jocks" beside them.

"He says he knows Loch Brendan. He took me along to their mess, introducing me as 'My friend, a Canadian-Scot—'"

That was the last direct communication from him.

The next news they had took them to Calgary; for Marjory would have it, too.

CHAPTER THIRTY-THREE
Blue Gentians

It was over at last, a year after Dan's sacrifice, and Angus's private opinion was that they had all, in every land, all the millions of them, died for nothing.

The war years he had felt not as four years but as a period of misery, as out of hell, driven into the world. Young men who had been in the Imperial Army were pouring into the country with the swagger taught them by old soldiers in the training camps; and most of them, by their manner, had individually won the war, and had a view that the Dominion was very much a British possession that they had come to possess. One day he read an article which stated this and that about the trouble and secret treaties predating it—and put it in the stove lest Fiona should see it. It was very depressing.

Fiona had never had an illness apart from the juvenile maladies of whooping-cough and scarlet fever. The last time she had a doctor in attendance was at the birth of Dan, and childbirth is certainly not an obscure disease, not even, rightly considered, an illness! After the death of Dan she failed, and when the war ended (or perhaps one should say when word came that Marjory in Calgary was engaged to be married to a young man who had recently arrived from the Old Country) there was a quiescence about her almost as of one defeated. Tulloch was constantly coming to the house to see her. He advised change of air, so she went off to Minnesota to visit Flora, but stayed only a week.

"I'm getting now," she said on her return, "so that I like to be near my own easy-chair."

People were kind to them, knowing how they would feel, the war over and Dan not back. Hector's elder child—not a child then—came up to spend a week with them, "a very sweet lass," said Angus. She reminded them both of Fiona's mother, even to the turn of wrist and neck. When she was gone Flora visited them for a month; and when they were thinking how nice it was to be alone again, much though they enjoyed seeing these two, Mrs. Chantelaine arrived in a car and was so kindly pressing that they packed suitcases and went over to the reserve to spend a few days there.

"I won't take no for an answer," Mrs. Chantelaine said, "unless you really don't want to come. The flowers are out along the coulee and I know you love the sight of them."

While they were at the agency Peter All Alone came home. He had been with a battalion detained at Rhyl, in North Wales, awaiting transports. They had made him a sniper, it appeared, but the old chiefs of the dwindling Warriors' Society in the tribe were disgusted with much he told them of how the white men fought over there, so he speedily became a silent veteran.

Much did they talk of the old days on the reserve; and in all the changes, the improvements, the better homes, the disappearance of neck sores on the children that had once worried him, Angus took deep and personal interest. Chantelaine, knowing his early story, considered that the fact of his eviction at an impressionable age had much to do with his sympathy for these people, not evicted but circumscribed. They talked of the Blackfoot Reserve that Nigel had visited when on a vacation, of the hospital there maintained out of the tribe's own funds, and of the agent the Blackfeet had, George Gooderham. Mention of that hospital brought them back to the All Alone family because of Louise, who was in those days a qualified nurse with a permanent position on the reserve.

"Louise All Alone," said Chantelaine, "is halfway between Peter and young Angus, your namesake. She's pretty, too, and a fine nurse—but there are lots of Indians these days on a level with her. Angus is outstanding, of course. I shouldn't be surprised if he ended in a profession. There have been professional men already among them, from the Six Nations Reserve in Ontario to the Gilas in Arizona. And if a Sioux can struggle up through the hell of their conditions that I've read and heard about in Dakota to a profession, there is nothing to prevent a lad like Angus All Alone. Gosh! See who comes!"

An agency truck had driven up to the door of the storehouse, and coming across from it was Angus All Alone, carrying a suitcase. His grandfather watched him from the window.

"He must have been coming back and got a lift," observed Chantelaine.

They heard voices in the outer office, the clerk talking out there. Then the door of the private room opened, and the new man (Murray had been transferred to another reserve) stepped in.

"Are you too busy to see Angus?" he asked.

"Send him in," replied Chantelaine.

Young Angus entered.

"Hullo, Mr. Munro!" he exclaimed. "I was going to call and see you in High Butte before coming out, but there was a truck just leaving, so I came on it." He looked very happy. "Just back from High School," he explained.

Just back from high school. How time was bridged ever and again at a scent, a sound, a word. Angus Munro recalled this stripling's father coming in at the front door with a policeman, back from doing time, recalled how he had been sitting there with a white-fatherly homily all prepared, and how it was scattered to the winds at a lively "Just back from college!"

"Sit down, my boy," said Angus. "Sit down and tell us all about it."

It was a heartening, and more an astonished than a boastful report. Young All Alone was top of his class in most subjects, near the top in all.

"I don't mind telling you now, sir," he admitted, "that I had considerable difficulties at first. The reserve school did not prepare me for everything at high school. I have had to think not as an Indian."

"In what way?"

"Well, take physics for example, sir. There isn't a word except one in Cree for all the new words I've had to learn for physics alone."

"Oh? And that word—?"

"Mystery."

"Quite," said Munro. "What do you think you will make of it all?"

"I don't know, but whatever I decide it has been a great experience. I've been thinking that I'd like to take up flying."

"Flying!"

"Yes. Oh, not for good—as a means to an end, to put myself through university. Flying is pretty well paid and I'd like to pay my own fees. I have a friend in Calgary. He's clerking in a drug store to make money to study for a medico. I want to go up with him."

"You want to be a doctor?"

"You bet."

A doctor! That was Dan's profession. Angus looked past young All Alone out of the window, meditatively. Where did this predilection originate? he wondered, and recalled his mother with her knowledge of herbs and medicinal roots, of simples, her prescriptions for ailing neighbours in the old days at Loch Brendan. Dan a doctor, Louise a nurse, and now this youth talking of wanting to be a medico!

"Well, I could speak to Sir Samuel Douglas about an aircraft job," he said. "You know, Sir Samuel Lovat-Douglas, chairman of Arctic and Border Airways."

"That's very kind of you. Mr. Munro. I've got a job for this summer, anyhow, a vacation job."

"You have?"

"Yes. A very interesting man came to lecture to us about the geology of the district, and I'm to drive a car for him for two months in the field—in the Red Deer River country."

"The Red Deer River! What's he doing there?"

"He's making excavations. They have discovered prehistoric creatures, fossilized, creatures of the pterodactyl sort—"

"They have!" exclaimed Angus, and his mind was back to the cabin at Rocky Mountain House, and he was listening to strange stories of Minota's—wild legends he had thought them. "They have!" he ejaculated again.

The door opened again and the clerk looked in.

"There's Dick Beaver going by in a rig," he said to young All Alone. "He goes your way, if you want a lift."

"Will you excuse me, Mr. Munro, if I beat it now?"

"Come and see me again," said Chantelaine.

"Sure! And I'll see you, sir."

"Oh, he'll be here some days yet," Chantelaine interjected.

"We mustn't stay too long," Angus told him.

"Well, I'll either see you here or at your home in High Butte," said young All Alone.

The clerk had dashed out and was shouting to Dick Beaver to wait.

"God bless you, my boy," said Angus, getting stiffly to his feet. He lifted both hands in air in the old sign, greatly moved, and looked after the lad as he ran, suitcase in hand, to the waiting wagon, Nigel watching his old chief and thinking how much he had his heart in the job.

They were happy days at the reserve for all. Fiona sat with Mrs. Chantelaine, a sewing-basket by her side, on the seat under the cotton poplar clump. From there she could see the pools and streamers of the wild flowers along the coulee bottom one way and, the other, the high peaks of the mountains, their promontories jutting into the foothills, for it was halcyon weather.

Mrs. Chantelaine took them for drives in the car away off the reserve and through the Mennonite settlement. It had been bald prairie there once, then there had been dotted houses and anon round each house little twigs of trees. No houses were visible as they came to the ridge overlooking the Mennonites' domain that summer, not even a twinkle of sun in a window to indicate where they were. The bunches of twigs of a few years back were trees, dotted copses (shelter brakes) round the homes. They were very happy, but even so Fiona was not loath to be back in her own easy-chair again.

As they had once noticed, on a visit to the old folk at High River, a sudden change in the Frasers, the static period over, so did the Chantelaines, on that visit, notice a change in them. Suddenly they had aged—but, then, there had been the war, and Dan's death. There had also been the speedy engagement (and marriage) of Marjory, which, perhaps, had hurt Fiona a little, though of that their friends knew nothing.

Talking over their visit, the Mennonites' farms and much else that proclaimed the flight of time, said Fiona: "All the changes make me feel old—near an end," she added.

That was a speech too serious to take seriously.

"Aye, aye," he replied, and laughed. "I may put you to bed yet, lass, though I'm over ten years older than you."

She laughed back at him, realizing that he felt the subject too deep to talk of save jestingly.

"I would like to be the last to go," thought he. "I would not like to leave her alone. One can make happiness but, the way things are now, it's often not a happy world. Yes," he went on, aloud, "I'd like to tuck you up for the night and see ye comfortably bedded, whatever."

"Oh, tut! And what would you do left alone with nobody to darn your socks?"

"Sit and smoke my pipe with none to bother me!"

"Well, we'll not talk about it," said she, suddenly veering from the view that its seriousness necessitated pretence of levity. "It's no matter to be joking on."

"It's too sad to do anything else but joke on, my lass. God bless you."

"Perhaps we'll go together," she said.

But the blue gentians had just faded and the prairie asters of that year were blooming again, as through ages they had bloomed there—ribands of them by the mile drawn along the sides of the motor roads for a wild border—when she went alone.

CHAPTER THIRTY-FOUR
Angus and Sam

They called him Old Man Munro after that. When we mourn for the dead, he told himself, we really mourn for ourselves, missing them. He was glad she had gone first. It was lonesome with one's partner away, but he had more faith in future than present, whatever followed.

He became as a certain group of elders among his late wards: he lived in the past—several jumps to rear. Every now and then an Indian's horse would be seen standing at the veranda's end, or a patched democrat wagon, signifying that he had callers from the reservation. One or two even came in cars sometimes, but not All Alone. He did a little business with the High Butte General Store in beaded moccasins or fringed gauntlets. Tourists passing through would buy a pair for two dollars. It was a "fifty-fifty" trade, the storekeeper paying the chief a dollar a pair or giving him credit to that amount for goods—and how he and his wife loved oranges! They never drove into High Butte with these things but they came to smoke with Angus—good friends, these, as the years passed. There was occult comfort for Munro in these visits of Minota's son.

"Mistah Chief All 'Lone and Misses Chief All 'Lone come see you!" Mah Yip would chant in the doorway, always glad to see them, knowing that their visits cheered the old man.

From his window one day he saw odd movements of two men, peered at them across distance. It looked as if one was threatening the other with fierce gestures, then the other waved his arms in air, and next they both moved on together. There was not another war; those were not recruits practising flag-wagging. The truth suddenly dawned upon him: He recalled that he had given a donation toward founding the High Butte Golf Club, helping toward initial payment on a course. Calgary and Edmonton had theirs long ago.

This shocked him. Stunned, the old man turned from the window, picturing that little play-ball bouncing among these undulations across which (not unprepared for having at least to temporize with some band of roving Blackfeet prowling north into Cree country for horses, if not for scalps) he and Sam Douglas had ridden—ages past.

It eased him somewhat to have Sam back again. Sam still had many "interests," was not only president of Western Oils Limited, the head office of which, demanding his presence there during the war years, was in London, but he was also chairman of Arctic and Border Airways, known as The A.B., and when he was elected to that position he returned to Calgary. There Angus discussed with him the possibility of getting young All Alone into the service.

"Certainly, certainly. I'll tell them to expect him and to take him on. It'll be mechanic's work at first, of course, but I'll tell them."

"He's a marvel in a motor car," said Angus proudly, "one of the finest drivers I've ever seen, and if anything goes wrong with one of the big combines at the harvesting out at the reserve he can crawl around and tinker it."

"Send him along. I'll tell them to keep an eye on him. Man, you are awful keen on your Indians! I'll see to it," he said with finality, and flung off into a tirade over a trifle perhaps to some but to him clearly not so.

He had been down to the coast, to Vancouver, and a train man in the Kicking Horse Pass had pointed out to him a rock there telling him it had given the place its name.

"He tried to make me see it was the shape of a kicking horse. 'Nonsense!' I says to him. I told him the true story that you and I know—how Dr. Hector (him that later became Sir James Hector, governor of the Windward Islands), when he was out in the mountains with Captain Palliser, got kicked over a cliff there by a baulky horse. But I doubted if I did any good. He'll keep that rock to show to the tourists. Och, aye! The old days are dust, Angus. The Ten Peaks in there that were named by the Stoneys in their tongue, one to ten, they are giving new fancy names to. It's as bad as that attempt a while back to obliterate the good old name of Medicine Hat. Medicine Hat—I hope they keep it to tell folks a thousand years hence what we won't be here to tell them."

"That's a long jump ahead," said Angus.

The next time Old Man Munro went to see Sam about Angus All Alone he did not go to his house. He went to the office, for he did not like the duty that carried him there. He walked slowly from his hotel, deep in thought. Motor cars in ribbons along the streets, came to a halt before silent policemen, and moved on again. The bells of electric streetcars clanged, adding their imperative clash to the honkings. The sidewalks were agog from shop-fronts to curb, and it seemed that all the languages of Europe were being spoken round him, from Finnish to Greek, from Gallician to Ukrainian. A metropolis! He recalled Douglas's prophesies that so it would be, made in days of long ago. A polyglot metropolis: that's what Calgary was!

Tall new steel blocks were being built to the din of electric hammers driving home the rivets. At a crossing he suddenly discovered that a car, turning into the side street there, was creeping slow behind him. He stepped on smartly, and in doing so, with a glance over his shoulder noticed that the driver was Marjory. She waved a hand to him, but of course could not stop, because other cars were close, taking the turn. He waved too, and bowed, standing on the curb. There was the Hudson's Bay Company's store, a tall block, very different from the log-cabin he had seen on his arrival to meet Sam, riding in from the Mountain House.

A few blocks further on he turned into a tiled hallway, where a revolving doorway was constantly spinning to exits and entrances, and glanced at the rubric on a wall. Yes: Second Floor, Arctic and Border Airways. Four elegant elevator doors gleamed in a row to one side. A trig young woman in uniform, wearing rakishly a jaunty cap, sang to him: "Going up?"

"Thank you. Second floor."

"Second floor!"

Angus stepped out of the lift and read the legends on the glass doors. General office. He entered and—

"Sir Samuel Lovat-Douglas in?" he asked a clerk.

"Have you an appointment, sir?"

"No. Tell him it is Mr. Munro—Mr. Angus Munro."

The clerk departed toward the inner corridor. As Angus waited he heard many typewriters clicking and the noise, without, of riveting.

"Come this way, please, sir."

He was ushered into Sam's room. The chairman sat in a revolving chair beyond a gleaming table.

"Well, Angus!" he exclaimed. "Sit ye doon. Grand tae see ye at any time. Sit ye doon—no, not in that chair. That's for business people and people wanting something out of me." He rose. "We'll sit down here," and he passed to a divan that stood between two bright windows.

There they subsided.

"There's something on your mind," said Sam, producing a cigar-case.

"Yes."

"What is it? Can I help?"

"Yes. It is about A.B. Airways' matters."

"Oh?"

"I've been hearing a lot about them from men who know. I can't think it's malicious gossip."

"Out with it, man!" Sam did not open his cigar-case but sat there playing with it, slapping a hand with it.

"They say"—Angus paused—"they say the machines go up not airworthy."

"Do they?"

"Yes. They say that A.B. buys discarded machines—"

"—and mends them, and mends them!" interrupted Douglas. "Makes them as good as new. What's all this about? Did you come to warn me for my good name's sake? If so—I've heard it all before,"

"Well, Sam, it's this way," said Angus. "You can get tri-motor all-metal planes, yet you are using one-engined, water-cooled planes."

"I know it. Do you think A.B. can afford these grand machines?"

"Maybe not," Angus replied, "but why send young men up in buses, as they call them, that are not guaranteed even for the rises they have to make in the over-mountains work? I forget the word."

"Ceiling, I believe," supplied Douglas.

"That's it."

"But what's—what's all this for? You will be wanting me to have wireless operators in them all and—"

"And they have to tinker their engines," went on Angus, "with hay-wire."

Hay-wire annoyed Sam, for there was a slang phrase of the land, A hay-wire outfit.

"Come to the point, man," he said, testily. "I'm thinking,

213

Sam, of Angus All Alone—that lad I got in with you about a year or so ago. He's flying now."

"Oh, that Indian lad! Well well. The pilots have the nerve to go up in anything. Fine boys, fine boys!"

"Because they have the nerve," demanded Angus, "should they be asked to do it, take such risks?" Sam cleared his throat.

"I'm sorry about this," he said. "I never expected it from you. You spoke for him, and he's been pushed along ahead of others, and now you come and talk to me as if I was ruthless. He's—all—right! The machines are safe enough. It's your Indian kink, Angus, run away with you."

"'Kink?' Well—" Angus paused.

"Aye?"

"He's my grandson—that Indian lad."

"Your grandson! Well, I'm—" Sam stood up. "Well, I'm—" he sat down. "What do you know about that!" he ejaculated in a phrase more exclamatory than inquiring. "Well, what do you know about that!" and he got up and walked to the wall, carefully straightening a picture that some part of him had amazingly noticed was a little out of plumb, unaware what he did. He came back and stood over Angus. "Yon bonny brown wench ye had in your cabin at the Mountain House—there was a child?"

"Yes."

Sam pointed a finger at him.

"Minota!" he chanted. "Minota!"

"Yes."

"I remember the name. It just came to me."

He felt in a pocket for his cigar-case, which had slipped down at the back of the divan, seated himself beside Angus again, gave up the quest for the cigars and laid a hand on his friend's forearm, pressing it in assurance.

"Angus," said he. "Now, honestly, I don't know—or I didn't—much about the machines. I'm only the chairman, after all, I'm not the engineer in charge. I know but little about the airplanes. I've never felt it was for me to inquire. But I tell you what I'll do. I'll have a chat with my executive head about it. I'll admit he has told me he hoped our political opponents would not get to know certain things, but I haven't troubled to inquire just what. Your grandson, eh? Well, you have kept your thumb on it." He paused, meditatively. "And I have kept my thumb on your having an Indian woman in the old days, seeing I never heard you mention it."

Somehow Angus was reminded, sitting there, of humping down beside Sir Ernest Reynolds on all that remained of the wall of the house where he was born by Loch Brendan.

"Aye," Sam continued, "I'll see about what you've been talking of. As a matter of fact, I've heard other hints and I have been thinking we'd better improve our machines before some paper gets noisy about it. I've got to thank you for coming to me with this, Angus. Have a cigar. Where did I put that case? Here it is. Cigar? No, no, it's lunchtime. We'll go and have lunch at the Club. My wife is away awhile visiting in Ottawa."

As a matter of fact, Angus All Alone, having sedulously saved his pence, left the Airways service on the next commencement at McGill, going to Montreal with that drugstore clerk who was then in a similar position with at least sufficient funds, if not affluence. He called on old Angus at High Butte before his departure,

"If I get through all right," he said, "some day I hope to be with the department, in one of the agency hospitals. I'd like to be in the service. I sometimes think, if you don't mind my saying so, sir, that the Indian blood—well, it has its own strength. I don't believe my people are a dying race, going out in misery everywhere."

It was a talk that, when the young man was gone, jogged Angus to many memories—memories of Dan's ambition (not ambition enough to please his friend Sam Douglas), memories of Buffalo Calf talking of how the Indian blood is strong. Recalling Buffalo Calf brought to mind Gus Atkins—and where, he wondered, was he? Once or twice they had met since '77. Gus must have retired from the police force long since. Angus wished they had kept in touch.

He passed into a reverie of men he had known and liked, yet lost touch with, thought of Buchanan of the old Red River flat-boats and the boat-building on Saskatchewan's headwaters. The last he had heard of him was from Sam, ratifying a rumour that he was piloting a stern-wheeler on the Fraser River, Douglas having seen him there when he first went to the Cariboo country. Buchanan, thought he, must be dead. "We've all got to come to it," as Sam had said, almost cheerfully, commiserating with him when Fiona's mother went.

Mah Yip came in, and seeing him sitting deep in thought, summoned him.

"No mo' ladio?" he asked. "Why you nevah listen ladio, Mistah Munlo? Ladio all same lot of people come alound. You tly! You no likee, all light—you tu'n off. You listen ladio!"

CHAPTER THIRTY-FIVE
Voice of the Prairie

The radio had been a present he had given to Fiona. They had never been able to take that small polished box for granted. Always it was Mystery, and they would often wonder what kindred and further marvels awaited in the future. Since she went he had hardly touched it, but to humour Mah Yip, recognizing kind solicitude in his manner, he switched it on.

"This is Calgary speaking—C.F.C.N.—the Voice of the Prairie. We regret to announce that the talk promised for this evening by Sir Samuel Lovat-Douglas on Reminiscences of the Old West"—(imagine Sam talking of the Past instead of the Future!)—"will have to be postponed, Sir Samuel having been taken ill suddenly this afternoon. We are sure that all his old friends wish Sam a speedy recovery."

The wish of his old friends was not gratified. In the papers the obituary notices read, Suddenly . . . at his residence in Calgary. But, sudden though it had been, that man of method had all arranged, even to a list of pallbearers and honorary pallbearers, and an additional list lest any of those named in the first should be unable to see him to the grave. Always a jump ahead was Sam.

Some of the newspaper headings disgusted Angus. He never liked such titles as Grim Reaper Takes . . . Old Timer Answers Last Call . . . Grim Reaper! Sam's own attitude to that inevitable was always so much to the tune of "It comes to us all," and he was of such an age that it was, as one old friend said, almost a cheerful funeral. He had lived his life, a full life, and was looked upon as somewhat of a Character by many which (despite his descent to a title) he would prefer to being considered a Personage.

There was no slow trudge of bearers, no halting at the intoning of Relief! He lay in his coffin in a dress-suit, and those who cared could pass in file to look their last on him. Angus did not. He wanted to retain other memories of Sam—of Sam alive, moving, throwing back his head to laugh, trying to coax the Glasgow bailies—to humbug them some would have said. The most expensive undertaker and the most fashionable clerics put him to bed. Angus wondered what, honestly if privately, he would have thought of the service. Sam, no doubt, had his own thoughts about much but he always did the established thing. They were far from each other in some ways, these two friends who had often come very close in the flying of the years. To Sam, he recalled, he had on an impulse divulged a secret he had not shared with his loved wife—the secret of All Alone.

When the body was resurrected would the dress-suit be resurrected, too? Thoughts of all sorts, queer and not queer, whimsical and serious, passed through Angus's mind during the formal ceremony. The pageant seemed ghoulish to old Munro and when he died he hoped there would be no such prolonged harrowing of any who might have cared for him. Death needed not that. He consoled himself by thinking that, after all, all the clerics had there was the body. The spirit was off and away. He remembered that Socrates said, when asked how he would be buried, "You will have to catch me first." Then somehow—perhaps in part, after all, because of the pageantry of it—the harrowing quality diminished. It became almost a genial funeral. Sam had lived his life, and he had died easy, not slowly in a weary sick-bed.

After all was over one of the other honorary pallbearers, who had glanced at Angus once or twice during the spectacle, stepped to him.

"I believe you've forgotten me," he said. He was a lean man of stiff erect carriage, with scanty gray hairs and gray face.

"Gus Atkins!" exclaimed Angus.

"Yes. Still alive but not kicking violently. I'm glad I didn't have to help to lift him even onto that butler's-wagon thing. Here's a car to take us back to town. Get in with me, will you?"

Both had commissions in the city's centre, so alighted there, Angus remembering at his shopping (his life going on as usual), Big Beaver's remark: "If I am not here next year I hope your hunting will be good." He felt as though he were somewhat of a ghost over these purchasings.

"That all?" asked Gus.

"That's all."

"All mine, too. Where are you putting up?"

"The Palliser."

"The Palliser. You used to go to the Alberta."

"Yes, and before that the Potter House."

"That's right, too—the old Potter House. Gosh, what changes!"

As they walked they talked easily of the dead, or Gus did and Angus listened.

"We've all got to come to it," said the graying Atkins. "It's good not to be bedridden long, and he was an old man, and he had a damn good time. He was a good boss and a good friend, and as years went on, a mellow and easy-oasy enemy. Bit of a humbug, perhaps, but another way of looking at that is that he liked to get

217

through without trouble. Plausible, some said, and others said genial. Some said all for himself. He really wasn't all for himself with everybody. I know that. Yeah, he was a great card. I'm sorry he's gone."

They moved on and came to the hotel. Angus liked it for many reasons, and one was its name. Palliser must really have been on his way west, across the plains and through the mountains, when the coronach by Loch Brendan played the Munros to their exile. True he had eventually presented a report against the building of a railway, but that was because he could see "no immediate advantage commensurate with the required sacrifice of capital." The words came back to Angus's mind, remembering the past.

But who, thought he, would have dreamt then (in the days when Palliser had to spend a winter with Old Sun of the Blackfeet, that the tribesmen might know him and let him be at his surveying) of this? Did even Sam Douglas with all his hopes and prophesies?

They had afternoon tea—Gus and Angus (Afternoon tea! How queer it seemed when thinking of the old days)—in the tall hotel of the reverie-creating name. Then it was time for Gus to go to catch his train. He had retired at Banff.

"Come and see me sometime," said he as they walked to the door. There he held out his hand, and added, imitating a voice they would hear no more: "It's grr-and tae have seen ye again, Angus!"

"Grand to have seen you, Gus."

Angus walked back into the long lounge and, sitting down there, told himself that he was old. Gus Atkins was much his junior, and he was gray. There he called up the ghosts, the shadows, from the years that had flown. Fiona he had no need to call. She, it seemed, was always with him—in a blessed dispensation of Providence. She retained for him, in her ghostly companionship, a feeling that all was not agley, despite the fact that the brief post-war sense of relief and hope had ebbed, leaving depression. The overflowing happiness of her youth remained with him, the dismissing gentleness of her middle years that made acrimony barren, her refusal to be implicated in acerbities. When, meditating there, he put a hand out to one side on the couch, it was as though he laid it on hers, she sitting there with him, though to the head-porter in his niche he was but an old man sitting alone, absently turning a collet ring round and round on his little finger.

Old man Buchanan was there. Fiona's father and mother were there for him. Minota of the dark, candid eyes, the views that to one of the twentieth century were naïveté's, the simplicities that to foolish folk would be foolishness—she was there. All these came to him in the beauty of remembered mornings and noons, of dusks that were eternal. He thought of the caulked cabin at Rocky Mountain House, heard the hum of the Franklin stove, heard again, in his other cabin beyond Jasper, the blue jays raucously demanding breakfast, recalled, across the years, his misery there on a certain regrettable occasion.

Some music broke out. He thought of a sea loch of Scotland, with a sense of instability, a sickness under his heart. He had no place—no place. There was no ground under his feet. The place of his birth was a tangle of bracken. He had no place—no place. There was no ground under his feet. A faintness came to him. Oh, well—we come and we go, through various vicissitudes, and it is all one where our bones lie at the end of the strange dream. He drew a long, trembling breath. He glanced this way and that, wondering where was the orchestra. A Japanese attendant came running to him.

"Is there anything you want, sir?" he asked.

"I wondered where the music was coming from," replied Angus.

"I shall find out, sir."

Had he never come to this land he would never have met Fiona, so he dismissed from his mind that memory, in the music, of a distant sea loch, its scents and sounds. After all, it was in the mind one lived, not on a certain given acre of the world.

The porter returned.

"New York, sir, relayed from Salt Lake City."

"Oh—radio."

"Yes, sir."

The music again took him far: He was in Edinburgh, sitting with Fiona and Dan at the Buffalo Bill show. It ceased and he remained there talking to Hill Burton. Outside there was a wind shrilling in the chimney pots of Auld Reekie. It would be nice, he considered, to live in one's own country. Still, he had grown to love this one, and Fiona, born at Red River, had come to love the west. The scent of crushed sage-brush she loved, aromatic sage.

Other music came, and he was riding up the north bank of the Bow with Gus Atkins (ruddy of hair, ruddy of face) after having unpacked the horses beside the Redcoats' camp. Then the lounge of the Palliser was full of voices for him, the voices of Sarcee Indians and of Stoneys (Minota's mother was a Stoney) riding through. They were all painted and feathered. Bells were on the horses' bridles. They came jogging from the ballroom to west toward the dining-room to east. People going in to early dinner did not see them, only he. The early diners surrendered their coats and hats to the tall girl at the cloak alcove, and the head-waiters received them with a bow and a salute of menu card; but the Sarcees and the Stoneys rode on, trailing travois, lodge-poles, raising the dust on their way to that great gathering at Blackfoot Crossing in '77. The elevators hummed up and down, with a smooth click opened to deposit those guests who descended and to receive those who waited—click and hum. The horses whinnied as they passed, or cleared their throats of a husk, and there was laughter in the cavalcade, "the sweet laughter of Indian women."

He came back with a gasp to the present, saw the reflected lights in tiles of the lounge between the rugs, the glow of the lamps on the polished woods.

"Shadows," said the old man, talking to himself, sitting there. "Shadows!"

Well, like Sam's, his life had been a full one, thought he, reviewing there the flying years. In his mind there was a sanctuary, with these for company. Soon he must be going. He looked up at the clock. How quickly time passed! He rose, a little stiffly, and went tapping over the tiles to catch his train home.

THE END

www.ingramcontent.com/pod-product-compliance
Lightning Source LLC
Chambersburg PA
CBHW031954040426
42448CB00006B/351